THE LIVING BUILDING CHALLENGE

ROOTS AND RISE OF THE WORLD'S GREENEST STANDARD

MARY ADAM THOMAS

FOREWORD BY DENIS HAYES

D1220685

A MANIFESTO IN THE GUISE OF A STANDARD

THE LIVING BUILDING CHALLENGE:
ROOTS AND RISE OF THE WORLD'S GREENEST STANDARD

An Ecotone Publishing Book/2016

Ecotone Publishing – an Imprint of International Living Future Institute

For more information write:

Ecotone Publishing
721 NW Ninth Avenue, Suite 195
Portland, OR 97209

Author: Mary Adam Thomas

Book Design: softfirm

Edited by: Fred McLennan

Library of Congress Control Number: 2016934655

Library of Congress Cataloging-in Publication Data

ISBN: 978-0-9972368-1-1

1. Architecture   2. Philosophy   3. Environment

First Edition

Printed in Canada on FSC-certified paper, processed Chlorine-Free, using vegetable-based ink.

4

In 2014, China produced 2.7 billion tons of cement. The manufacture of one ton of cement produces nearly one ton of carbon dioxide. Cement — used in essentially all our buildings and foundations — accounts for about 5 percent of all anthropogenic CO_2 released each year.

Wood could be a less destructive, more sustainable building material than cement. Forests can capture atmospheric carbon, protect topsoil from erosion, and provide habitat for a rich variety of species (including the last 450 wild Siberian tigers). But voracious logging companies have for the last century been harvesting the world's old growth boreal forests and fragile rainforests with no more care and selectivity than a combine brings to a North Dakota wheat crop. Although such ecological pillaging is illegal in most of the world's forests, the governments of wood-exporting states are often too poor or too corrupt to enforce the law. Importing countries turn a blind eye in return for rock bottom prices.

The environmental impacts of the built environment are enormous, and they reach far beyond the local sites of our buildings, neighborhoods, and cities.

In the late 20th century, a variety of efforts were undertaken to encourage more sustainable buildings. There are now approximately 600 building certification programs in effect globally — some serving neighborhoods and others spanning continents. Many, like the Forest Stewardship Council, Energy Star, and Water Sense focus on a single attribute of buildings. Others, like Passivhaus, the USGBC's LEED standards, Green Seal, BREAM, Cradle to Cradle, Pharos, CASBEE, Green Mark, Green Star and Pearl review multiple aspects of buildings or building materials.

Such programs represent steps in the right direction. But they all tend to focus mostly on the construction of a building, not its subsequent performance. From the developer's viewpoint, that is very attractive. A developer who is willing to spend the money to incorporate the required features can guarantee the building's rating. Developers treasure such certainty.

From society's viewpoint, however, this approach has a major fault. The actual performance of buildings sometimes does not correlate with the sum of its features. Many LEED Silver buildings, for example, have better real-world performance than LEED Platinum buildings. These lower-rated buildings often have superior design and better construction, but they contain fewer of the attributes that are awarded "points."

I am a strong supporter of green certification. LEED, in particular, has had an enormous impact in nudging architects, developers, and banks in a greener direction. Even the most basic LEED standards have created a demand for smarter designs, more efficient equipment, and better materials. The growing consumer demand for LEED Platinum, Passivhaus, Cradle-to-Cradle, and others has led to very significant innovations.

But for those of us who seek a deeply transformational approach to buildings — one measured by long-term performance — the Living Building Challenge filled a void. The Living Building Challenge re-conceptualizes buildings as organisms, nested within an urban ecosystem that reflects the climate and the geophysics of its immediate environment. The Challenge is based upon hundreds of millions of years of beta testing of habitats by Mother Nature.

The Living Building Challenge began, not with the standard green question of "How can we minimize harm," but rather with the much more profound question, "How can we maximize good?" Like a beaver pond or a coral reef, the creation of a new Living Building should actually improve the world.

An extremely green conventional building might reduce the amount of energy used for space conditioning, lighting, and other building operations by two-thirds or more. A Living Building, in contrast, is so spectacularly efficient that it is able to generate more energy on its site than it uses for all purposes — not just to run the building but also to meet the plug loads for the computers, printers, refrigerators, toasters, etcetera of its tenants.

The Living Building Challenge does not merely apply these leapfrog challenges to energy or water or materials or siting or transportation or carbon impact or any other single feature. Instead, it takes a holistic approach to the health, resilience, and sustainability of human habitat.

When my team and I first began to explore the possibility of a six-story speculative office building in Seattle that would meet all the Petals of the Living Building Challenge — and also be affordable, beautiful, and fully tenanted — every major real estate developer I talked with said it could not be done.

That is why Jason McLennan's advocacy of this visionary new approach was an act of raw professional courage. He bet his professional reputation on a set of attributes that he saw as essential to the future of the species and that therefore had to be achieved. Metaphorically, he made a calculated leap off a cliff for something he believed in. At the time that he announced the Living Building Challenge, Jason could not name a single developer anywhere on earth who was willing to construct such a building, or a single bank willing to finance one. Yet Jason was committed, to the core of his being, to making it happen.

Significant progress often follows the public declaration of an almost-impossible stretch goal. Such goals, when coupled with someone possessing a determination to bend the world to reach them, are the stepping stones of human progress. They got us to the moon, unlocked the mystery of DNA, and eradicated smallpox. They offer our best chance of diverting society from its current slow spiral toward oblivion into a new trajectory that affirms life.

Jason never wavered, never doubted, never compromised. He recruited a talented team that shared his values, gave them the necessary freedom to find creative solutions, and raised enough financial support to sustain a critical mass.

As a result, after many years of passionate creativity and tireless work, Living Buildings now are beginning to sprout up across the globe. The process is much slower than I would like, but it is inexorable.

If we are to have a sustainable future, Living Buildings must swiftly become the default standard for human habitat.

AUTHOR PROFILE

MARY ADAM THOMAS is an independent writer and editor with a deep and varied portfolio of published work. She has been helping tell the story of the Living Building Challenge and the important efforts of the International Living Future Institute since 2006.

Mary is the author of two titles in the Living Building Challenge Series – *The Greenest Building: How the Bullitt Center Changes the Urban Landscape* (2016) and *Building in Bloom: The Making of the Center for Sustainable Landscapes at Phipps Conservatory and Botanical Gardens* (2013). She collaborated with Jason F. McLennan on his collection of essays, *Zugunruhe: The Inner Migration to Profound Environmental Change*, and contributed the introduction to his follow-up book, *Transformational Thought: Radical Ideas to Remake the Built Environment*. In addition, she provided editorial support for *Living Building Education: The Evolution of Bertschi School's Science Wing* and *Busby: Architecture's New Edges*. Mary is also the collaborative author, with Andrew Schorr, of *The Web-Savvy Patient: An Insider's Guide to Navigating the Internet When Facing Medical Crisis*. She has also contributed feature articles and essays to numerous print and online publications.

Mary lives outside of Seattle, where she and her husband wait for their two young adult children to have the time to join them on weekend hikes.

ACKNOWLEDGEMENTS

As I neared the end of this project, I opened a fortune cookie at a restaurant one evening and unrolled its enclosed prize. "A challenge will help strengthen your spirits," it said. This simple seven-word missive, stamped onto a tiny strip of paper, felt like a secret and profound message written just to me.

After nearly a decade of writing about the Living Building Challenge and proudly trumpeting the efforts of Jason F. McLennan and the International Living Future Institute, I was deep inside the world's greenest standard. I had authored two case study books, polished several other writers' manuscripts, contributed to various ILFI marketing pieces, edited numerous articles, conducted hundreds of interviews, and absorbed the wisdom of many Living Future unConference speakers. Now, I was wrapping up this very volume exploring the backstory of the Challenge itself. Individually and collectively, the assignments had been enormously fulfilling and extremely difficult, all at the same time.

And that little fortune connected me to the global community of people who have walked in those same green shoes. A cookie-encased message, randomly selected by me, captured the emotions experienced by anyone who has ever taken on the Living Building Challenge: a crazy mix of exhilaration, exhaustion, inspiration, and exasperation. It's very hard work, but it is oh-so worth it. Just when you think you can't do more, you find a way to break through; a path that leads you forward toward truly sustainable solutions. And it feels fantastic when you do.

Sure enough, the Challenge helps strengthen the spirits.

So I express my gratitude to Jason F. McLennan for his original vision, and for inviting me to join the Living party way back in 2006. It has done nothing less than strengthen my spirits. To Amanda Sturgeon for her graceful willingness to make time for me and this book, even during the very busy early phase of her transition to ILFI CEO. To Michael Berrisford at Ecotone Publishing for championing my efforts at every step of the process and for, once again, keeping me sane along the way. To Fred McLennan for making sure my words all fell in the right order. To Erin Gehle and Johanna Björk for creating dazzling art out of plain text. To the ILFI staff for providing their attention and resources to help fill in the blanks. To the dozens of people I interviewed (listed on the Contributors page), who selflessly shared their stories about the Living Building Challenge and without whose passionate participation neither this book nor the Challenge would be what it is. And to the countless professionals, unnamed in these pages, who are committed to a Living Future and willing to make big changes to achieve it.

Finally, to my family and friends who strengthen my spirits most powerfully of all. Together, you are my true fortune.

MARY ADAM THOMAS

LIVING BUILDING BLOCKS

DISTRIBUTED THROUGHOUT THIS BOOK
ARE INSET PAGES EXPLORING THE
THEORY OF CHANGE THAT SHAPES THE
LIVING BUILDING CHALLENGE. IDENTIFIED
AS "LIVING BUILDING BLOCKS," THESE
ARE THE FOUNDATIONAL PHILOSOPHIES
THAT WORK INDEPENDENTLY AND IN
COMBINATION TO INFORM THE WORLD'S
GREENEST BUILDING STANDARD AND
INSPIRE THE MOVEMENT THAT IT SERVES.

01

"Those who contemplate the beauty of the earth find reserves of strength that will endure as long as life lasts. There is something infinitely healing in the repeated refrains of nature — the assurance that dawn comes after night, and spring after winter."

RACHEL CARSON

FIRST IMPRESSIONS

A BOY EXPLORES
HIS SURROUNDINGS

A modest cabin sat on a densely wooded one-acre island in the Ottawa River in Northern Ontario. Few people would think much of this small, inconspicuous structure if they happened upon it. But it was paradise for a young Jason F. McLennan, who spent family vacations enjoying and studying the direct relationship this unconventional building had with its natural environs.

Hand-built with local materials by McLennan's aunt and uncle, the cabin used only the sun for its light, the river for its water, and the breeze for its ventilation. Art graced the interior walls and a sky unpolluted by city lights offered celestial nighttime entertainment (including regular displays of the aurora borealis that helped remind one wide-eyed young stargazer of his tiny scale within the context of the cosmos).

The structure itself was not beautiful according to classical measures, but it enabled its inhabitants to experience the splendor of nature in all its forms. It emerged from its very surroundings, built from river rock and timber gathered from nearby and adorned with salvaged windows and doors delivered to the site from the mainland. It was glorious in its messiness; harmonious in its randomness. To those who created and used it, the cabin embodied pure beauty.

Preparing for trips to the cabin required forethought. Since it was separated from "civilization" by a long boat ride and many driven miles, resupplying mid-visit was not an easy task. All food and provisions had to be hand-carried from the boat to the property, then back again (along with any accumulated refuse). It was an exercise in examining one's definitions of need and want. What was really necessary? What really mattered? What were the limits within which a person could happily exist?

Once on the island, where there was no television, radio, or electricity, visitors relied on one another and the setting for inspiration, entertainment, and companionship. Circadian rhythms dictated routines while wildlife and insects supplied the soundtrack. To McLennan, the tiny island felt limitless in its scope. Everything about the cabin and its place on the land — even the outhouse, which generated compost in an inelegant but productive fashion — felt comfortable and right to him. The experience was primal, which proved to be immensely important to the curious and eager future designer. It was his first exposure to a building that emerged from — rather than competed with — the natural world.

"Aunt Rita's island," as McLennan refers to it today, is surely one of the earliest inspirations for the green building standard he developed years later. It is irrelevant that the cabin bore little resemblance to the 21st-century structures that have since met the stringent requirements of the Living Building Challenge; what matters is that it is one of countless seeds from which the Challenge organically grew. It is among the many buildings, ideas, and thinkers McLennan readily credits with helping the Challenge take shape and evolve.

LEFT:
The cabin on "Aunt Rita's island" in the Canadian wilderness left an early and profound impression

RIGHT:
Jason F. McLennan and his father, Fred, canoe on the Ottawa River near the cabin

Since its 2006 introduction, the Living Building Challenge has continued to mature and adapt as more projects accept it, more buildings achieve it, and more people become aware of it. The first Living Buildings were certified within just four years of the Challenge's introduction, with several more projects following quickly on their heels. Just five years post-launch, there were hundreds of commercial and residential projects registered all over the world, thousands of engaged practitioners, numerous manufactured items being reconfigured to comply with Red List requirements, and countless new technologies being developed to adhere to Challenge Imperatives.

From the beginning, the Living Building Challenge has been less about certification than about philosophy — specifically, an important re-telling of how we *can* and *should* live on the planet. It's about what the built environment is capable of being, what revolutionary change we are capable of creating, and what wisdom a committed community is capable of sharing. Ultimately, the world's greenest building standard is about our role as a species on the planet.

The story of the Challenge itself features a long list of characters, all passionately devoted to a set of goals they agree are exceedingly difficult to attain but arguably essential to our survival.

Inco Nickel Smelter with its Superstack, Sudbury, Ontario, Canada
PHOTO: WIKIMEDIA COMMONS

SETTING THE SCENE

To know the Living Building Challenge is to know its creator and primary author, Jason F. McLennan. To know McLennan is to know where and how he grew up. We look back at his childhood not to paint an idyllic portrait, but to reveal what was going on in and around Sudbury, Ontario when McLennan was a youngster. *That* place during *that* time shaped him, influenced him, inspired him, and infuriated him, eventually driving him toward a career that has had many of the same effects on the entire design-build industry.

The largest city in Northern Ontario, Sudbury sits above Lake Huron's Georgian Bay approximately 300 miles northwest of Ottawa and 240 miles north of Toronto in what is known as the Canadian Northern Shield. The city grew up around its mines, which drove the local economy throughout the 20th century and continue to employ tens of thousands of people today.[1] Platinum, silver, tin, iron, copper, and other minerals have been found in the area since 1883, but Sudbury is best known for its lumber and nickel supplies[2] and for being home to a 1,247-foot smokestack — the world's tallest when it was erected in 1972.[3]

By the early 1970s, decades of deforestation and nickel mining had turned parts of Sudbury into one of the most toxic places on earth. For decades, the air was thick with sulfur dioxide and soot, the soils and water acidified, the natural surfaces blackened. Re-growth had become virtually impossible, with approximately 10,000 hectares (the equivalent of nearly 25,000 acres) reduced to desolation likened to a moonscape.[4]

THROUGH A CHILD'S EYES

McLennan, born a year after the smokestack took over Sudbury's skyline, had no other frame of reference for his hometown. He came of age surrounded by the ecological fallout of the local industry just as the environmental movement was gaining speed. As he enjoyed a happy, busy childhood in what he describes as "a great place to grow up," pioneers — many of whom he would come to call his mentors — were busy pushing the early environmental agenda forward. (Denis Hayes, national coordinator for the first Earth Day in 1970, was one of them. In a wonderful historical coincidence, Hayes lived briefly during his childhood in the small Canadian town of Espanola, less than 50 miles from Sudbury. One of Hayes' first teachers was likely none other than Annie McLennan, Jason's paternal grandmother, who taught in the local school. It was 2010 before Hayes and McLennan dis-

1   www.greatersudbury.ca/living/about-greater-sudbury

2   www.uwaterloo.ca/earth-sciences-museum/what-earth/rockhound-and-rocks-and-minerals-canada-magazine-articles/mining-history-sudbury-area

3   The Inco Superstack is still the tallest freestanding chimney in the Western Hemisphere and the second tallest in the world after the GRES-2 Power Station in Kazakhstan. It reaches 184 feet higher than the Eiffel Tower

4   www.canadiangeographic.ca/atlas/themes.aspx?id=shield&sub=shield_features_greening&lang=En

covered this connection — one of many ways in which the two men's lives and trajectories have intertwined. They have been influenced by some of the same people, they share the same passion for ecological stewardship, and they have been driven by the same commitment to advocacy. Today, the Bullitt Foundation that Hayes oversees owns and occupies the world's first Living office building, Seattle's Bullitt Center.)

McLennan spent his grade school years focusing on what most children do at that age: family, sports, and exploring the world around him. His parents often took their three children on driving and camping trips, helping to expose them to what lay beyond Sudbury's boundaries. It gave McLennan many opportunities to contrast his community's desolation with the pristine wilderness that surrounded it. These treks also got him thinking about how different other communities seemed from his own: less polluted, more architecturally inviting, more elegantly planned.

In third grade, he developed a friendship with a fellow student whose family had relocated to Canada following a military coup in their African country. This young boy brought stories from his homeland that offered a sense of adventure and otherworldliness. As he introduced Jason to tales of Africa, Jason introduced him to Northern Canada.

The boys were part of a group of local youngsters who shared a love of the outdoors and a willingness to jump on their bikes to seek out undiscovered places in the woods and swamps that abutted Sudbury. They feasted on home-made lunches and fresh-picked blueberries, which grew in wild abundance in the acidic soil. On one foray to a favorite hill in "the bush" (as the woods are known to Canadians), Jason and his new friend climbed to the crest to peer out at the expansive view they had enjoyed on so many previous journeys to the same spot. But on this visit, they got their first glimpse of what industrialized creep looks like when seen from above. The local dump had expanded and was beginning to encroach on what they boys considered their sacred, natural hideout. Seagulls circling above the trash piles added a three-dimensionality to what already felt overwhelmingly catastrophic. How long would it take for the garbage to reach their beloved overlook? How could adults allow such a thing to happen?

WATCHFUL

By middle school, McLennan was gaining greater — albeit untrained — awareness of design aesthetics, due in part to his ability to visit the older, grander cities of Toronto and Ottawa. As new commercial developments were erected back in Sudbury, he watched with interest only to feel disappointed that these buildings and neighborhoods looked just like all the others around them. Sudbury, he began to notice, seemed like nothing more than an endless strip of inexpensive construction projects sorely lacking in planning and grace — he

23

McLennan wondered why his community wasn't as beautifully
designed as other places he visited, such as Ottawa, ON
PHOTO: PIXABAY / DEZALB

and his friends referred to it as a "vinyl village." He knew his hometown was geologically and ecologically unique, but he couldn't understand why its fast-growing developments ignored these distinctions. Even as an adolescent, McLennan was frustrated by his city's lack of architectural vision. He had seen beauty and spirit in two of Canada's greatest cities; why couldn't those qualities be incorporated into Sudbury's built environment?

Meanwhile, Sudbury was garnering international attention for its efforts to right some of its own environmental wrongs. The now-legendary regreening of Sudbury began in earnest in 1978,[5] bringing together citizens, students, scientists, and ecologists all focused on a common goal: to return this nearly-ruined place to its former glory as a Boreal forest. To this day, it is considered one of the most successful environmental reclamations in history.[6] (Regreening maintenance efforts in Sudbury are ongoing as of this writing.)

Sudbury's student community of the late 1970s and 1980s — McLennan included — participated in the regreening undertaking, which gave every citizen an opportunity to contribute to the revitalization of their landscape.[7] Young children took field trips to plant trees. High schoolers spent whole days on work retreats. People of all ages got involved, then watched as their efforts yielded results. Formerly blackened hillsides slowly sprouted small green trees that grew in tandem with the very children who helped put them there. Sudbury literally came back to life during those years, proving nature's regenerative capacity and making quite an impression on the young people who watched it bloom.

But Sudbury's economy was subject to the up-and-down cycles of nickel prices, which meant that building patterns followed suit. Residential and commercial developments tended to be built quickly and inexpensively, and architectural styles reflected the aesthetic and material trends of the era. When McLennan was still in middle school, a developer purchased a tract of land that had benefited from the community's efforts and where young replanted trees were beginning to spread their branches. The greenery was in the way of the developer's plans, though, so the trees were bulldozed, the amended soil was scraped, and the geologically unique rock was blasted — all to make way for a boxy new strip mall and parking lot.

It was yet another seminal experience for McLennan, as he realized that this devastation could not be blamed on the mining industry. Instead, the fault for such carelessness lay with commercial entities that put no thought into how, where, or why a building gets plunked into a place. He viewed it as an irresponsibly casual approach to development, particularly when what it offered to his community was so disproportionate to what it

5   www.jswconline.org/content/42/4/228.extract

6   www.find-great-leaders.com/environmental-success-stories.html

7   Noted Canadian designer Bruce Mau also grew up in Sudbury and participated in student regreening efforts, although he and McLennan did not meet until the 2000s.

took away. Worse yet was McLennan's realization that the shopping mall housed stores that his family would undoubtedly patronize. In other words, this wasn't just about distant corporations or oversized mining operations; this toxic pattern could be linked directly to him. He, too, was culpable, along with every member of the consumer culture. It dawned on him that as a species, humans are capable of destroying our environment, regenerating it, then undoing our efforts as soon as necessary to serve our insatiable consumptive needs. This pattern, he decided, reflects poorly on humans' sensitivity to place, process, and plan.

FROM THE GROUND UP

McLennan continued to ponder the juxtaposition between the man-made and natural worlds that surrounded him in Sudbury; the inherent beauty of the woods, rivers, and trails he explored an hour outside the community stood in stark contrast to the planless developments he watched being built in and around his community. By the time he enrolled in his first drafting class in high school, he had already begun to devour books about architecture and planning. Combined with what he studied at home, the curriculum opened up a world he knew he wanted to enter — one where he could shape how built structures would look, how people would behave in their spaces, and how these constructed things would relate to nature. From that point forward, his high school schedule always included at least one class devoted to design, environmental studies, or other disciplines related to his future pursuits.

The next step for McLennan would be a formal education that would take him away from Sudbury and into the United States. However, this "great place to grow up" — this so-called moonscape — had left its indelible mark. For better *and* for worse, it had served as the ideal first classroom and McLennan its fervent budding student. If anywhere can be considered the birthplace of the Living Building Challenge, it is Sudbury, whose rocky, blackened hills provided the figuratively fertile ground for one of the most important design-build innovations of the 21st century.

SETTING AUDACIOUS GOALS
A LIVING BUILDING BLOCK

The Living Building Challenge rests squarely on the idea that real and profound change requires raising expectations dramatically higher than they've ever been set.

When the Challenge was introduced in 2006, it asked the design-build industry to take buildings far beyond what were then considered to be the farthest limits of sustainability. It intentionally pulled people well outside of their comfort zones and the realms of their previous experience, demanding them to abandon preconceived notions about what was truly feasible in green design.

Offering Living Buildings as the new ideal empowers people by requiring them to innovate and collaborate on new approaches. Transformative solutions then often take on a life of their own and can lead to additional unintentional discoveries.

While drafting the Living Building Challenge, Jason F. McLennan was inspired by the words of Goethe: "Boldness has genius, power, and magic in it." He was also reminded of the British runner Sir Roger Bannister, who refused to accept what was presented at the time as fact: that human beings were incapable of running a mile in less than four minutes. Bannister began to work toward this seemingly outrageous goal, training as if it were a common target. In May 1954, when he crossed the finish line at 3:59:40, he also crashed through long-held assumptions of what was possible. When he broke that tape, he forever changed the sport. It was widely assumed that his previously unfathomable record would stand for decades, if not forever. But it took only 46 days for another man to unseat Bannister as the fastest mile runner. Since then, athletes have continued to drive down the time — all because one individual chose to believe he could do something that had never been done before.

Setting a higher bar can be frightening, as it makes us question what is even possible and can feel like a set-up for failure. But the Living Building Challenge also reminds us that we no longer have the luxury of time. Global issues such as climate change and the worldwide loss of habitat demand that we stop taking baby steps and begin leaping toward answers. Why self-limit by setting low, safe, predictable goals?

Living Building Challenge project teams frequently report being surprised by what they accomplish on their journey to meet the Standard. Even when they don't achieve the ultimate audacious goal — full Living Building certification — they almost always create structures whose designs and systems far surpass anything that could have been done by using a lesser target. Many net zero energy and LEED Platinum projects get to the point of energy self-sufficiency by aspiring to the Living Building Challenge but "only" achieve that Petal's requirements. In the context of the Challenge's audacious goals, these projects have succeeded wildly.

02

"Education is the most powerful weapon which you can use to change the world."

NELSON MANDELA

THE OREGON TRAIL
AN EDUCATION

In the early 1990s, as Jason F. McLennan weighed his college options, the University of Or- egon Department of Architecture had a reputation as one of the only architecture schools with a focus on environmentally-friendly design practices. While a handful of other programs around the United States had single professors who lectured on sustainability, Oregon was making an effort to elevate the discussion in a cohesive, cross-disciplinary way.

From its founding in 1914, Oregon's architecture department was structured differently than its counterparts on other campuses. Then, as now, it was based on a non-competitive, individualized approach to learning with curriculum that is deeply tied to the allied arts. By the 1920s, department head W.R.B. Willcox infused his philosophy that architecture reflects the values and personality of society itself. Architecture students, Willcox believed, should study cultural topics just as diligently as they study design. The department has continued to honor that foundational goal as it has adapted to the changing face of the discipline, promoting its faculty's flexibility with regard to innovation, collaboration, and research.[8]

Although McLennan considered several schools, Oregon's pull was strongest. The small city of Eugene was a long way from Sudbury, Ontario, but McLennan knew he wanted to be in the epicenter — or at least in the closest thing his chosen discipline had to one — when he decided where to study. With his family's support, McLennan headed south of the Canadian border to begin his education.[9]

8   From the University of Oregon Department of Architecture website. Source: architecture.uoregon.edu/about/history

9   When McLennan left for college, his parents actually accompanied him to Oregon to begin a new academic adventure of their own.

> "In education, the aim, it would seem, should be the development of one's own endowments, and not to surpass another, merely, who strives for the same goal. What higher motive than the first can there be, and why should a lower one be accepted as a necessary stimulus? With such an aim, the goal is open to all at the same time; it is not an arbitrary fixed standard of excellence, but a relative one. Its attainment can be measured only with respect to growth, not with respect to another's attainments."[10]
>
> **W. R. B. WILLCOX,**
> **UNIVERSITY OF OREGON DEAN OF ARCHITECTURE 1922-1947, 1923** *AIA JOURNAL* **ARTICLE**

SETTLING IN

The University of Oregon architecture department's individualized structure served McLennan well, as he was the kind of student who craved more than what was offered via classroom curriculum. He read voraciously, supplementing required reading with whatever he could find that could broaden and deepen his knowledge of how, why, and with what to build green. He was always on the lookout for mentors, especially those who could get him involved in demonstration projects.

As an underclassman, McLennan also managed to enroll in a few courses typically reserved for upperclassmen and graduate students, getting a jump on more advanced architecture curricula. (Since sustainable design concepts were relatively new and untested at that time, they tended to be introduced only to older, more experienced students.) There, he first learned about alternative building materials, including straw bale homes, cob buildings, rammed earth structures, and Earthships.[11] He was introduced to technologies that allowed buildings to operate off the grid. He studied experimental on-site water treatment systems. In other words, he gathered his earliest data on what would later develop into Living Building Challenge Imperatives.

Being in the Oregon architecture program at that time gave McLennan the opportunity to interact, directly and indirectly, with some of the green building movement's early

10 From an article Willcox wrote for the AIA Journal, 1923. Source: architecture.uoregon.edu/about/history

11 Pioneered by Michael Reynolds in the 1970s, Earthships are passive solar daylit houses built from a combination of natural and recycled materials, most commonly dirt-filled recycled tires. McLennan was more enamored of the ecological concept than he was of the architecture.

University of Oregon in the early 1990s

"In the early 1990s, there weren't a lot of other departments doing what we were doing. To be there when that was happening was exciting."

JOHN REYNOLDS,
UNIVERSITY OF OREGON

leaders. Several individuals who are now lauded for their valuable contributions to the sustainable design industry were on the Oregon faculty at some point during McLennan's tenure as a student. John Reynolds, a pioneer in the world of solar design, co-wrote *Mechanical and Electrical Equipment for Buildings*, the definitive textbook used by architects to understand environmental control systems. G.Z. "Charlie" Brown authored *Sun, Wind, and Light: Architectural Design Strategies*, which shows architects how to design to carbon-neutral performance targets. Charles Rusch introduced students to the philosophical side of green, creating a holistic training ground in alternative design that explored the relationships between people and place. Robert Peña (who would later play an important role with the Bullitt Center) partnered with Reynolds to delve deep into curriculum on environmental control systems. Virginia Cartwright taught students how to incorporate daylighting strategies into their designs. Will Sturges served as the students'

Jason F. McLennan at University of Oregon

supportive, nurturing champion. Kevin Matthews, who showed the students how to use software for analysis, demonstrated the power of out-of-the-box thinking. Other ground-breakers rounded out the impressive faculty roster.

Through these teachers and their connections, McLennan was exposed to the ideas and inspiration of such pioneers as Sim Van der Ryn and Pliny Fisk III, both of whom have since become close allies of McLennan's and vocal evangelists for the Living Building Challenge.

McLennan's fellow Oregon students — present-day practitioners Gunnar Hubbard, Sandra Liebowitz, Jason Wilkinson, Narda Golden, Ross Leventhal, Matthew Swett, and Larry Wikander among them — contributed to the eager, enthusiastic mood of the department

"I was experimenting with rammed earth around that time, so I made a little structure at my house in Eugene and invited students to work on it with me. There they were with rods and sledge hammers, ready to ram earth by hand, and Jason was right in there. It was a great ensemble and a great reminder of just how many kids in that department — Jason being one of them — were leading this charge."

ROBERT PEÑA, UNIVERSITY OF WASHINGTON

> "I was learning about all this cutting-edge stuff and I was learning it directly from the pioneers — the guys I refer to as the 'Solar Rollers.' Even when I wasn't working on projects directly, I was exposed to the ideas through these great professors and visiting lecturers. A lot of this stuff was experimental and didn't work well. But I could see the potential and I kept thinking, 'This has to be the future.'"
>
> **JASON F. MCLENNAN, INTERNATIONAL LIVING FUTURE INSTITUTE**

as a whole. It helped, too, that sustainability discussions spread outward from the campus and into the community, where citizens and builders were equally excited about the concepts being taught in the classroom. Cob cottages, straw bale homes and projects made from other alternative construction approaches were cropping up throughout Eugene. University students, McLennan among them, were paying attention.

ADVOCACY AND LEADERSHIP

McLennan got involved early on with the Solar Energy Center, a collaborative of University of Oregon students and faculty that studied, discussed, experimented with, and built awareness about green building innovations and renewable energy.[12] Although the Center was officially a student group, its educational impact rippled outward from the campus and into the community at large. The Center published a newsletter, stocked a rich resource library, and hosted a well-attended speaker series.

Put in charge of the Center's speaker series as a sophomore, McLennan took advantage of the opportunity to reach out to the trendsetters of his newly adopted movement and bring them to Eugene. The eclectic roster of speakers ranged from photovoltaic technology innovator Steve Strong to Ecological Design Institute founder Sim Van der Ryn. McLennan also added faculty and fellow students to the speaking calendar to create yet another forum where eco-design ideas could be exchanged. (A former Oregon landscape architecture professor by the name of Richard Britz once spoke for the Solar Energy Center. Years later, McLennan commissioned Britz to create a series of cartoons that evolved into the Living Building Challenge Petal icons still being used today.)

12 Fellow students Hubbard, Liebowitz, Wilkinson, Golden, Leventhal, Swett, and Wikander also served as the Solar Energy Center's director at some point during their stints in Eugene.

"When I started designing houses and remodels for people in Eugene, my professors thought I was nuts. But I was both naive and fearless. I was always honest with my clients about what I knew and what I didn't know. They liked that I was hungry and probably that I cost a fraction of what they would pay a more experience professional. But I knew that I had to learn by doing and practicing, not just by reading and dreaming."

JASON F. MCLENNAN, INTERNATIONAL LIVING FUTURE INSTITUTE

McLennan's affiliation with (and eventual leadership of[13]) the Solar Energy Center gave him more than a network of like-minded environmentalists. It also connected him with members of the local community who were willing to give eager students an opportunity to put their ideas to work in the residential sector. McLennan began consulting on small sustainable design jobs in Eugene, helping homeowners green up their remodels and, in some cases, their new construction projects. It helped him pay his living expenses while giving him some real-world experience. Nobody ever told him he was too young to perform such services. He was willing, enthusiastic, and came with good credentials; as long as

"Rob Peña had just joined the faculty and he and I were sharing the lecture load in the department's Environmental Control Systems course. The one not teaching was expected to interrupt, clarify, and make humorous remarks. This was highly technical material dealing with heating, cooling, lighting, acoustics — we joked that if it moves, we teach it — yet at the same time there are heavy social implications about comfort and privacy that go along with these subjects. So there's an opportunity to be technological and sociological. We addressed the triumphs and failings of these buildings and how they related to the subject matter. There weren't a lot of good examples yet, but there were lots of negative ones."

JOHN REYNOLDS, UNIVERSITY OF OREGON

13 McLennan served as co-director of the Solar Energy Center for two years.

"Oregon is interesting because of all of the political and policy-making activity that goes on around here, particularly in Eugene. As president of the Energy Trust of Oregon, I saw it first-hand. It broadens your view because it's not just about numbers. It's about the whole attitude toward promoting conservation. That culture has been alive and well in Eugene since we stopped the nuclear plant in 1970."

JOHN REYNOLDS, UNIVERSITY OF OREGON

"Most schools of architecture, Oregon included, are organized around the design studio. What's different at Oregon is that all of the faculty, whether they teach building science or structures or history, also teach design. So unlike other schools, the design cadre are not a separate group driving the agenda of the school. It's a much more horizontal structure where all faculty are design instructors plus they teach environmental controls, theory, history, and structures. So the culture was different, and more supportive of building science at a high level as opposed to schools with strong technical faculty operating at the perimeter of the school."

ROBERT PEÑA, UNIVERSITY OF WASHINGTON

35 ——

"During my years in Eugene, I was aware of the jarring juxtaposition of what was fashionable in architecture — glass boxes and other really resource-wasteful stuff that appeared on the covers of magazines — and what I was learning about sustainability from these new role models of mine. My passion was really about realigning our relationship with nature and building buildings that fit into the landscape."

JASON F. MCLENNAN, INTERNATIONAL LIVING FUTURE INSTITUTE

"What distinguished Jason, particularly in his later years at Oregon, was this wonderfully inquiring mind. He was just always asking; always seeking."

JOHN REYNOLDS, UNIVERSITY OF OREGON

> "My experience in Glasgow blew my mind. The main professors were all concrete brutalists and not always a very nice group of people. But they were considered the top of the architectural heap. It taught me that there's no sacredness to these so-called experts or in the way things are done."
>
> **JASON F. MCLENNAN,**
> **INTERNATIONAL LIVING FUTURE INSTITUTE**

the customer referrals came in, he continued to take clients. He considered it yet another way to gain experience and experiment with workable green solutions, many of which were still unknown to the general architecture community.

Looking back, those who were in Eugene in the early- to mid-1990s acknowledge that there was something special happening on and around campus with regard to green building. Between the faculty, the students, and the community, there was passion for sustainability and a fervent desire to test conventional boundaries. Some characterize it as a temporary alignment of forces that powerfully propelled people and ideas forward in a manner not seen before or since.

A STUDENT OF THE WORLD

As a fourth-year student, McLennan studied abroad at the Mackintosh School of Architecture at the University of Glasgow. Named after the Scottish architect Charles Rennie Mackintosh, referred to as "the father of Glasgow Style,"[14] the school celebrates its namesake's modern design sensibilities. In the mid-1990s, however, it had not yet embraced the value or importance of sustainability. Instead, it offered McLennan a traditional British education based on what he recalls as a "confrontational, hierarchical" approach — one that stood in stark contrast to the collaborative style of the University of Oregon department.

The North American student challenged his European instructors by introducing environmentally-friendly elements into his work and suggesting that the professors weave similar ideas into the curriculum. While it allowed McLennan to be true to his green principles, the tact did nothing to endear him to the Mackintosh faculty. He received and maintained lower-than-his-usual grades, in spite of (or perhaps because of) his impassioned attempts to convert the department to his way of seeing things. Few of his Mackintosh professors were very interested.

Still, Glasgow itself provided an inspirational backdrop for the official focus of McLennan's study abroad: urban theory.[15] McLennan intensely studied the city — its back alleys, its

14 www.crmsociety.com (the Charles Rennie Mackintosh Society)

15 McLennan received an Urban Theory Certificate for successful completion of the course.

Glasgow, Scotland

architecture, its infrastructure, its culture. As the former "second city of the empire" and future European City of Design, it had a great deal to teach.

During breaks from school, he backpacked throughout the continent and studied the design and layout of some of Europe's oldest cities. Immersing himself in Paris, London, Amsterdam, Berlin, and Barcelona allowed him to look at how centuries-old buildings behave and serve people within the context of the grand cities in which they stand. He was curious about how and why certain urban structures endure, and in what ways a great city's built environment can best serve people and the planet simultaneously. Europe showed him that architects and planners are capable not just of building cities, but also of delivering beauty and inspiration to the communities they support. Many of McLennan's ideas around Living Communities were born at this time.

"Jason was one of many students who were wildly enthusiastic about a career and a future dedicated to a built environment that doesn't harm people or the planet. In that regard, he was not a stand-out. What did distinguish him was a certain kind of earnestness and a kind of 'why not' attitude and, in some ways, a lack of pragmatism. Other students look at the other side of an issue, saying, 'I see why we can't do that.' But Jason had a kind of naivety; he didn't look on the other side and say 'that can't be done.' There was an unabashedness about him."

ROBERT PEÑA, UNIVERSITY OF WASHINGTON

A PROPHETIC FINAL PROJECT

When he returned to Eugene for the final phase of his college tenure, McLennan worked closely with Professor Robert Peña, who was then one of Oregon's younger faculty members and later joined the architecture department at the University of Washington.[16] Peña advised McLennan on assigned work and helped him get class credit for independent extracurricular work.

Ultimately, Peña oversaw McLennan's thesis studio (referred to at Oregon as a terminal studio), the last and most substantial requirement of the five-year professional degree. The assignment was to design an environmental resource center and McLennan was determined to create a truly sustainable building. He didn't know it at the time, but he was conceptualizing a structure that would now qualify as a Living Building. He incorporated into the design everything he had learned about sustainability up to that point: net zero energy, water independence, and local non-toxic materials. The deeper he got into the project, the more it became clear to him that this was all he ever wanted to do with his career. Nothing less than the deepest green designs would suit him.

16 Peña was instrumental in the creation of Seattle's Bullitt Center, the first office building to achieve Living Building status. More information on the Bullitt Center is included in Chapter 13.

POMP AND CIRCUMSTANCE

Upon graduation from the University of Oregon in 1997, McLennan faced what many recent graduates do: the great unknown of post-college life. As focused and driven as he was as an enrolled student, he had no specific career plans in place when school ended because he did not want to compromise. He knew he wanted to put his architecture education to work, but the industry did not yet offer many opportunities for deep green practitioners and he simply was not interested in conventional practice. While researching his options, he stayed in Eugene and continued consulting with local clients.

The idea of how best to pursue his passion without diluting it nagged at him. There had to be a way, he told himself, to bring together the various innovations and grassroots efforts to which he had been exposed so they could be integrated and employed on a grander scale. He did not just want to design buildings; he wanted to change the industry. He was inspired even by the many failed attempts at greener approaches that had been introduced since the 1970s, as they yielded crucial data that could ultimately guide the concepts toward successful implementation.

He kept returning to a single reality: the design and construction industry was a major contributor to the planet's ecological decline. In order to move the industry toward greener solutions, there needed to be a more elegant and inspiring paradigm from which to build. There needed to be a new vision that would ask more of architects, engineers, planners, and clients. How, though, could an idealistic 20-something make a real and lasting difference?

The answer came in the form of a phone call from Kansas City in the early summer of 1997. Things were about to change drastically for one young architect and for the green building movement at large.

STARTING WITH THE END GAME

A LIVING BUILDING BLOCK

40

The Living Building Challenge clearly defines its end goal — a truly regenerative built environment — and leaves it up to the genius of each project team to determine how best to get there. There is no prescriptive path; no single rigid set of steps laid out or checklist to meet — only high-reaching performance requirements. The destination is the only fixed element and it provides an unwavering guidepost for course corrections through the design process.

The Living Building Challenge clearly defines its end goal — a truly regenerative built environment — and leaves it up to the genius of each project team to determine how best to get there.

This "end game" approach does more than allow for innovation — it requires it. Teams adjust and "tack" to the destination as they go to stay true to their projects' missions. Jason F. McLennan is fond of using a sailing ship as a metaphor to explain the concept: If one stands on shore watching a vessel approach, it can appear from that vantage point to be traveling directly toward land. But unless the ship itself has its sights set on a specific onshore target, it can easily wander far off course due to navigational variations of only a few degrees. Without a definite marker guiding it toward where it wants to end up, it veers. Those steering the ship must know where they are going and take the longer view.

Many Living Building project teams incorporate "backcasting" to support this philosophy. Pioneered in the context of sustainable design by The Natural Step, backcasting is a planning tool that begins with the end in mind then asks, "Moving backward from that successful outcome to the present, what steps must be taken?" In reverse order, a plan emerges that suits the specific characteristics of a project.

Keeping the end game in clear view provides a reference point to identify what success looks like.

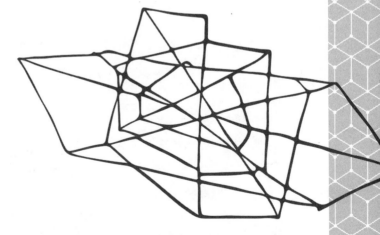

03

"Choose a goal that seems right for you and strive to be the best, however hard the path. Aim high. Behave honorably. Prepare to be alone at times, and to endure failure. Persist! The world needs all you can give."

E. O. WILSON

GETTING TO WORK
A FIELD OF OPPORTUNITIES

No exploration of Jason F. McLennan's work would be complete without mention of Bob Berkebile. While McLennan is the author of the Living Building Challenge, it could be argued that Berkebile provided the figurative pen and paper.

Throughout the 1990s, Berkebile watched with interest as the University of Oregon Department of Architecture was gradually changing its academic model, transitioning its students to more sustainable approaches. As a founding partner of Kansas City-based Berkebile Nelson Immenschuh McDowell, Inc. (BNIM), Berkebile was considered the spiritual leader of what was still a fledgling green design movement. (In spite of valiant efforts by the movement's 1970s pioneers, there was virtually no green design activity in the decade that followed. Berkebile was one of the industry's few notables who used his voice to try to regain some sustainable momentum in the 1990s.)

In 1997, BNIM initiated a national search to populate the firm with like-minded practitioners. Specifically, they sought an associate to join Berkebile's team; someone who would work closely with him on the firm's modest but promising sustainability practice. BNIM cast a wide recruitment net to look everywhere potential new hires might be, but focused on the places where a higher concentration of suitably green candidates might be found.

Berkebile reached out to Oregon faculty member Robert Peña, who provided him with several names, McLennan's among them. Alongside overviews of the students' academic achievements, Peña gave Berkebile a sense of each young architect's passion for environmentalism and a summary of his or her practical sustainable design experience. McLennan's qualifications quickly elevated him to the top tier of Berkebile's list of prospects. After the requisite interview process, all of which occurred over the phone, BNIM formally added McLennan to its ranks. He moved sight unseen to Kansas City in July 1997 and went straight to work (in a position he describes as "right hand man to Bob's right hand man").

McLennan and Berkebile immediately forged a strong bond; McLennan found an inspirational mentor while Berkebile found an eager protégé. They quickly discovered important parallels in their lives that influenced them personally and professionally. Both studied under dynamic teachers (McLennan with the earliest pioneers in sustainability who served as faculty and guest lecturers at the University of Oregon, and Berkebile with the great Buckminster Fuller himself in the early 1960s).[17] Both felt their work was more a calling than a job. And both felt an urgent sense of responsibility to change the nature of architecture.

INFORMED BY TRAGEDY

Much of Berkebile's drive stemmed from a single devastating episode that abruptly changed the course of his career 16 years before he ever met McLennan. One night in July 1981, Berkebile's work got extremely personal when two skywalks collapsed at the Kansas City Hyatt Regency, a structure he designed. When the dust settled, 114 people were dead and 216 were injured — many of whom Berkebile personally carried out of the building after rushing to the scene to help with rescue efforts. Although the accident was shown to have been caused by

"The accident at the Hyatt changed my career and my life in many ways. When I was recovering from the experience of that long night helping the rescue team, important questions came up. The first was: Did I kill all of these people? Once that was answered, the one that emerged and challenged me was: What is the real impact of our designs on the people we intend to serve?"

BOB BERKEBILE, BNIM

17 This thread reappeared when the Living Building Challenge won the 2012 Buckminster Fuller Challenge, called "Socially Responsible Design's Highest Award." For more information on the award, see Chapter 12.

Laura Lesniewski, Bob Berkebile, Jason F. McLennan, and Skip Backus at the Omega Institute

"When Jason got to BNIM, I discovered right away his energetic, inquisitive mind. He asked more questions than his contemporaries... and I liked that."

BOB BERKEBILE, BNIM

a grievous engineering error, not an architectural problem, the incident haunted Berkebile. He began to consider the various ways buildings affect people; the actual human and environmental consequences of design, engineering, and construction decisions.

Following the accident, Berkebile started to shift the focus of his practice and gradually helped redefine the culture of BNIM. As Berkebile transitioned to a new way of thinking, his work would forever more seek to align the business of architecture with what he refers to as "the eternal truth that emerges within each of us."[18] In the context of his architecture practice, Berkebile interpreted the eternal truth as environmentally, socially, and culturally responsible design.

18 Berkebile credits Leon Shenandoah, head of the Six Nations of the Iroquois Confederacy, with introducing him to this concept. Shenandoah, elevated to Tadadaho or "chief of chiefs" of the confederacy in 1969, met Berkebile during the difficult time immediately following the Hyatt accident. The chief counseled him not to get so engaged in distracting background noise (including advice offered by well-meaning advisors) that he would be unable to hear the eternal truth.

TAKING THE MESSAGE TO THE INDUSTRY

Berkebile got increasingly interested in and vocal about new design approaches throughout the years following the Hyatt incident. By 1990, he was an American Institute of Architects (AIA) leader and an outspoken environmental advocate calling for industry-wide change. Berkebile served as the first chairman (from 1990 to 1992) of the AIA Committee on the Environment (COTE) national advisory group. In 1993, Berkebile was instrumental in helping form the U.S. Green Building Council (USGBC), led by David Gottfried, Rick Fedrizzi, and Mike Italiano. By March 2000, Berkebile was one of many professionals across the disciplines who were responsible for introducing the USGBC's flagship initiative: the Leadership in Energy and Environmental Design (LEED) green building rating and certification system.

LEED is an unquestionably important aspect of the Living Building Challenge story, mostly because of the ground it helped to break. With LEED, the USGBC distributed a standard that tested the industry's interest in green. It codified goals related to energy and water efficiency, responsible materials sourcing, sustainable sites, indoor quality, and other categories. In all of those ways, LEED was a crucial and necessary advancement. But for purists like McLennan, whose sustainable design career was in full swing and who had already begun experimenting with the even greener concept of Living Buildings by the time LEED hit the market, the standard just wasn't enough. It seemed antithetical to the thinking, he felt, and it provided a flawed set of solutions.

But before there was LEED and before anyone could form an opinion about it, there was a recent architecture school graduate starting a new job at a firm in Kansas City.

> "I remember Bob asking me to read over an early draft of LEED Version 1.0. It was interesting, and in the end we got behind it because it was generally the right idea from a business perspective — to get an industry moving in the right direction. But it was entirely the wrong philosophical approach to getting us where we ultimately needed to go."
>
> JASON F. MCLENNAN,
> INTERNATIONAL LIVING FUTURE INSTITUTE

THE NEW EMPLOYEE

Upon joining BNIM in the summer of 1997, McLennan was placed on any of the firm's projects that had even the slightest green components. While the sustainability practice was steadily growing, it represented a small fraction of BNIM's overall billings. Still, McLennan shadowed Berkebile and Berkebile's so-called "right hand man," Chris Kelsey, on every job. McLennan was young and had virtually no professional experience, but he was passionate

> "When Chris Kelsey announced he was leaving BNIM, he placed a pile of papers on my desk and said, 'Well, it's up to you now. Good luck.' I was completely underqualified from an experience perspective, but I did have several years of sustainability training in college, which was more than most people had at that point. And *how* I thought was the differentiator."
>
> **JASON F. MCLENNAN, INTERNATIONAL LIVING FUTURE INSTITUTE**

and devoted to the cause. Six months after McLennan joined BNIM, Kelsey left the firm. The vacancy allowed McLennan unfettered access to Berkebile. He relished the proximity.

Berkebile had no qualms about thrusting McLennan directly into any and all projects that called for — or could potentially incorporate — a sustainable approach. It was where Berkebile wanted to take the firm and it was unquestionably where McLennan wanted to be. Within just a few months of the young associate's arrival, Berkebile had him working nearly full-time on a particular project in Montana: one that would prove to change the careers of most of the people involved, would bring together the future leaders of the green design movement, and serve as the breeding ground for the Living Building Challenge.

BIG SKY COUNTRY

By the time McLennan joined BNIM, the firm had been involved in a revolutionary endeavor on the Bozeman campus of Montana State University for a few years. With the help of a $1.2 million grant from the National Institute of Standards and Technology, the university was asked to identify cutting-edge green building technologies, establish research goals to study them further, and hand-pick a team to design and build a 10,000 square foot building where the ideas could be tested and demonstrated. The project was overseen by the esteemed Kath Williams, a sustainability visionary whose resume would later include top leadership roles at the USGBC and the World Green Building Council.

Dubbed the EPICenter (Educational Performance and Innovation Center), the building was meant to be a structural laboratory for sustainable design and engineering. The goal was to create a building that operated like an organism; one that fit into and coexisted with its environment by being self-sustaining, non-toxic, and beautiful.

Berkebile's leadership of the EPICenter team was practical, historical, spiritual, and motivational. He reminded his colleagues that they were working in the very region where Lewis and Clark had traveled nearly 200 years earlier, and he wanted the EPICenter to recapture the pristine nature of the Gallatin Valley as it may have been during the explorers' early 19th-century journey. Readings from *The Journals of Meriwether Lewis and William Clark* opened up most design charrettes, which was motivating and alarming at the same time as their descriptions of the valley provided important evidence that humans had radically altered the face of the place in the intervening years. If that was true on the relatively undisturbed Montana landscape, Berkebile argued, then it was true everywhere. It was up to this team, if not all design-build teams, to find a way to change this pattern by rethinking the systems at work in the built environment.

"I began finding alignment between what I'd earlier thought was design intuition and these new ideas of doing the right thing, which informed my actions and the things I was doing for the firm. I was operating on that new energy and insight when I met Jason. He was younger than a lot of the people I shared these ideas with, so he didn't have as much life experience but he was more open to the potential of it. The more senior professionals I talked to about it saw all the reasons why it couldn't or wouldn't happen. They'd say, 'Great idea, but we could never do this.' But Jason said, 'Great idea; now how should we do this?'"

BOB BERKEBILE, BNIM

"The BNIM team leaders ... knew what the Latin term Plus Ultra meant ... and pushed every concept in that direction. Once Jason McLennan joined BNIM, the push became a shove. It was: identify the state of the art, find the barriers, and move beyond."[20]

**KATH WILLIAMS,
KATH WILLIAMS + ASSOCIATES**

Berkebile also introduced the concept of "Plus Ultra" (Latin for "more, beyond") to guide the EPICenter team toward goals that had never before been established in the built environment. It became both the mantra and the methodology of the project. Fundamental to the Plus Ultra philosophy was the coming together of all the disciplines and stakeholders — architects, engineers, landscape architects, scientists, community members, government representatives, and others — to enable joint discussion and decision making regarding the design of the building and it systems.[19]

19 Today, this group approach is much more common; integrated design is written into the Living Building Challenge.

20 From Williams' "Pioneering the Living Building" published in EDC Magazine.

"When people ask, 'What would it mean for a city to function like a forest?' the answer should be an actual metric, not just a metaphor. You start by comparing the city to a reference habitat — the closest and healthiest native ecosystem you can find. A biologist can tell you how many tons of carbon are being stored per acre, how many liters of water and air are being purified, how many inches of soil are being built, how many degrees of cooling is occurring, and so on. This generous outpouring of services is happening right next door, so you know it's possible for the city to match or exceed it. Then, to collect design ideas, you ask the organisms that live there, 'How do you clean the water here, store water, build soil, hold soil, cool the air, clean the air, etcetera?' We call this catalogue of best practices the "Genius of Place," and it's truly vernacular. As a process, biomimicry references nature not just as measure, but as model and mentor too. The outcome is a generous city and an evolutionary leap. When our cities are functionally indistinguishable from the wildlands next door, we'll finally be home. We'll be a welcome species in our watersheds."

JANINE BENYUS, BIOMIMICRY 3.8

Indeed, the EPICenter was aptly named, as it brought together a group of people who are now recognized internationally as the movement's best and brightest; the visionaries at its very core. In addition to Kath Williams, Berkebile, and McLennan, the EPICenter was touched to some degree by such notables as Pliny Fisk III, Gail Vittori, Ron Perkins, Peter Rumsey, Phaedra Svec, Greg Norris,[21] David Gottfried, John Todd, and Steve Selkowitz. Janine Benyus, whose trailblazing 1997 book, *Biomimicry: Innovation Inspired by Nature*, had made an enormous impression on both Berkebile and McLennan, served as a sort of inspirational guide on the site. Even actress Jane Fonda, who owned property nearby, got into the act by visiting the site on occasion. It was a community of thinkers whose powerful ideas were made even more potent by the spirit of collaboration. McLennan refers to most of these practitioners and advocates as among his own greatest mentors.

21 Greg Norris joined the International Living Future Institute in 2014 as Chief Scientist, and played an instrumental role in the development of the Living Product Challenge.

Many of those involved directly or indirectly in the Bozeman project also had a hand in forming early drafts of LEED. In fact, the EPICenter helped influence LEED's language related to the initial materials radius credit (500 miles from any project) and it eventually served as a pilot project for LEED Version 1.0 (well before that building standard was broadly recognized by the industry).

The complete story of the EPICenter is complex and nicely detailed elsewhere.[22] In the context of how the Living Building Challenge came to be, the EPICenter project is significant because of its primary goal: to be the first truly sustainable building ever designed. It did nothing less than inspire the philosophical framework of what evolved into the world's greenest building standard. The EPICenter team was actually designing a Living Building nearly a decade before the Challenge was formally introduced.

> "At the EPICenter, all of us were really learning together about what it actually means to make a truly sustainable building. There had been early ideas like the Integral Urban House,[23] but nothing of the EPICenter's size had ever been considered before."
>
> **JASON F. MCLENNAN,**
> **INTERNATIONAL LIVING FUTURE INSTITUTE**

McLennan arrived on the EPICenter site at a critical time, infusing new energy into the project when the original team was beginning to feel fatigued by the process. His primary job was to oversee the project's sustainability aspects, although he wanted to know as much as he could about every aspect of the effort. He researched systems, reached out to people he knew (such as his contacts at Oregon's Solar Energy Center) who could weigh in on possible strategies, and engaged scientists researching new technologies that might apply to the project. He and Berkebile stayed up late talking about the social and economic systems that were damaging the environmental health in the Gallatin Valley and how they might be able to modify them to create better outcomes.[24] They even tried to rethink how to put local mining byproducts to better use as locally harvested building materials — some of the first use of flyash in concrete on any project.

50

22 See McLennan's *The Philosophy of Sustainable Design* and Kath William's article, "Montana's EPICenter: Pioneering the Living Building."

23 Sim Van der Ryn's 1970s experimental self-reliant urban homestead in Berkeley, California.

24 Berkebile jokes that McLennan arranged to have them stay in adjacent rooms at the bed-and-breakfast where the design team was housed so that he could pepper his mentor with questions hours after the workday ended. They would stay up sometimes until 3:00 a.m. discussing issues of sustainable design, then have to return to the job site first thing in the morning.

"As it turns out, we ended up doing all of the Living Building Challenge Petals at the EPICenter. Had the building gotten built, it would have ended up being the first Living Building. It would have been amazing."

JASON F. MCLENNAN, INTERNATIONAL LIVING FUTURE INSTITUTE

"With the EPICenter project, we were taking a big risk and we were getting pretty far out there. But ever since then, the way the industry refers to that project is like the building did happen. People think of it as the root of the Living Building Challenge, even though it never got built. It showed that it's possible to stretch."

KATH WILLIAMS, KATH WILLIAMS + ASSOCIATES

"All those people who ended up creating USGBC and launching LEED and those of us who went on to create the Living Building Challenge — we all tested these ideas in the soup that was being created in Bozeman mostly over the breakfasts, dinners, and beers that were had before or after the workday for that project."

JASON F. MCLENNAN, INTERNATIONAL LIVING FUTURE INSTITUTE

"There were several elements of the EPICenter project that made it way ahead of its time. One was a real understanding of regionalism — from a material sense, a byproduct sense, and the use of local academic and business know-how. Also, we were able to implement cutting-edge research related to global warming and materials issues and apply it as a model for the nation. A third thing, which was very profound, was that Jason and I began to map out cycles of life within the building. It was the first time that happened on that kind of structure. It was cool."

PLINY FISK III, CENTER FOR MAXIMUM POTENTIAL BUILDING SYSTEMS

Eventually, the EPICenter got bogged down by political, bureaucratic, and funding issues. The building itself was never built. However, the people who helped conceive of it and the movement they were establishing while doing so were forever changed by the experience. The EPICenter challenged a group of professionals to push past real and perceived barriers in sustainable design; it proved that changes were possible; it planted theoretical seeds.

A GRAND DESIGN

During the same timeframe, a second so-called failure provided McLennan with critical experience he would call on later when working to convince the industry that nothing is impossible when it comes to environmentally-friendly design innovations.

As BNIM's work in Bozeman continued, the firm was hired to design Canyon Forest Village, a 272-acre model sustainable mixed-use community near the Grand Canyon that would feature affordable housing, retail, hotel accommodations, a medical facility, fire and sheriff substations, a school, and other community amenities. McLennan was named the project manager and project lead in Arizona while still actively working on the EPICenter. Focusing on both endeavors at once gave him an opportunity to test ideas at two scales simultaneously.

"Canyon Forest Village really influenced my thinking about water systems. It was all about, 'If we can do net zero water in the desert, why couldn't we do it everywhere?'"

JASON F. MCLENNAN,
INTERNATIONAL LIVING FUTURE INSTITUTE

Canyon Forest Village, like EPICenter before it, was a LEED Version 1.0 Pilot Project and was the first project that attempted to apply LEED principles beyond the scale of a single building. Notably, Canyon Forest Village was to be designed as a water-independent community on the semi-arid Colorado Plateau in northwestern Arizona. In other words, it would have been an eco-district before that concept even existed.

The BNIM team conducted then-revolutionary research into how to reach net zero goals for water, energy, and waste at scale across multiple building types in a challenging climate. On paper, their calculations worked.

Although, once again, politics eventually prevented it from moving past the conceptual stage, Canyon Forest Village gave McLennan yet more evidence that these ideas were possible. Sustainability, even on the community level and even in harsh desert conditions, was feasible.

"Bob was so generous in introducing me to all the leading thinkers. I had 30 mentors at once, all influencing my thinking around what was possible. We were all fighting together to keep this idea of sustainability alive, since it wasn't considered very cool at that time."

JASON F. MCLENNAN, INTERNATIONAL LIVING FUTURE INSTITUTE

AN IDEA THAT CONTINUED TO GROW

Between the EPICenter and Canyon Forest Village — as well as dozens of other BNIM projects that successfully incorporated individual high-performance systems that did get built — McLennan was earning what he calls his "virtual Ph.D." in green design and systems thinking. Although neither EPICenter nor Canyon Forest Village took physical shape, each was akin to a practicum. Both got him thinking more about combining design and engineering strategies into a comprehensive system that supported larger environmental goals. He kept coming back to the idea of biological organisms, their systemic interdependencies, and their performance efficiencies.

"I didn't have an architecture chapter in *Biomimicry* (I started to write one, but there were space limitations), so it was interesting to me that so many architects picked up on it. Bob Berkebile was the second person ever to ask me to speak on the subject. (Jane Jacobs was first.) I addressed the AIA Committee on the Environment in October 1999 — the same month Bob and Jason's piece in *The World and I*[25] came out. I remember everyone fell very, very silent afterwards and then rushed to their feet like a whoosh. When Bob spoke the next day, he held up scribbled sheets of yellow legal paper and said he had completely rewritten his talk to incorporate what he heard. I remember feeling that biomimicry had found its home community."

JANINE BENYUS, BIOMIMICRY 3.8

McLennan had studied and admired John Todd's waste-treating Living Machines as a college student, but he was always bothered by the name. He was drawn to the term "living," but felt that having the word "machine" describe a biomimicking system was wrong, and struck him as yet another moniker that catered to a mid-century paradigm. Entire buildings, he believed, were capable of functioning as efficiently and self-sufficiently as biological organisms themselves. McLennan considered Janine Benyus' work on biomimicry to be profound and definitive, although he (and Berkebile also) wondered why she had omitted architecture from her first book on the subject. She included chapters on how energy, food, and business could factor into a biomimetic future — but said nothing about the built environment.

On a growing number of completed BNIM projects, several individual performance systems were operating successfully. And if the Montana and Arizona projects had moved from paper to three dimensions, they would have been the first structures to "live" with all systems working in concert with one another. Better than living machines, why couldn't there be living buildings? Why couldn't sustainable design be cast in a biological rather than a technological light?

The best way to describe the ideal high-performing, self-sufficient, beautifully inspirational structure was to refer to it as a Living Building.

PUTTING WORDS TO PAPER

The more he ruminated over the idea, the more eager McLennan was to spread the word about Living Buildings. He began to organize his thoughts in writing, outlining early drafts of a document that captured the underlying philosophy of Living Buildings and summarized all their necessary performance areas. In addition, McLennan and Berkebile promoted the idea of Living Buildings to any project teams that would listen.

McLennan and Berkebile co-authored several articles on the topic that appeared in national architecture and engineering trade journals. After a piece was published by the American Council for an Energy-Efficient Economy (ACEEE), McLennan was asked to address that organization's 1998 conference in Monterey, California and speak to a live audience about the Living Building concept. During a break in conference activities, McLennan took a walk on the beach. There in the dunes, buffeted by wind, sand, and salt, were carpets of bright purple flowers. These hardy blooms grew in abundance up and down the coastline in spite of terribly inhospitable conditions. This natural species, McLennan marveled, found a way not merely to exist but to thrive. He decided that this diminutive flower would serve

25 More information on this article appears later in this chapter.

> "Jason came to me early on and said, 'I want to be doing what you're doing; I want to be a national voice.' I told him it would take time, but it was possible, and he was all over that. I took him to conferences but he was too young to get a keynote spot. Sometimes I could negotiate with organizers to get Jason included with me on presentations. So there was a bridge period when we were billed as 'Bob with Jason.' But it didn't take long before it was equal billing, and not long after that I got to go back to doing what I loved to do and he was the road warrior."
>
> **BOB BERKEBILE, BNIM**

as the symbolic depiction — the mascot — of Living Buildings.[26] Like the philosophy it would represent, the flower was resilient and beautiful.

The following year, McLennan and Berkebile received a swell of attention for "The Living Building," another co-authored article that ran in *The World and I Journal* in October 1999. There, in addition to painting a portrait of the Living philosophy, they offered up what they respectfully suggested was the content missing from Benyus' *Biomimicry* — the chapter devoted to architecture. The hugely positive post-article response led to more invitations to write and speak and helped broaden the awareness. It also strengthened the men's resolve to pitch the Living Building concept to as many clients as possible. It was still considered revolutionary — impossible, even — but McLennan and Berkebile were undeterred by any skepticism they encountered. They considered all forms of feedback to be valuable, as it helped answer outstanding technical questions and hone the underlying message.

Now all that was needed were a few Living laboratories where the concept could be taken past the theoretical stage and put to the actual test.

55

26 Later, the flower mascot used for the Living Building Challenge was changed to a gerbera daisy, but the symbolism of the small but sturdy bloom remains.

RECOGNIZING THE TRUE LEADERS

A LIVING BUILDING BLOCK

As the green building movement first gained popularity and became more mainstream, it became difficult to distinguish those who were accomplishing real change from those who were simply claiming to be green because it was fashionable to do so. Promotional "greenwashing" efforts suddenly touted everyone's commitment to sustainability, but it wasn't always easy to find data that proved authentic achievement. The movement's celebrated practitioners and projects were sometimes those with the deeper marketing pockets rather than those with better actual performance.

As an extremely rigorous, performance-oriented, third-party-validated program, the Living Building Challenge was designed to eliminate the possibility of greenwashing and to focus attention on the most substantive areas of potential environmental impact. Projects either achieve all the Petal Imperatives to become a Living Building or they don't. The same is true for the people who design, engineer, and build them. Energy engineer Peter Rumsey is fond of quoting William Edwards Deming, who said, "In God we trust, all others bring data."

This objective framework based on proof, measurement, and inspection reveals the true leaders who innovate their way forward and emboldens them to push ahead toward whatever solutions their next projects might require them to discover. The pioneers help the entire industry understand what genuine success looks like. They illuminate the path, pulling others into the light with every step forward.

"In God we trust, all others bring data."
WILLIAM EDWARDS DEMING

04

"All things are possible until
they are proven impossible."

PEARL S. BUCK

TESTING GROUNDS

SMALL SIGNIFICANT SUCCESSES

After EPICenter and Canyon Forest Village came to an end, Jason F. McLennan and Bob Berkebile were acutely aware of what those projects *might* have been; the many ways in which they could have demonstrated the viability of Living Building concepts. They did not want to see all of that knowledge wasted. McLennan in particular was determined to find other opportunities to apply Living Building principles — not just to improve single buildings, but to elevate the entire industry.

McLennan came up with an idea to create a new business unit that would allow BNIM to guide other firms toward green design solutions. He wanted to establish a sustainability consulting division that would work side-by-side with architects, engineers, and developers to "green up" their work. He wrote up a business plan, pitched it to Berkebile and BNIM's other senior partners, and convinced them it would be both financially and environmentally valuable for the firm.

ELEMENTS OF CHANGE

In 2000, McLennan was named the founding head of Elements, a new division of BNIM that he pitched to the partners via an unsolicited but convincing business plan. It was unconventional at that time for an architecture firm to offer consulting services to benefit its competitors (as well as its own in-house teams still getting up to speed on sustainable design), but it illustrated how strongly BNIM felt about preaching the green gospel and how hungry the industry suddenly was for such expertise. McLennan was influenced by the Rocky Mountain Institute's[27] green consulting division run by Bill Browning — the first example of an organization providing such services to its industry counterparts (although not as an architecture firm). Indeed, within a few short years, many firms followed suit with their own sustainability consulting divisions as demand for green design began to rise.

Through Elements, McLennan was involved, either directly or indirectly, in many of the cutting-edge projects that hit the market in the early 2000s. In addition to influencing BNIM's portfolio, he also weighed in on projects being developed by other firms around the country. These various interactions allowed McLennan to help numerous designers, engineers, and planners put environmentally-friendly systems into place. Both the State of California and the City of Seattle asked Elements to consult on green issues, which put McLennan at the forefront of the strategic sustainability planning process.

> "Jason proposed the idea of Elements, was its founding director, led the effort, and grew the team. It was a way for him to accelerate his learning and to develop the tools and the skills for the entire firm to do a better job of systems design on all our projects."
>
> **BOB BERKEBILE, BNIM**

(Interestingly, the Seattle work introduced him to Amanda Sturgeon, who served as that city's sustainable building specialist from 2002 to 2005. She first met McLennan and learned of the Living Building concept when he presented Elements' capabilities to her team. It was the beginning of a strong professional connection, as Sturgeon was a founding board member of the Cascadia Green Building Council and would cross paths with McLennan again when he interviewed for his position there in 2006. In 2010, she formally joined McLennan on the Living Building Challenge team, eventually rising through several positions until she was named CEO of the International Living Future Institute in 2016.[28] Sturgeon's impact on the movement, the Challenge, and the Institute is covered in more detail in later chapters.)

---

27 The Rocky Mountain Institute was co-founded by Amory B. Lovins, with whom McLennan would later collaborate on the Packard Sustainability Matrix and who occupies a prominent spot on McLennan's roster of mentors.

28 When she and McLennan first worked together, Sturgeon introduced him to Bainbridge Island — the naturally beautiful small town where she and her family lived just 35 minutes by ferry from downtown Seattle. When McLennan came to the region from Kansas City in 2006, he and his wife also chose to set down roots on Bainbridge Island.

"We were proposing stuff that Bob and I were mostly envisioning but had not yet done anywhere, but we'd present ideas with a straight face and people would take them seriously because Bob was pitching them. And people usually said yes to Bob. His gravitas got any crazy idea considered, including mine. After meetings, I'd ask him how the hell we were going to do these things, and he'd say, 'God, I don't know! It's up to you to figure it out, and I have confidence in you.' It was all about not being afraid to fail and believing that change is possible. That's the underlying philosophy I later wrote into the Living Building Challenge and it has some of Bob's incredible spirit baked in."

JASON F. MCLENNAN, INTERNATIONAL LIVING FUTURE INSTITUTE

One by one, for structures of all kinds built in various climate zones, these projects began to prove the viability of the Living Building concepts. Whether through responsible site selections, net zero energy or water strategies, locally harvested materials, naturally ventilated interior spaces, or the simple incorporation of beauty into a green design, McLennan could see his Living Building ideal taking shape in pieces. Projects were finally demonstrating elements of Living Building design with true restorative qualities, just as he knew they could — one strategy, one idea, one performance area at a time. It was only a matter of time before a single project would be able to incorporate them all.

WORKING EXAMPLES

Among the projects that came to life during that time were these selections, noted because of one or more of their deep green features that tested Living Building principles:

ANITA B. GORMAN CONSERVATION DISCOVERY CENTER, KANSAS CITY, MO: This BNIM design for the Missouri Department of Conservation incorporated multiple sustainable features, the most dramatic of which was a water capture and waste treatment system inspired by John Todd's Living Machine and designed by 2020 Engineering.[29] Elegant and efficient,

---

29 Mark Buehrer, owner of 2020 Engineering, would go on to serve on the boards of the Cascadia Green Building Council and the International Living Future Institute.

"I paid attention to a lot of examples that had to do with water, like things Pliny Fisk III was doing with rainwater collection in Texas and other places. These things showed me anything was possible in any climate, as long as you design appropriate to time and place. As long as you think like a flower."

JASON F. MCLENNAN, INTERNATIONAL LIVING FUTURE INSTITUTE

the strategy was one of BNIM's earliest aspirations toward net zero water and a certain inspiration for what would later become the Living Building Challenge's Water Petal.

UNIVERSITY OF TEXAS, HOUSTON, TX: Several projects on the University of Texas campus achieved LEED Platinum status (with certain features that came close to Living Building standards) while also winning prestigious design awards. These buildings, designed through a partnership between BNIM and Lake|Flato Architects, were among the first to demonstrate that high performance and beauty could coexist; that one need not diminish the other.

MISSOURI DEPARTMENT OF NATURAL RESOURCES, JEFFERSON CITY, MO: This 100,000 square foot state office building, whose design began in 2002 and whose doors opened in 2005, achieved LEED Platinum status with zero cost premium. It proved that effective design and engineering decisions made through an integrated process could yield the highest levels of performance within real-world budget parameters. McLennan used this project's data to ask the important question, "If LEED Platinum can be built for the same amount of money as a traditional building, isn't it time to move beyond it?"

HEIFER INTERNATIONAL HEADQUARTERS, LITTLE ROCK, AR: McLennan served as lead sustainability consultant for this 94,000 square foot office building, which was initiated in 2000 and first occupied in 2006. He coordinated the design and planning efforts of the project's architects and engineers, none of whom had any previous green experience (other than Peter Rumsey, who mentored the engineering team alongside McLennan). Together, the team produced an elegant high performing building with sophisticated systems that eventually earned LEED Platinum status and multiple design awards.

"The success of the Heifer International building helped me understand that the market was ready. With the proper coaching and tools, we could really transform the design process past what a lot of people were thinking."

JASON F. MCLENNAN, INTERNATIONAL LIVING FUTURE INSTITUTE

GREEN DIRT FARM, WESTON, MO: Perhaps the most significant testing ground for Living Building concepts was Green Dirt Farm outside of Kansas City. Working side-by-side with fellow architect Chris DeVolder, McLennan embarked on what he now calls a "Living Building lab before there was even a Living Building Challenge." The house and barn he was asked to create for Green Dirt's eager and courageous owners, Sarah Hoffmann and John Spertus, allowed him to test how Living Building ideas worked in concert with one another. The relatively small scale of the project also gave McLennan total design control, which allowed for greater flexibility than a larger structure with a deeper roster of players. By the time the job was complete, the structures were designed to be water- and energy-independent, built from locally sourced and reclaimed materials, laid out to nurture family togetherness, and crafted to honor the Missouri River bioregion.

63

Green Dirt Farm, Weston, MO

THE PACKARD SUSTAINABILITY MATRIX

Amid all of the BNIM projects, all of the Elements consulting, all of the Berkebile/McLennan speaking engagements, and all of the preaching about sustainable design, there was one assignment that yielded the most tangible, credible, quantifiable evidence regarding the value of Living Buildings.

Building For Sustainability: **Sustainability Matrix**

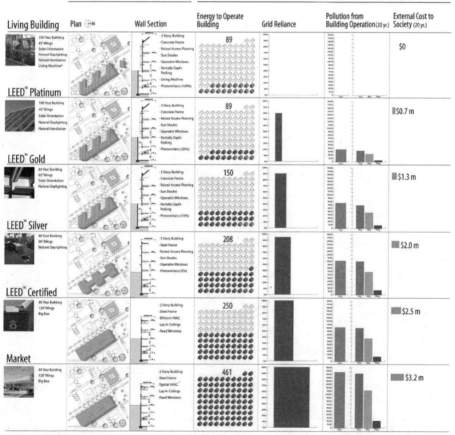

In the spring of 2001, BNIM was invited to bid on the design of a new 90,000 square foot headquarters building for the David and Lucile Packard Foundation in Los Altos, California. The Foundation had followed the firm's progress on the EPICenter job and was interested in incorporating as many green elements as possible into its new main offices. Berkebile and McLennan felt confident that most, if not all, of the concepts they had experimented with in Bozeman could succeed on the Packard job, given the client's demonstrated support of environmental solutions. They assembled a team, which included Kevin Hydes, then CEO of Vancouver-based KEEN Engineering.

Schedules

- ■ = Additional Research
- ■ = Design
- ■ = Construction

Short and Long Term Costs

All of these figures are based on cost estimates created for each conceptual building model. All costs shown have been adjusted from actual cost estimates to reflect a $10 million Market Building as a baseline. The Net Present Values indicated represent 30-, 60- and 100 year cost models that are based on 5% cost of capital, 1-1/2% inflation rate and 5% annual increase in energy costs.

Schedule	Construction Cost	Furniture, Fixtures and Equipment	Design and Management Fees	Net Present Value	
	$50.5 m — Living Machine, 45' Wings, Increase in Photovoltaics (100%), Design for Deconstruction, Reduce Life Cycle Impacts of All Building Materials	$6.6 m	$7.6 m	$72.2 m (30 Year Model); $75.6 m (60 Year Model); $80.2 m (100 Year Model)	**Living Building**
	$47.4 m — 100 Year Building, 45' Wings, Increase in Photovoltaics (20%), Additional Window Shading, Additional Concrete Massing	$6.4 m	$6.6 m	$70.9 m (30 Year Model); $92 m (60 Year Model); $241 m (100 Year Model)	**LEED™ Platinum**
	$45.2 m — 80 Year Building, 65' Wings, Increase in Photovoltaics (10%), Concrete Frame Building, Partially Daylit Parking	$6.3 m	$5.9 m	$71.4 m (30 Year Model); $106.9 m (60 Year Model); $370.8 m (100 Year Model)	**LEED™ Gold**
	$44.3 m — 60 Year Building, 90 Foot Wings - 3 Stories, Raised Access Flooring, Sun Shades on South, Photovoltaics (5%)	$5.8 m	$5.8 m	$76.3 m (30 Year Model); $142.2 m (60 Year Model); $645.5 m (100 Year Model)	**LEED™ Silver**
	$39.5 m — Efficient HVAC, Collect 50% of Rainwater, 50% of Materials that are Removed from Site are Recycled or Salvaged, Material Selection Based on LEED™	$5.6 m	$5.1 m	$75.4 m (30 Year Model); $175.4 m (60 Year Model); $915.4 m (100 Year Model)	**LEED™ Certified**
	$39.2 m — Typical Class "A" Office Building	$5.1 m	$5.1 m	$87.9m (30 Year Model); $243.5 m (60 Year Model); $1,349m (100 Year Model)	**Market**

The David and Lucile Packard Foundation   Los Altos Project

> "In our first conversations with the Packard Foundation, we asked them: if they spend so much of their resources on environmental issues, why would they stop with LEED Platinum — a building that simply does less damage. Why wouldn't they go beyond that? They asked us what that would look like, and then commissioned us to answer that exact question; to quantify how a Living Building would compare to all of these other modalities. It was huge."
>
> **BOB BERKEBILE, BNIM**

In an early meeting with the client about project goals, Berkebile, McLennan, and Hydes learned that the Foundation aspired to create an economically replicable example of sustainability with their new headquarters, which they hoped would be built to LEED Platinum standards. But the BNIM team leaders pushed back. They argued two things: 1) that simple economic replicability would be impossible to achieve if the economic design and construction paradigm itself was flawed, and 2) that there was no reason to stop at LEED Platinum if an even greener option were available and financially preferable over the life of the project. Yes, they wanted to help Packard create a deeply green building, but they insisted that only a true Living Building would be economically replicable and ecologically restorative over time.

The Packard Foundation people responded favorably to the point, which led to a shift in the nature of the project. They were so intrigued by the idea of measuring the near- and long-term costs of different types of buildings and by exploring the possibilities of net zero systems that they put the headquarters design on hold, choosing instead to prioritize a study exploring the economic impacts of varying degrees of sustainable design. BNIM had a new assignment, and it was exactly what the burgeoning green design movement needed at the time.[30]

Over the next several months, the BNIM and KEEN teams supervised work on what became the Packard Sustainability Matrix, first released in 2001 then updated for a re-release in 2002. They schematically designed and priced a single structure conceptually built on

---

30 Although the Packard Sustainability Matrix emerged from this process, the Foundation headquarters building project was put on an extended hold following the burst of the dot-com bubble soon thereafter. The project was later resumed and a 49,000 square foot structure designed by EHDD was completed, earning LEED Platinum certification in 2012 and Net Zero Energy Building certification in 2013.

the same site to each of six levels of building performance: standard market rate, LEED Certified, LEED Silver, LEED Gold, LEED Platinum, and a Living Building (even though the program had not yet been formally written). For each, they estimated required operational energy, grid reliance, pollution, external societal costs, schedule, construction (first) costs, equipment costs, design and management fees, and net present worth (payback) when different envelopes, systems, and operational strategies are used. Data were calculated for costs and values at the 30-, 60- and 100-year marks. Throughout the exercise, they asked the question: What changes and why throughout a building's lifecycle when it goes from tradition-al market rate up the sustainability ladder all the way to Living status?

> "When we said to the Packard people that we should all be thinking more deeply about this question of economic replicability, they agreed. They said, 'If you're so sharp why don't you answer your own question about the economic implications of green buildings?'"
>
> **JASON F. MCLENNAN,**
> **INTERNATIONAL LIVING FUTURE INSTITUTE**

Even the layout of the Matrix became a strate-gic decision. Hydes drafted initial sketches of the summary document placing the market rate building at the top of the page, with LEED's four rows below that and, finally, the Living Building data running across the bottom. As an engineer, Hydes recalls being focused on the incre-mental reduction, which would make the descending categorization logical. But McLennan suggested a different sequence, noting that the aspirational building needed to be on top because it was the methodology most worth celebrating. The Matrix layout was adjusted and the Living Building now sits in its celebratory position at the top of the page.

Many answers emerged from the data. Market rate buildings, which filled the majority of the built environment at the time, were clearly least expensive to build when it came to first

> "At the beginning of this conversation about the Packard Matrix, I was only thinking about net zero energy because that's how my engineering world was constrained. But I could see the twinkle in Jason's and Bob's eyes. They had been exploring this idea of Living Buildings and they wanted to take the building comparisons broader. So instead of just including a net zero building, they included a Living Building in the Matrix."
>
> **KEVIN HYDES, INTEGRAL GROUP**

68

"After the Matrix was completed, Bob and Jason and I went all around the continent presenting it along with this idea of Living Buildings. The Matrix really introduced Living Buildings publicly and helped to arouse curiosity — regionally, nationally, with the AIA, everywhere."

KEVIN HYDES, INTEGRAL GROUP

costs. As buildings got greener, first costs gradually rose. However, over a 30-year period, Living Buildings provided the best economic performance and market rate buildings the worst. Over 60- and 100-year lifecycles, the market rate approach was staggeringly more expensive to operate and maintain. Economically, Living Buildings were a much more strategic choice. Environmentally, they were unquestionably the better option, as shown by the Matrix's pollution rate analyses for the different building types.

The team knew that the integrity of the report's data was a key factor in its success and adoption, so they had it peer-reviewed by leading architects, engineers, academics, and scientists. Between the respected Packard name and the verification of noted experts, the Matrix was quantifiable, credible evidence that green solutions made undeniable economic and environmental sense. Living Buildings had passed their first test, even before their namesake standard was fully formed.

> "Some people would say that the Packard Matrix changed everything, even though there were lots of other things happening in the industry simultaneously. For some projects, for some clients, that report made the difference. It meant that an in-house architect could justify to a CEO or a board that going this direction makes sense because, 'Here's the proof, and it comes from Packard, and it's peer-reviewed.'"
>
> **BOB BERKEBILE, BNIM**

Looking back, it is possible to point to various projects from the 1990s and 2000s that sported one or more characteristics of what would come to be incorporated into the Living Building Challenge. The technology was there to accomplish these goals, even a decade before the formal launch of the Challenge. But political and cultural barriers usually stood in the way, as did the perception that green solutions were prohibitively expensive.

Gradually, though, as more buildings began to sprout sustainable features and more professionals began to talk about the wisdom of these approaches, the climate began to change. The industry, along with its paying clients, started to tilt ever so slightly toward the deeper green end of the spectrum.

> "I first heard about the Packard Matrix while I worked for the City of Seattle and Jason presented it to us. It was exactly what we needed and we hired Elements because of it. It was an easy tool we could give to green building project managers so they could assess the different strategies and benefits based on the building types they were working on."
>
> **AMANDA STURGEON, INTERNATIONAL LIVING FUTURE INSTITUTE**

70

MOTIVATING WITH INSPIRATION, NOT GUILT

A LIVING BUILDING BLOCK

For a long time, the environmental movement attempted to disturb or shock people into action; to motivate with guilt and sometimes even fear. Images of environmental destruction were used to try to shake people into changing their behaviors and actions yet often left people feeling numb or hopeless. Solutions to the problems presented were often equally dour. "Put on a sweater, turn off the heat, and suffer" was the prevailing sentiment — one that was hard to compete with in the face of the much more compelling consumer messages being broadcast. The environmental rhetoric spoke only to those who were already committed to the cause but turned off a substantial portion of potential advocates because of the message's underlying negativity.

The Living Building Challenge is built from different DNA. As Buckminster Fuller was fond of saying, "To change something, build a new model that makes the existing model obsolete." In other words, provide alternatives that are more compelling and better in all ways than the paradigm that is leading civilization down the wrong path. The Living Building Challenge rejects the notion that doom and gloom are powerful enough motivators for success. It relies instead on beautiful images of what can be; an aspirational goal to spur action. It invites people to build more comfortable, beautiful, healthy, and cost-effective structures that are superior in all ways to normal buildings being built today.

The International Living Future Institute has created a culture whereby all of its programs and products are inspiring, beautiful, and pleasant to engage with. Tough issues are discussed yet people are not left in a place of despair. They are instead armed with tools, metrics, standards, and strategies to envision a completely achievable Living Future.

05

"Man's mind stretched to a new idea never goes back to its original dimension."

OLIVER WENDELL HOLMES

THE SHIFT
A MARKET ADJUSTS ITS ATTITUDE

The story of how the Living Building Challenge came to be and came to thrive is not a linear one. Yes, there are specific dates when certain milestone events occurred, but the overall tale of the Challenge's gestation, birth, and maturation is difficult to tell in a strictly chronological fashion. In fact, it could be said that the Living Building Challenge evolved when and how it did because of the very imprecise nature of the market it intended to serve.

The green fervor that grew quickly in the design-build industry during the 1970s and early 1980s inexplicably died down and remained relatively dormant well into the 1990s. During that quiet period, there were a handful of vocal practitioners (Berkebile among the loud-est of them) touting the importance of environmentally sensitive architecture, but those advocates were in the extreme minority. The U.S. Green Building Council (USGBC) wasn't founded until 1993 and it took another seven years to launch LEED in 2000.[31]

By the turn of the millennium, both the supply and demand sides of the industry — design-ers and clients alike — finally seemed open to the idea of sustainability. People were ready to talk about change, and LEED unquestionably helped start the conversation.

---

31 The first LEED Pilot Project Program, referred to as LEED Version 1.0, was introduced at the USGBC Membership Summit in August 1998. That draft received extensive modifications and evolved into LEED Version 2.0, which was rolled out in March 2000. The USGBC refers to 2000 as the year when LEED was launched. (Source: www.usgbc.org/sites/default/files/Foundations-of-LEED.pdf)

LEEDING THE WAY

As one of the first-ever codified programs, and the first to be introduced on a national scale in the United States, LEED helped define and identify the benefits of green design. It created a preliminary common language for a movement that was not exactly young, but was only just getting organized. It also helped prove that green buildings did not have to be strange looking or cost-prohibitive. In short, LEED legitimized practices that were previously categorized in the periphery.

But as more project teams pursued LEED certification for their buildings, a handful of architects — Jason F. McLennan among them — felt that the standard fell short. He was pleased to see more professionals getting exposed to green technologies and systems in order to comply with LEED requirements, but it only proved what he and others of like mind had been saying for years: that accomplishing these goals was not terribly difficult to do when knowledgeable teams of people applied the proper techniques on behalf of engaged clients. If LEED Platinum was the farthest-reaching green standard and it was designed only to do less environmental damage, then it was time to extend the boundaries. The industry was ready for a standard that was actually curative.

AN UNFOLDING TOPIC

McLennan was not the only person considering alternatives to LEED during that time. Bill Reed, himself a founding USGBC board member, spoke often of regenerative design concepts. William McDonough was simultaneously writing about many similar ideas, releasing his seminal collaboration (with Michael Braungart) *Cradle to Cradle: Remaking the Way We Make Things* in 2002. Sim Van der Ryn and Pliny Fisk III continued to write and lecture on related topics, with McLennan always paying very close attention to their work.[32]

Berkebile, too, believed that the industry could do better. Even as one of LEED's original authors, he recognized the standard's inherent constraints. But it was all a matter of taking the market along a journey one step at a time, and LEED paved the way forward.

So McLennan decided that there needed to be a bridge between LEED and the industry's next great thing. He wanted to convert the philosophy of Living Buildings into some sort of written standard; one that was somewhat reminiscent of LEED but was capable of codify-

---

32 McLennan and Bill Reed have since co-authored several articles. During a conversation in preparation for one of them, they found themselves comparing the green design movement to martial arts, with its many disciplines all teaching restraint and control through distinct methodologies. They pondered how practitioners take a variety of routes, but all aim for the same destination. Similarly, LEED, the Living Building Challenge, and other schools of sustainable thought may use distinct languages, but they are founded on a common philosophy.

"LEED is a great tool for showing people how to do less harm, but it stops short of being restorative. It can never get to that ideal because the construct is inherently limiting."

JASON F. MCLENNAN, INTERNATIONAL LIVING FUTURE INSTITUTE

"The really hard thing about LEED is that it's about points, which means that everyone ends up chasing points, whether they admit it or not."

KATH WILLIAMS, KATH WILLIAMS + ASSOCIATES

"We knew at the time we were creating LEED in the 1990s that the consensus model brought serious limitations. The first is that it assumes the whole planet is one bioclimatic region, which is, of course, not true. Secondly, there's no lifecycle analysis programming in it. Third, even LEED Platinum stops short of net positive results; you're just doing less damage to the environment."

BOB BERKEBILE, BNIM

"LEED's big gift to the industry was that it started to shift the way people thought. As teams were pulling off LEED certified projects that weren't weird or scary, it proved that this stuff wasn't just pie in the sky."

JASON F. MCLENNAN, INTERNATIONAL LIVING FUTURE INSTITUTE

"If you look back at the original goals set by the founding LEED steering committee, the vision was to move the market forward by setting a high bar and then challenging the community to reach higher. The Living Building Challenge occupies the bleeding edge; the far forward front of leadership and sustainability. It helps demonstrate what's possible and challenges people to do more, which ultimately helps create more room for technological advances and big ideas to be adopted."

MICHELLE MOORE, GROUNDSWELL

ing a truly regenerative built environment. He knew it would have to be done in a way that appealed to rather than alienated the "LEEDers," using the existing paradigm as a starting point, then continuing onward.

A MATERIAL WORLD

McLennan had already embarked on a complementary endeavor related to building materials. During his early stint at Elements, he began to develop what would later become Pharos, a type of ingredients label for building materials. Pharos was intended to counter the problem posed by single-attribute green certification for the building industry at a time when multi-attribute analysis — otherwise known as lifecycle analysis — was gaining ground. It would be the first foray into product disclosure and transparency.

McLennan moved the Pharos idea forward by collaborating with Bill Walsh, founder of the non-profit Healthy Building Network, to whom he was introduced by Gail Vittori, co-director of the Center for Maximum Potential Building Systems and founding chair of the USGBC. He outlined a white paper on the topic, drafted a business plan for how to codify the idea, and sketched a visual that would appeal to the graphically-minded architectural audience. He and Walsh, along with the Healthy Building Network's Tom Lent and Jack Geibig, a lifecycle analysis expert from the University of Tennessee's Center for Clean Products, distributed the Pharos message however and wherever they could. They received enthusiastic responses from designers, builders, and manufacturers devoted to the idea of materials transparency.

McLennan, though, was working full-time at Elements, and he knew the Pharos idea required sufficient resources and personnel to help it blossom. He handed the idea to Walsh, who incorporated it into the operations at the Healthy Building Network and raised all the initial funds to get the idea off the ground. Today, the Pharos tool is used by dozens of companies and promotes the importance of total transparency in the materials market. The thinking behind Pharos greatly influenced the original thinking around the Living Building Challenge Materials Petal.

"The Pharos project was probably the first time I wrote what could be considered a standard. I had admired the Healthy Building Network from afar, so I knew they could do more with the idea than I could from my position at BNIM."

JASON F. MCLENNAN, INTERNATIONAL LIVING FUTURE INSTITUTE

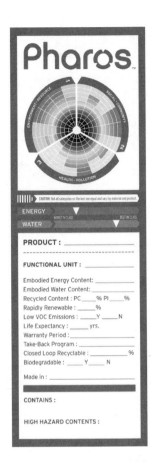

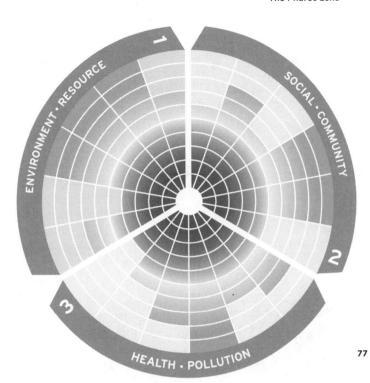

GETTING PUBLISHED

Also during his Elements years, McLennan sought additional ways to tap into the new curiosity about sustainability. There were individual books and articles devoted to the topic, and one leading green design magazine (*Environmental Building News*, founded in 1992), but no single book publisher dedicated to chronicling the movement or its leaders.

In 2003, McLennan borrowed money from a close friend and took out a second mortgage on his Kansas City home in order to launch Ecotone Publishing Company.[33] Ecotone would give him and others a professional method with which to inform, educate, and inspire all tiers of the market. (Early titles included *Green Dollhouse*, *The Dumb Architect's Guide to Glazing Selection*, and *Women in Green*.)[34]

33 Bob Berkebile later became a co-investor.

34 In 2011, McLennan sold Ecotone Publishing to Cascadia Green Building Council. It is now a division of the International Living Future Institute.

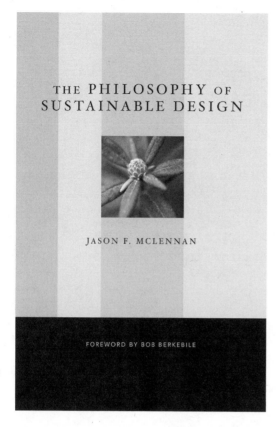

THE PHILOSOPHY OF
SUSTAINABLE DESIGN

JASON F. MCLENNAN

FOREWORD BY BOB BERKEBILE

"Ecotone was never intended to be a money-making venture. It has always been about getting ideas out there in the hope that they will change the world."

**JASON F. MCLENNAN,
INTERNATIONAL LIVING FUTURE INSTITUTE**

In 2004, Ecotone released McLennan's *The Philosophy of Sustainable Design*, which he had been writing after-hours for the previous few years. In it, McLennan quietly introduces the Living Building concept, but mostly in the context of other subjects — as a component of the Packard Matrix, as a recommended fifth level of LEED, and as the most viable option in a sustainable future. The fact that he takes only two of the book's 325 pages to define Living Buildings helps us understand how young the idea was, even to McLennan, just a few short years before it would evolve into a full-scale standard.[35] Perhaps more significantly, it reflects the fact that true restorative design had not yet captured much of the industry's attention.

In the preface of *The Philosophy of Sustainable Design*, McLennan spells out his intent:

I wrote this book because I believe it is possible to change the way we design and build our buildings, communities and cities. I want to see each community discover what is unique to it, as I have with Sudbury, and to respect these unique qualities in the places we make. I believe it is possible for us to live in our environment, both natural and of our own making, in ways that are healthy, nourishing and restorative. Through this book I want to contribute to the advancement of the sustainable design movement.

35 *The Philosophy of Sustainable Design* was well received from the start, and still serves as required reading in academic architecture programs throughout the world.

MOTHER NATURE WEIGHS IN

As McLennan and Berkebile wrote and spoke on the subject of sustainable design in general and Living Buildings in particular, global issues were helping to build widespread environmental awareness. In 2003, Europe experienced a deadly record-breaking heat wave that scientists attributed to climate changes caused by human influences.[36] The 2004 tsunami in Southeast Asia shone new light on the links between global warming and natural disasters.[37] The Kyoto Protocol went into force in February 2005, calling for industrialized nations to reduce their collective emissions of greenhouse gases.[38] In August of that same year, Hurricane Katrina slammed into America's Gulf coast, exposing deadly flaws in built and social infrastructures. Al Gore's 2006 documentary, *An Inconvenient Truth*, prompted climate change discussions everywhere from household dinner tables to Hollywood's red carpets.

Amid all of this activity, one thing became increasingly clear to McLennan: However primed the world was for a new sustainability paradigm, however positively people responded to the idea of Living Buildings, and however much all sides of the marketplace were shifting, a green design philosophy on its own would never accomplish real and permanent change. This big idea, he realized, needed to become a standard that provided specific performance goals and required measurable results while retaining its philosophical roots.

Evangelizing was no longer enough. It was time to create a call to action. It was time to issue a challenge.

36 www.nature.com/nature/journal/v432/n7017/abs/nature03089.html
37 www.worldclimatereport.com/index.php/2005/04/21/tsunamis-and-global-warming-who-would-dare-connect-them
38 www.kyotoprotocol.com

80

GETTING TO THE ESSENCE OF THE MESSAGE

A LIVING BUILDING BLOCK

The Living Building Challenge is the most difficult green building standard in the world to achieve, yet it is presented clearly and succinctly in a way that is easier to understand and digest than any other program. Practitioners are drawn to its elegance, even when it seems daunting. This clarity helps the Challenge stand apart from other programs, some of which are so complex that they turn people away from sustainability altogether.

Flowing through the Challenge is the wisdom of Antione de Saint-Exupery, who said, "Perfection is achieved, not when there is nothing more to add, but when there is nothing left to take away." With that in mind, the Challenge is presented as simply and directly as possible. Each new version further hones both the message and the intent, even when the subject matter is complicated. When McLennan first authored the Challenge, he found ways to distill down each category to as few requirements as possible — always seeking to find "the essence" of the performance level required that would have the maximum positive impact.

The Red List is a perfect example. Trying to understand all the thousands of chemicals used in the building industry is incredibly daunting and requires toxicological expertise to begin to understand how to build free of harmful chemistry. Figuring out where to begin with an industry that didn't disclose or even always understand what was in their own products presented an infinitely complex problem. So McLennan did something simple — he worked with experts to identify the worst offenders ubiquitous in the building industry that had almost no safe exposure limit and coded them with the word "red"— a color universally associated with one thing. Red means stop. People instantly understand that the Red List is a collection of chemicals to *stop* putting in buildings. This simple mechanism has now gone on to reshape the building manufacturing sector.

The Living Building Challenge does not bog down its message by diving deep into the various ways people can accomplish certification. Instead, it relies on the intelligence of those who accept the Challenge to figure out their own ways forward, provided they meet the performance standard. This has the outcome of making things no more complex than they have to be and no simpler than they should be.

06

"You can't cross a sea by merely standing and staring at the water."

RABINDRANATH TAGORE

WRITING IT DOWN
A MANIFESTO TAKES SHAPE

Jason F. McLennan has never been one to let the clock dictate the end of his workday. Nor has he ever been the type to kick back in front of the TV after a long day at the office. Anyone who has worked with him has witnessed the same pattern: daylight hours are devoted to his primary job while evenings, nights, and many weekends are spent pursuing other professional and personal endeavors. The concept of "downtime" is foreign to him. While attending college, he supplemented study and class time landing small design gigs in and around Eugene. While meeting his obligations as an associate at BNIM, he wrote articles on Living Buildings and early drafts of his *Philosophy* book. While running Elements, he designed and built Green Dirt Farm. Throughout it all, he devoured books on a variety of topics that inspired him to do, create, and be more.

In fact, the various projects he juggled during those busy and eye-opening early years of his career gave him the practical experiences he needed to put pen to paper for the initial draft of the Living Building Challenge. Montana's EPICenter, the Packard Matrix, Green Dirt Farm — everything McLennan touched served as a Living Building laboratory, yielding data about what was feasible, sustainable, and measurable. Whenever he stumbled across a new piece of critical information related to the potential of Living Buildings, he jotted it down. Nothing, not even perceived failures, was irrelevant to his research. After several years of experimenting, writing, preaching, and proving, McLennan was ready to turn the Living Building concept into a performance-based standard that challenged the industry to raise the bar.

NIGHT OWL

By 2002, McLennan was married with a family. He and his wife, Tracy, had purchased a small house in Kansas City equipped with a modest office that served as McLennan's late-night getaway. After he helped tuck his kids into bed and said goodnight to Tracy, McLennan would steal away to his study and get back to work, sometimes until the early morning hours. It was there where McLennan drafted much of what he initially dubbed the Living Building Standard.

McLennan, of course, had written extensively about Living Buildings in the years leading up to that point. On his own and in collaboration with Bob Berkebile, he had amassed a robust collection of formal and informal Living Building content that he could use as part of the new Standard. All of it was useful and relevant; it just needed to be re-purposed and re-organized into something that would codify the concept and give the industry an alternative to LEED. However it took shape, it needed to be no more complicated than necessary, no more simple than possible, and it needed to fix the inherent problems in LEED.

> "I had this cool little office in our Kansas City house, and that's where I would go to read or write or create or draw. It was like my own little evening workshop."
>
> **JASON F. MCLENNAN,**
> **INTERNATIONAL LIVING FUTURE INSTITUTE**

Early renditions of the Living Building Challenge logo

He began by turning to his favorite metaphor: the flower. Dating back to the publication of his *Philosophy* book, McLennan had referred to the flower as the perfectly simple symbol for the ideal built environment. In the book, he wrote:

Flowers are marvels of adaptation, growing in various shapes, sizes and forms. Some lie dormant through the harshest of winters only to emerge each spring once the ground has thawed. Others stay rooted all year round, opening and closing as necessary to respond to changing conditions in the environment such as the availability of sunlight. Like buildings, flowers are literally and figuratively rooted to place, able to draw resources only from the square inches of earth and sky that they inhabit. The flower must receive all of its energy from the sun, all of its water needs from the sky, and all of its nutrients from the soil. Flowers are also ecosystems, supporting and sheltering microorganisms and insects just as our buildings support and shelter us. Equally important, flowers are beautiful and can provide the inspiration needed for architecture to truly be successful.

Although he penned those words several years before he sat down to write the Living Building Standard, they foretold the Standard's very framework. As he wrote the Standard, he deepened the significance of the flower metaphor, choosing to use "Petals" to represent the six performance areas. The flower explanation he had written years earlier would prove to be prophetic as he clarified those six key aspects:

SITE   "Like buildings, flowers are literally and figuratively rooted to place ..."

ENERGY   "The flower must receive all of its energy from the sun ..."

WATER   "... all of its water needs from the sky ..."

MATERIALS   "... and all of its nutrients from the soil."

INDOOR QUALITY   "Flowers are also ecosystems, supporting and sheltering microorganisms and insects just as our buildings support and shelter us."

BEAUTY & INSPIRATION   "Equally important, flowers are beautiful and can provide the inspiration needed for architecture to be truly successful."

THE LIVING BUILDING CHALLENGE: ROOTS AND RISE OF THE WORLD'S GREENEST STANDARD

TRACES OF THE FAMILIAR

The six Petals of the Living Building Standard were intentionally reminiscent of LEED's original six credit categories (sustainable sites, water efficiency, energy and atmosphere, materials and resources, indoor environmental quality, and innovation in design). McLennan agreed that LEED focused on some of the correct categories of environmental design (even though he felt they should be approached holistically, not separately), so he didn't feel the need to stray from this fundamental six-part construct. In addition, he knew that any new standard had to seem at least familiar to LEED if it had any chance of gaining traction among architects and engineers who were only just beginning to adapt to LEED itself.

Still, it was extremely important to McLennan that his Standard relied on the head *and* the heart; the left brain *and* the right. So he added a performance area that helped the Living Building Standard stand well apart from LEED: the Beauty and Inspiration Petal.

Calling for aesthetic performance in a building standard, McLennan believed, would help dispel the assumptions that green buildings were unavoidably and consistently unattractive. He had seen first-hand how beautiful sustainable structures could be and wanted to bring others over to his way of thinking. He also knew that for Living Buildings to be successful, they had to convey beauty so that all tiers of the market would embrace them. So he included the "unquantifiable" among the more tangible aspects of Living Buildings that would need to be measured and proven in order to be certified. Doing so shed light on the notion that even though certain things are hard to quantify, failing to count them at all means giving them a value of zero. And beauty in the built environment, according to McLennan, should always be assessed, appraised, and prioritized.

87

"When people first realized that Beauty was included as a performance area, some of them told me that stuff like that didn't matter and couldn't be measured. But for most people, it really resonated and was very well received. Including Beauty as its own performance area proved to be a major innovation that added huge value to the Standard."

JASON F. MCLENNAN, INTERNATIONAL LIVING FUTURE INSTITUTE

Across the six Petal areas, McLennan wrote 16 "prerequisites." (Later, after the Standard had evolved into the Challenge, the term "prerequisites" was changed to "Imperatives." But the industry was accustomed to LEED's prerequisite concept, so McLennan opted to include that familiar terminology in the earliest iteration of his manifesto.) However, unlike LEED, the Living Building Standard was not structured around credits. Its prerequisites were not designed as an à la carte menu from which architects, engineers, or owners could pick and choose according to which aspects of the standard they felt they could achieve. The problem with that approach, McLennan felt, was that it tended to entice people to pick the points that were easiest to attain. Instead, all 16 of the Living Building Standard's prerequisites were required and had to be solved in an integrated, holistic fashion — thus dissolving the idea in practice of there even being categories. In other words, for a structure to be considered a Living Building, it had to meet every one of the 16 performance area prerequisites.[39]

But it was up to each team to determine *how* to reach those performance goals. Unlike LEED, the Living Building Standard was not prescriptive and relied on the genius of each team to uncover the best solutions for a given problem.

SEPARATE BUT COMPLEMENTARY

It appealed to McLennan to distance the Living Building Standard from LEED's credit-oriented and more prescriptive format because it would ensure that the two codes stood apart from one another — not as competitors but as tools serving different purposes. McLennan had seen LEED inspire true greatness and had watched deep green projects rise as a result. (He even published an article several years later — in 2011 — called "Defending LEED," in which he supports the USGBC's program while acknowledging that any such effort is always a work in progress.)

> "Do I think that LEED is perfect? Absolutely not. No system is perfect. And yes, some criticism is deserved – and *needed* to keep improving what has become the most dominant green building program in the world. But there is a big difference in criticism that is intended to make the program stronger – so that it can continue to contribute to lowering environmental impact and changing the building culture – and criticism that is intended to tear down and destroy something that I believe has done a lot of good in the world. The former is essential – if not always appreciated – the latter is destructive and typically self-serving of particular corporate or individual interests."
>
> **JASON F. MCLENNAN, FROM "DEFENDING LEED,"** *TRIM TAB*, **SPRING 2011**

---

39 Later, projects could apply for individual Petal certification. But Version 1.3 — the first version used by project teams — required that all 16 prerequisites be met for full Living Building certification.

Still, McLennan believed there was room for improvement. His ideal green building standard was, by design, much more challenging. He had seen too many project teams hand-select elements of LEED that were easier to accomplish but environmentally insignificant, just to earn the credits and publicize the so-called sustainability of their buildings. Many of those close-to-mainstream projects, he observed, were slapped with green labels they had not rightly earned. He felt that LEED in the right hands was an undeniably powerful tool but was written in a way that made it easy to abuse. Since receiving official LEED certification relied more heavily on paperwork than proven performance, McLennan felt that teams were beginning to spend a disproportionate amount of their overall budgets working to "prove" their LEED credits through reports instead of investing in ideas and technologies that could actually improve the environmental performance of their buildings.

McLennan wanted to ask more of the design-build community. Rather than issuing a set of goals that was easy to document and relatively easy to achieve, he wanted a tool that was easy to document and *extremely difficult* to achieve. He sought to put an end to greenwashing; to prioritize true restorative design over point chasing.

POLISHING

As McLennan fine-tuned the Standard, he drew mostly from his own experiences and knowledge about the Living Building ideal. Then, when technical questions arose for which he needed specialized expertise, he sought counsel from his rapidly growing team of mentors and advisors. For example, to home in on realistic waste targets for the Materials Petal, he turned to his friend and Elements colleague Brad Nies, who had recently completed a substantial construction waste study. Then Bill Walsh, Tom Lent, and others at the Healthy Building Network weighed in on the nuances of supplies and materials as McLennan fleshed out the Red List for the Materials Petal.

"There has to be poetry in this kind of thing; passion and poetry. And that's what Jason brought when he created the Living Building idea."

**SIM VAN DER RYN,
ECOLOGICAL DESIGN COLLABORATIVE**

Gradually, the Living Building Standard took shape, growing and blooming like the flower it meant to emulate. But even as the draft now commonly referred to as "Version 1.0" neared completion, McLennan kept it largely under wraps. He continued to promote the idea of Living Buildings to any clients and colleagues who would listen, but he remained quiet about the Standard he had written that supported the concept. The reason, he now explains, was that it was still only half-baked; not yet ready to be released to the world at the ideal three-quarter-baked stage.[40] He felt so strongly that the Standard had the power to usher in profound change that he wanted to help it find its rightful home; it needed the proper platform and he was committed to finding it, even if it meant delaying the idea's release.

PONDERING OPTIONS

He considered turning it into a book. He had already launched Ecotone Publishing, so he wouldn't need to shop the concept to agents or publishing representatives in order to get it into print form. He and Michael Berrisford (his Ecotone partner and also his brother-in-law) even attempted in 2005 to launch a design competition for any project team interested in designing and creating a Living Building. The winner would receive a book contract to produce a case study on their work. But there were no projects of Living Building status either pending or in progress, and Ecotone did not have the networking power at that time to publicize the idea to the national design-build community.

McLennan naturally assumed as he was writing the Living Building Standard that the concept would eventually land at the USGBC. As the sole national green design advocacy group and the owner of the movement's only widely used standardized code, the USGBC was the logical entity to adopt the Living Building Standard and promote it as the next big thing. McLennan and Berkebile (who was one of the few people privy to the details of the Standard as McLennan was composing it) even discussed with USGBC leaders the idea of creating a new rung on the LEED ladder that would exceed the requirements of LEED Platinum, the highest level both then and now. There, they felt, was where the Living Building Standard could get the traction it deserved.

> "It only made sense for USGBC to adopt this thing. They had LEED, which was exploding in the marketplace; they were a third-party entity; they were an NGO. I knew that the Living Building Standard could not be run by a for-profit or it would not have any credibility. That's why BNIM or Elements could never oversee it, because they weren't non-profits."
>
> **JASON F. MCLENNAN, INTERNATIONAL LIVING FUTURE INSTITUTE**

40 McLennan has always ascribed to the notion that ideas are at their peak of readiness when they are "three-quarter-baked" — mostly formed but needing additional input from the larger community. The most successful innovations, he believes, are those that are begun by their authors, then released into the world to be finessed and completed by a greater pool of contributors. McLennan devotes an entire essay to this concept in *Zugunruhe: The Inner Migration to Profound Environmental Change*.

McLennan and Berkebile soft-pitched the idea to people at the USGBC in the early 2000s, but they were met mostly with indifference. McLennan recalls a USGBC board member referring to the Living Building concept as a "pie in the sky idea" that was too impractical to implement. Besides, LEED was gaining ground quickly and demanded the full-time attention of USGBC staff and resources. Living Buildings, at least for the time being, would not come to rest at the USGBC.

So the greenest standard remained the sole intellectual property of McLennan, who continued to strategize how to release it. Little did he know, the fate of his manifesto was indeed in the hands of the USGBC — not the national entity but a smaller regional faction of the organization that would end up planting the Standard in its own garden with McLennan cultivating its growth.

92

RELEASING 3/4-BAKED IDEAS

A LIVING BUILDING BLOCK

Many ideas are best unleashed at the point when they are mostly — but not fully — formed. The world is full of "half-baked" ideas that are not well thought through and fatally flawed or "overcooked" and extremely rigid, appropriate only for certain settings and conditions.

The Living Building Challenge has instead always relied on the three-quarter-baked philosophy.[41] It was intentionally launched with a clear and inspiring vision but a slightly incomplete programmatic structure as a way of inviting the larger industry to participate in its evolution. It was crafted but not stiff; framed but not closed; finessed but not finished. It was up to the user

41 This philosophy first appeared in McLennan's 2010 book, *Zugunruhe: The Inner Migration to Profound Environmental Change.*

community to determine what else it needed. No idea can be polished to the point of perfection, especially by any one individual or even a large group. People and processes must be allowed to do their part as a community.

Quality and timeliness suffer when too many people with potentially competing interests attempt to sculpt concepts into pristine shape.

Similarly, ideas and visions that are developed by committee — even when extremely intelligent people band together to hone them — can fall victim to over-analysis and a syndrome of solving for the lowest common denominator.

Quality and timeliness suffer when too many people with potentially competing interests attempt to sculpt concepts into pristine shape. Slight messiness can be uncomfortable, but far more fruitful. The Living Building Challenge was conceived and almost entirely formed by a single individual, yet has matured and been strengthened by a community of thousands.

The project teams that embraced the first (deliberately unfinished) version of the Living Building Challenge helped round it out. And each new version of the Challenge reflects the feedback and discoveries of those who have since put it to the test. Members of the green design movement have refined the standard that has redefined their own industry. As such, the Challenge belongs to everyone who uses it.

07

"Life calls the tune, we dance."

JOHN GALSWORTHY

MAKING A MOVE

A MAN AND A STANDARD
BOTH FIND A NEW HOME

By 2006, Jason F. McLennan occupied what anyone — himself included — would describe as an enviable professional position. Still only in his early 30s, he was the youngest-ever partner at a respected architecture firm recognized for its excellence in general and its green design leadership in particular.[42] He was the presumptive successor to his greatest mentor, Bob Berkebile, and an important future steward of BNIM. He ran the firm's consulting business, which gave him visibility throughout the movement and access to game-changing ideas and people. Independent projects allowed him to put previously theoretical design concepts to the real-world test.

On paper, he had the career he had dreamed of. And he continued to savor his work and colleagues at BNIM, never taking his professional fortune for granted. Still, he couldn't help feeling there was something else that he was meant to be doing. Instead of changing the built environment one structure at a time, he had a growing sense of urgency about making a more comprehensive difference on the industry at large.

42 In 2011, five years after McLennan's departure, BNIM won the coveted Architecture Firm Award, the
    highest honor given by the American Institute of Architects.

"I had this feeling that what I was supposed to do was make cutting-edge change. It's hard to talk about without making it sound like it was a religious calling, but it was almost like that. There was just this voice in my head telling me I had to do more than what I could do from inside one firm."

JASON F. MCLENNAN,
INTERNATIONAL LIVING FUTURE INSTITUTE

It wasn't clear to him exactly how or where or from what position he was supposed to effect this change. He just felt drawn to do more. And the subsequent agitation about this bigger mission began to be a distraction.[43] Meanwhile, he continued to hold onto the Living Building Standard, waiting and watching for the right context in which to offer it to the community.

Thinking that a position with the U.S. Green Building Council (USGBC) might offer an opportunity to weigh in on national issues and perhaps give the Living Building Standard a home, McLennan ran for a seat on the board in 2005. From within the framework of the country's governing green design body, he assumed, he may be in a better position to make a difference. But he lost the election to the seat's incumbent, his friend and occasional collaborator, Kevin Hydes. So he stayed busy with his work at BNIM/Elements, although that nagging feeling kept getting stronger.

A SIGN MEANT TO BE SEEN

One evening in the spring of 2006, McLennan returned home to Kansas City very late after an out-of-town trip that had left him frustrated by a slow-going project, a slow-to-change client, and the glacial pace of the movement itself. He was becoming increasingly convinced that the bureaucratic processes that bogged down the progress of individual buildings was symptomatic of the bigger issues that plagued the industry. Something had to change.

With his family already in bed and feeling too wound up to sleep himself, McLennan turned on his computer and began a search. He entered such non-specific terms as "sustainability" and "green building" looking for nothing and everything all at once. He was on some sort of a quest, but he had no expectations or hopes of finding anything in particular.

He scrolled through the results that filled his computer screen. Wikipedia offered a link to its page where sustainability was defined and explained. Magazines offered links to arti-

---

43 McLennan's first collection of essays, *Zugunruhe*, is named after the word biologists use to describe the sense of agitation displayed by a species just prior to a great migration. He likens this state to the way environmentally-minded humans behave when we know we must make substantial change in order to correct the damage we have done to the planet but we do not know quite how to make that shift. This is how he describes feeling himself during those months in 2006 leading up to his great migration from Kansas City to Seattle.

cles on green design innovations. A few manufacturers offered links to their sites where environmentally-friendly products were available for sale. Then one item among the search results jumped out at him. Not far down the list, there appeared a link to a job posting: "CEO, Cascadia Green Building Council."

McLennan quickly clicked through to explore further. The Cascadia Green Building Council, which operated as the Northwest regional chapter of the USGBC and the Canada GBC, was looking for a new chief executive officer. The ideal candidate would have design and managerial experience, along with a passion for the growing and changing green building industry. He or she would be capable of expanding the scope and relevance of the Cascadia chapter's impact. Interested applicants should contact the head of the search committee, Ms. Debra Guenther at Mithun.

At this, McLennan sat straight upright in his chair. He knew Deb Guenther. They had worked together in 2003 when they had both been hired as consultants by the City of Seattle to develop a new sustainability policy with Amanda Sturgeon.[44] They had forged a strong, mutually respectful bond during the course of that project. When it came to their green convictions, they were of like minds.

Although not a particularly superstitious guy, McLennan felt that this was nothing less than a sign. It was one thing for him to even sit down and conduct such a search — something he had never done before without a specific research purpose. It was another for this job posting to pop up so prominently amid such relatively benign search results. It was quite another for such an ally to be listed as the point of contact for the job itself.

He read and re-read the posting. Was this the opportunity he'd been waiting for? Would this be the platform that would allow him to effect change on a broader scale? Would he

> "I decided to search the Internet just to see what was out there. For whatever reason, because of the key words I used in the search, this job posting came up very quickly. It was like, 'Here — look at this one!' The whole sequence shouldn't have happened the way it did, but it did. There was a certainty about it all."
>
> **JASON F. MCLENNAN, INTERNATIONAL LIVING FUTURE INSTITUTE**

44 As the City of Seattle's staff sustainable building specialist, Amanda Sturgeon oversaw the project to which McLennan and Guenther contributed their expertise in 2003. Sturgeon was a founding Cascadia board member. She joined the staff of the International Living Building Institute in 2010 as vice president of the Living Building Challenge, was named executive director of the International Living Future Institute in 2014, and became CEO in 2016.

CASCADIA
GREEN BUILDING COUNCIL

be the best person for the job operating a cross-border GBC chapter, given his roots in both countries? Would running a small non-profit with a tiny operating budget be too big of a professional shift after occupying his plum position within BNIM?

All of those questions swirled in his head. But they kept bumping into one very clear thought: from that position in that chapter of that international organization, McLennan could give the Living Building Standard a home.

"As soon as I saw that job posting that night, it spoke to me. I knew right then what the whole chain of events was going to be. I was going to get that job and I was going to launch Living Buildings all over the world. I knew all of that in that one moment staring at that screen and it gave me chills."

**JASON F. MCLENNAN,
INTERNATIONAL LIVING FUTURE INSTITUTE**

McLennan found Guenther's personal email address (not the Cascadia address where she would receive responses to the ad) among his contacts and dashed off a note to her. As someone who knew him, she might have some thoughts about whether he should even pursue such a job. Perhaps she would give him additional context missing from the job posting that would shed more light on the position. Maybe her perspective could save him a lot of time and effort. He turned off his computer and went to bed.

First thing the next morning, McLennan checked his messages. Among his new emails was one from Guenther that was short and sweet and undeniably enthusiastic. She asked him to call her immediately so they could talk in more detail.

"Deb's email just said, "Oh my God," with a million exclamation marks. And I thought, 'Oh shit. This must really be something.' In my brain, I knew this didn't make a lot of sense. But the emotional part of me knew this was what I had to do."

JASON F. MCLENNAN, INTERNATIONAL LIVING FUTURE INSTITUTE

> "I was so excited by that first phone call with Jason. It was terrific to hear he was interested, and it was fortuitous that he'd seen the announcement because we'd just opened it. I knew he'd be perfect because I knew him as someone who's able to tell stories, paint a vision, and build analogies. And he'd been in the trenches at BNIM, so he was making these green buildings happen while figuring out the policy and economic obstacles that we all struggled with."
>
> **DEB GUENTHER, MITHUN**

DIGGING DEEPER

When they spoke later that morning, Guenther told McLennan that the job posting had only just gone public. Cascadia, she explained, was searching for a new CEO. (She was its board chair as well as its search committee chair.) The new hire would oversee branches throughout Washington, Oregon, and British Columbia and could choose where in the region he or she preferred to be based. If he wanted to pursue it — and she hoped he did — he would need to go through several rounds of interviews, first on the phone with a smaller committee and then, if he got this far, in person in Vancouver with the entire board and all three staff members.

McLennan opted to see where this would lead, knowing that if he got the offer, it would mean making some difficult personal and professional choices. He quietly participated in the early rounds of phone interviews and a quick out-and-back one-on-one meeting in Seattle with Guenther without discussing it with his colleagues — not even Berkebile (which made him feel very conflicted). But when all of those interactions went well and it came time to travel to Vancouver to sit in front of the entire board and staff for the final round, McLennan knew he needed to share this news with his partner. When he did, Berkebile, not surprisingly, was extremely supportive. He encouraged McLennan to pursue Cascadia, if for no other reason than just to make new connections within the movement through the interview process. If he ended up with an offer, they would address that as it came. Either way, Berkebile reassured McLennan that the Living Building Standard was his to do with what he felt was best.

"When Jason interviewed for the job, we were changing a bit as an organization. From a funding perspective, we had already proven that we could grow and support our staff and programs. What we needed was a legitimate character who was a champion of the green building and sustainability movement, not just another fundraiser. When Jason's resume and portfolio came to us, we were really hopeful we could lure him our way."

DALE MIKKELSEN, SFU COMMUNITY TRUST

DUE DILIGENCE

During those busy weeks, McLennan researched everything about the Cascadia Green Building Council. He learned that the chapter's culture was in a state of change. It was moving from its youthful beginnings as a growth organization hungry for funds to one with a steadier constituency and brand. It needed a leader who could guide more than development efforts. It sought a face, a voice, and a visionary for the cause.

Cascadia had a distinctive personality that appealed to McLennan. Founded in 1999, it existed autonomously as a private non-profit advocacy group until it formally affiliated with the USGBC as one of the first regional chapters in 2000. Cascadia then expanded into a cross-border entity when it became a member of the Canada GBC in 2005.

Even as it joined both national networks, Cascadia remained fiercely independent, earning a reputation as a slightly roguish operation. Its members were regarded as activists, working alone and together to push for aggressive solutions to the environmental problems facing the design-build industry. Cascadia acknowledged the value of LEED, but did not regard it as the movement's be-all and end-all tool. It was willing to support and further the efforts of the USGBC, but not at the expense of shutting out other possible programs or approaches to sustainable design.

LIKE MINDS

McLennan came to learn that he and Cascadia had a lot in common. Both were fiercely driven to seek change and impatient with the pace of the industrial process. Neither cared much about political fallout if the net result meant a greener built environment. This organization, he felt certain, would be the ideal nesting ground for the Living Building Standard. He pursued the Cascadia job not because he had any great desire to run a non-profit, but

"Out of all the USGBC chapters, the Cascadia people were the troublemakers who didn't follow the rules. They were willing to stand up to the USGBC or anyone because of what they believed in. They were the diehards; the green warrior camp. So I knew I had to be there."

JASON F. MCLENNAN, INTERNATIONAL LIVING FUTURE INSTITUTE

"Cascadia was very opinionated and we were organized to voice our opinions effectively. We've always been deep believers in what we were doing, always very interested in where we should be going from a visionary standpoint."

DEB GUENTHER, MITHUN

"We were rogue in that we were explicitly not tied to the USGBC and LEED as a traditional branch or chapter. We recognized that LEED was a great program, but we were open to all comers when it came to sustainable building."

DALE MIKKELSEN, SFU COMMUNITY TRUST

"The working relationship between Cascadia and USGBC has always been strong, but there has always been a bit of tension too. Are we siblings, are we a child of the USGBC, or what?"

MARK FRANKEL, NEW BUILDINGS INSTITUTE

because he felt he had found the platform he had been seeking. He envisioned operating from within the framework of the movement, changing things from inside the machine. He felt certain that Cascadia would embrace the Living Building Standard and help it move up the USGBC chain until it settled within the construct of the national body, where it would be adopted as the new greenest standard at the level above LEED Platinum.

"When he interviewed for the job, Jason was kind of an eye opener. We wondered why someone like him would want a position like this. But he wanted it because he recognized that he could have more influence than in any other single position in the country if he came here with this intent. Cascadia gave him an established organization, a great community, and a pulpit to do what he felt he needed to do."

MARK FRANKEL, NEW BUILDINGS INSTITUTE

The Vancouver interview resulted in an offer, which McLennan knew he would take in spite of a cut in pay, a gut-wrenching departure from Berkebile, and complicated implications for his family. Upon returning to Kansas City, he told his BNIM colleagues individually about his plans. (He even asked them to leave the figurative door open for him in case things didn't work out and he returned in a year or so.) When his fellow partner in the firm, Kathy Achelpohl, asked him why he was making this radical change, he had an easy answer: "Because I'm going to launch the level above LEED Platinum and change the building industry."

GEARING UP

In the months between May 2006, when he accepted the position as Cascadia's new CEO, and August 2006, when he began the job, McLennan operated in two worlds. As he brought work and family life to a close in Kansas City, he started organizing his thoughts in preparation for his inaugural meeting in the Pacific Northwest.

His tenure would kick off with an all-hands gathering in Tacoma, Washington, where he would officially take the reins of the Cascadia Green Building Council. The agenda would contain all the expected topics for a meeting of that kind: committee reports, strategic plans, budget reviews, etcetera. But McLennan intended to add a bit of a surprise to the program: the gift of the Living Building Standard.

During the interview phase, McLennan had discussed his various portfolio projects where he had tested Living Building principles. He had reported on his experience with the EPI-

Center, the Packard Sustainability Matrix, UT Houston and Green Dirt Farm. The Cascadia board had come to understand his fervor for the Living Building concept. But they did not know he had created a standard that codified the idea; nor did they know until he addressed them as their new CEO that he intended to gift the Standard to the organization.

> "I couldn't give away the idea if they didn't pick me for the job, so I didn't unveil it until the first board meeting. That was a conscious decision. I knew Cascadia was the place for it, partly because I got a good sense that these people were a bunch of rabble rousers."
>
> **JASON F. MCLENNAN, INTERNATIONAL LIVING FUTURE INSTITUTE**

A GIFT

As he addressed the attendees of the Tacoma meeting, McLennan opened by saying "I have some surprises for you." He laid out his offer to give the Living Building Standard to Cascadia, along with his vision for how implementing such a program would transform the chapter's impact on the international green building industry. He clarified that he was not interested in being paid for the idea, but that the organization would need to put all of its weight behind it if it had any chance of succeeding. If Cascadia's mission was to change the built environment, and its board wanted McLennan to lead that effort, then this had to be the fulcrum that pushed that change. They knew him well enough already, he pointed out, to understand that he would never be satisfied leading the chapter using just the tools that were already in place. Embracing the Living Building Standard as its core offering would be consistent with Cascadia's innovative and pioneering approach. Besides, McLennan knew the Standard had to be housed within a non-profit entity in order to maintain its integrity. The higher ideal, not personal or corporate financial gain, had to be its driving force.

Still, there would be political ramifications for Cascadia if it chose to adopt the Challenge. Cascadia had to carefully consider the Living Building Standard's relationship to LEED. Regardless of whether the USGBC might later incorporate it into its own framework, it might be viewed as competition. This new Standard was bold and aggressive — much more so than anything that had come before it. It would unquestionably strengthen Cascadia's reputation as a pioneering entity, but was it a feasible set of goals to present to the industry? Would it stimulate the change the organization sought, or would its ultra-challenging nature undermine all of Cascadia's hard-fought efforts and credibility leading up to that point?

"[The Living Building Standard] was a stake in the ground, way out there. When we looked at it we said, 'This is a great thing but it's going to be really hard. And can anybody even do this?'"

MARK FRANKEL, NEW BUILDINGS INSTITUTE

"It was always clear that Jason was going to bring provocative thought to the board. So when he brought the idea of this new Standard to us in Tacoma, it wasn't a surprise to me. The board met this as an opportunity. It was a very clear, definable opportunity to allow Cascadia to be the organization we all wanted it to be — not just another delivery agency for existing models."

DALE MIKKELSEN, SFU COMMUNITY TRUST

"At that first board meeting, Jason really wowed us all with the idea of the Living Building Standard. His presentation was simple and very compelling. There was an overwhelming sense in the room that this was an idea that was going to help invigorate the organization — but everybody knew that it was much bigger than that."

JESSICA HALE WOOLLIAMS, FIRST CASCADIA BRITISH COLUMBIA DIRECTOR

"There was genuine and deep support in the idea that we would be able to put that tool forward. It's very compelling for folks to really understand the end game and be able to picture that and work toward it, even if it's challenging; even if people say it's impossible. The fact that it's not impossible is the whole purpose of having it. You have to chip away at making it possible."

DEB GUENTHER, MITHUN

Guenther asked for a show of hands. Who was in favor of accepting McLennan's gift of the Living Building Standard and shifting Cascadia's focus toward it? Without hesitation, every person in the room raised a hand. The group unanimously agreed in the power of this idea and in the value of folding it into the organization's mission. The Living Building Standard had found a home at the Cascadia Green Building Council.

Now what?

GETTING READY FOR PRIME TIME

McLennan had just witnessed the potential enthusiasm his Standard could create. If this forward-thinking assembly was inspired enough in the course of an eight-hour board meeting to endorse the Living Building Standard and knit it into its ongoing mission, wouldn't the larger green building movement likely respond proportionately? Cascadia needed a way to promote the Standard's value on the largest possible stage, where sheer audience numbers might make up for a woefully miniscule promotional budget. And there was only one event that fit that description; one annual three-day meeting of the minds where virtually every member of the movement gathered to share best practices and drive the cause forward: Greenbuild, the USGBC's yearly conference.

The 2006 Greenbuild International Conference and Expo was to be held in Denver in mid-November — just three months down the road. McLennan knew that the event's expected 12,000-person crowd[45] would offer just the targeted audience the Living Building Standard needed and exactly the international attention it deserved. In the 2006 world of sustainable design, Greenbuild was where things got done.

> "Once we decided to launch at Greenbuild, I had from August to November to figure out how to get a major slot on the meeting's agenda — which was pretty much impossible because it's pinned down so far in advance."
>
> **JASON F. MCLENNAN,**
> **INTERNATIONAL LIVING FUTURE INSTITUTE**

Together, Cascadia's board and staff — including its new CEO — discussed the notion of scrambling for a formal launch in only 90 days' time. Although it was ambitious (even for the envelope-pushing Cascadia), they collectively opted to take a shot.

But first, they decided to "audit" the standard internally so that the board members could vet it before staking their organization's reputation on it. Only minor revisions were suggested for the bulk of the content. However, board member Mark Frankel, technical director of the New Buildings Institute,

45 http://communicate.usgbc.org/greenbuild/2006/06.14.06_news5.3/news5.3.html

> "Who the hell wants to do L-E-E-D? It doesn't even matter what it stands for. But Living Buildings? Unbelievable. The name was brilliant. This was going the next step in words; in branding."

PLINY FISK III, CENTER FOR MAXIMUM POTENTIAL BUILDING SYSTEMS

recommended a strategic change that would prove to have lasting effects on the brand: converting the name from "Living Building *Standard*" to "Living Building *Challenge*." The program was all about the challenge of the process, he pointed out, so why not reflect that in its very name? It also tied thematically to the "2030 Challenge," a net zero carbon initiative launched by Ed Mazria and Architecture 2030 earlier in 2006 that was already gaining traction throughout the industry. The group agreed on the name change as well as the Greenbuild unveiling.

With that, the Living Building Challenge had a name, a home, a platform, and a miniscule amount of time in which to prepare for its formal launch. McLennan felt confident in the Challenge's readiness for the market; it was in the ideal "three-quarter-baked" form, ready for the user community to help polish it to completion. He only hoped the industry would agree on its value.

> "Even the name makes perfect sense. Calling it the Living Building Challenge — that explains it all. Living. Building. Challenge. It's beautiful. Just take a look at other programs' language. 'Leadership in Energy and Environmental Design?' Give me a break."

**SIM VAN DER RYN,
ECOLOGICAL DESIGN COLLABORATIVE**

AN EXPEDITED PRE-LAUNCH

In those frantic three months, McLennan and his Cascadia team covered every base they could think to cover. Financial support came from reliable donors, supplemented by a dramatically expanded donation from The Russell Family Foundation (RFF), Cascadia's first-ever and continuously loyal funder. The RFF's Grant Officer Nan McKay felt so strongly that the future of the Cascadia Green Building Council — and the movement itself — lay with the Living Building Challenge that she garnered the largest grant the foundation had ever given.[46] The funds allowed McLennan to hire a new staff member late that summer and invest in much-needed promotional tools that would accompany the team and the Challenge to Denver that November.

46 As Cascadia's original funder, the Russell Family Foundation earned a seat at many board meetings. Grant Officer Nan McKay was invited to attend McLennan's debut board meeting in Tacoma, where he introduced the Living Building concept. From that point forward, she fervently backed the idea and pledged her philosophical support along with her foundation's financial support.

> "The future success of Living Buildings will have to come out of the hearts and minds and spirits of project teams and committed owners. That's what will get us where we need to go. We're not there yet. That's why it's a challenge; otherwise, you'd have to change the name. They didn't call it the 'LEED Challenge.'"
>
> **KATH WILLIAMS, KATH WILLIAMS + ASSOCIATES**

Still, they needed to do more than merely *attend* Greenbuild. They needed to make a *serious splash* at Greenbuild. McLennan needed to find a way to get on an already-locked agenda, preferably immediately prior to or following a high-profile speaker who would draw a large crowd. So he called on some allies.

Kevin Hydes, one of McLennan's Packard Sustainability Matrix collaborators, was in the midst of his USGBC chairmanship in 2006, serving from the board seat for which he and McLennan had both run. (Hydes, coincidentally, had also served as Cascadia's first-ever board chair so he was familiar with the chapter's pioneering spirit.) While on a late summer family vacation, Hydes received a cell phone call from a very animated McLennan who was intent on persuading Hydes to release a spot on the Greenbuild agenda. No matter how many times Hydes assured McLennan that the meeting's presentation schedule was closed, McLennan pushed back. The conversation continued through several dropped calls, which McLennan repeatedly reinitiated. Finally, Hydes said he would see what he could do.

> "When Jason called me on my cell, he told me he had this idea that was really big. When I asked him what he wanted me to do about it, he said, 'I want you to help me launch it in Denver.' Jason's job is to be a provocateur. He was sort of using guerilla tactics, but that's what we love about him. To him, it was all about getting some major airtime for the Living Building Challenge."
>
> **KEVIN HYDES, INTEGRAL GROUP**

McLennan understood that he was placing his friend in a potentially difficult position, but he knew that if anyone could make this happen, it would be Hydes. Sure enough, Hydes convinced USGBC CEO Rick Fedrizzi to allocate 30 minutes to Cascadia, even though neither knew precisely what was going to be introduced. McLennan would appear on stage on Tuesday, November 14 just prior to that day's featured speaker, renowned scientist and environmentalist David Suzuki. It was poetic scheduling for McLennan, who grew up idolizing Suzuki and credits his television show, "The Nature of Things," with providing him and many young Canadians with an early environmental education.[47]

"It wasn't totally Kevin's call, but he made it happen. And to his credit, he never asked me for a lot of details on what it was I wanted to present. He managed to convince Rick and his team to let me have this time slot. It wasn't until the event that they started to get nervous, wondering what I was going to do. It could not and would not ever happen again."

JASON F. MCLENNAN, INTERNATIONAL LIVING FUTURE INSTITUTE

McLennan took this news to the Cascadia board, urging everyone to be in the room for the presentation. They were flabbergasted that he had managed to find a way onto the Greenbuild agenda — immediately preceding such a prominent speaker as Suzuki, no less — but had come to expect such behavior from their new CEO.

108 The Cascadia team spent the last few weeks leading up to Greenbuild fine-tuning the Living Building Challenge and their launch strategies. Two key improvements were made to the language of the Standard between when McLennan arrived at Cascadia and when he introduced the Challenge to the industry in Denver:

1. The "Habitat Exchange" prerequisite was incorporated into the Site[48] Petal, per the suggestion of Deb Guenther. As a landscape architect, she was especially concerned with the notion of preservation as a way to support critical ecosystems while also offsetting the potential harmful effects of the built environment.

2. A 16th prerequisite ("Inspiration and Education") was added to the original list, housed under the Beauty and Inspiration Petal. Suggested by Cascadia's brand new British Columbia Director Jessica Hale Woolliams, the first staffer hired under McLennan's leadership, the prerequisite allowed for a critical feedback loop that complemented and expanded on the intent of the one Petal that was most difficult to measure objectively.

47 Suzuki appeared as a keynote speaker at Living Future in 2013.

48 Effective with the launch of Version 3.0, the Site Petal was renamed to the Place Petal.

> "The Challenge is about looking at the end game so clearly. In order to get true ecosystem services to support our lives, we really have to think about preserving effectively functioning habitats somewhere else in the watershed. It was very exciting to be able to contribute to the Challenge the idea of a one-to-one ratio of habitat protection and development."
>
> **DEB GUENTHER, MITHUN**

Finally, mid-November rolled around. It was time for the team to pack up its new idea, raw as it may have still been, and head to Colorado. By then, McLennan was thoroughly convinced that he had made the right choice in joining Cascadia. He had always believed in the dual power of timing and platform to propel any idea forward, and he felt sure that he had both on his side as he set his sights on Denver. Greenbuild was the time, the place, and the moment for the Living Building Challenge to be released. The Standard may not have been the most refined at that point, but it was undeniably the greenest. And McLennan knew in his heart that it was what the movement needed most.

RIGHTSIZING
A LIVING BUILDING BLOCK

The Living Building Challenge is an antidote to an oversized, ill-fitting modern society. Centralized energy, food, water, and waste systems; monoculture agriculture and mass consumer goods; cities based on the automobile; and an International Style approach to design (to name just a few) have led to a built environment tilted out of scale relative to the quality and impact that structures have on humans and all living things.

The Living Building Challenge was written to shine a light on the concept of "rightsizing" — working to identify the ideal scale (environmentally, economically, socially) to solve a particular problem.

The International Living Future Institute believes that individual buildings, the neighborhoods they populate, and the larger communities they occupy must be built to suit the culture, climate, and place where they stand while honoring a healthy human scale and enhancing community and personal development. The scale must work not only for human life, but for all life, ultimately leading to ecological restoration. Project teams are encouraged to work within a watershed as well as a "lifeshed," use only current solar income for energy generation, and create on-site waste treatment systems.

By allowing scale jumping, the Challenge asks design teams to seek out the best scale for any given problem first by thinking as small as possible and then moving outward only as far as needed.

The mission is to return proper balance to buildings, neighborhoods, and communities by finding the sweet spot of size and scale for the maximum benefit of local species, local economies, and local residents. Living Buildings rely on the genius of project teams to find the right way forward.

The International Living Future Institute believes that individual buildings, the neighborhoods they populate, and the larger communities they occupy must be built to suit the culture, climate, and place where they stand while honoring a healthy human scale and enhancing community and personal development.

08

"The best time to plant a tree was 20 years ago. The second best time is now."

CHINESE PROVERB

ROCKY MOUNTAIN HIGH

THE INDUSTRY MEETS
THE CHALLENGE

The 2006 Greenbuild International Conference and Expo was the fifth annual U.S. Green Building Council (USGBC) gathering of architects, engineers, landscape designers, and other professionals committed to changing the nature of the built environment. The inaugural event had been held in 2002 in Austin, Texas and drew just over 4,000 attendees. Registration numbers climbed each of the three following years — 5,284 attended in 2003, 8,122 in 2004, and 9,724 in 2005.[49] With more than 13,000 people formally registered for the 2006 meeting in Denver,[50] it was clear that Greenbuild had become the place to find the people, projects, and ideas that were pushing the green building movement in new directions.

There was recognized buzz leading up to the Denver meeting. LEED had been in place for six years, during which time more than 6,000 buildings in 50 states and 16 countries had registered for certification.[51] Just ten months earlier, Ed Mazria and Architecture 2030 had launched the 2030 Challenge, which provided specific carbon neutrality targets that the industry could strive to meet. And it was no secret that the USGBC planned to announce important LEED updates in Denver, including requirements that would increase energy performance and reduce carbon emissions in certified projects.[52]

The industry had momentum and the Cascadia Green Building Council planned to take full advantage of it.

CREATING A BUZZ

Upon arrival in Denver, the Cascadia team immediately set out spreading seeds of curiosity around the grounds of the event. All staff and board members sported buttons displaying the bright orange gerbera daisy now emblematic of the Challenge, handing out hundreds more to attendees but not explaining what the buttons were meant to promote. They also found a corner of the exhibitors' hall and stealthily set up a small booth where they planned to display information about the Challenge following Jason F. McLennan's appearance at the podium. Meanwhile, individual board members were responsible for reaching out to key attendees to ensure that they would be in the room when the announcement was made.

Among the thousands of people in attendance at the 2006 conference were representatives from every facet of the green building movement. National GBC leaders from the United States and Canada, chapter leaders and members from throughout North America, and non-affiliated "green warriors" from all over the world all showed up to learn everything they could about sustainable design. People were there for a reason and their shared purpose created a sense of camaraderie.

> "At the Denver meeting, it felt like the green building industry was finally going to lurch forward. With Ed Mazria's 2030 Challenge already out there and gaining traction all the time, and LEED announcing the minimum energy requirements, and the Living Building Challenge about to be announced, it felt like there was a serious shift happening; like we were getting new wind behind our backs."
>
> **JASON F. MCLENNAN, INTERNATIONAL LIVING FUTURE INSTITUTE**

52 www2.buildinggreen.com/article/climate-change-dominates-greenbuild-conference-agenda

"I was going for it. I had quit my job and left my BNIM partnership to join Cascadia and launch this idea. You don't go into something like that and give it the old 'Gee, gosh, golly' approach. If you're trying to make change, you have to make change."

JASON F. MCLENNAN, INTERNATIONAL LIVING FUTURE INSTITUTE

FILLING THE ROOM

A sizable percentage of these devotees made their way to the ballroom to hear David Suzuki speak on that year's "USGBC Member Day" — Tuesday, November 14 — and there was palpable enthusiasm circulating through the crowd prior to his scheduled start time. What they didn't know was that another speaker, whose name was listed nowhere in the program, would take the stage just ahead of Suzuki.

"There was a lot of stuff going on to get people prepared for something exciting to happen. I recall it being very euphoric."

DEB GUENTHER, MITHUN

As guests made their way to their seats in anticipation of Suzuki's keynote, McLennan was off-stage preparing for what he considered to be the most important presentation of his career to that point. Everything he had studied, practiced, lobbied for, and gambled on was coming down to those next few moments. But he felt prepared, supported, and ready. His slideshow was well rehearsed and his remarks well crafted. Even his allergies, which had plagued him throughout his life and had been bothering him more than usual in the preceding few days, suddenly dissipated, further clearing his head as he approached the platform.

It took only about ten minutes for McLennan to summarize the Living Building Challenge to his captive audience. He stuck to the most important messages: the Standard's regenerative aspirations, its nods to biomimicry, and its performance-based framework. He reiterated the distinction, "no credits, just prerequisites." Beautiful images from nature splashed across the screen to accompany McLennan's animated overview of the Challenge and his impassioned calls for audience members to get involved in the change this greenest Standard was capable of making.

GREENBUILD 2006
FACTS & FIGURES[53]

DATES:
NOVEMBER 15-17, 2006

LOCATION:
DENVER, COLORADO

VENUE:
COLORADO
CONVENTION CENTER

TOTAL REGISTERED:
13,329

EXHIBITORS:
477

EXHIBITOR BOOTHS:
751 BOOTHS
27 TABLES

EXHIBITOR SPACE:
187,000 SQUARE FEET

COUNTRIES REPRESENTED:
43

CONFERENCE SESSIONS:
77

53 www.greenbuildexpo.com/Footer/
    PastEvents and www.asla.org/ppn/
    article.aspx?id=3924

REACTIONS

Those present that day report that the immediate response in the room was mixed, although predominantly positive. Most attendees recognized the Living Building Challenge as the logical next step that could take the industry past LEED Platinum and embraced it wholeheartedly. Others, though, were unsure and even nervous about how, if at all, it might fit into the existing USGBC/LEED structure. And only a very small percentage of the people in the room were familiar with McLennan, who, in spite of his resume, was still young and relatively unknown among the broader green design community.

But McLennan had allies throughout the room, including the venerable Bob Berkebile. The instant McLennan concluded his scripted comments, he invited Berkebile to join him on the stage as a way of associating a more recognizable and well-respected face with the concept. Berkebile eagerly took the figurative reins from McLennan, applauding the idea and turning to face the audience directly. With everyone's attention, he called them to action — serious, committed, game-changing action. "Who will join us in this giant leap forward?" he asked. "Who will rise to this Challenge?"

Gradually, people throughout the room rose to their feet. Soon, thousands of people were joining the standing ovation and adding to a noisy round of applause for a building standard they had only just been introduced to moments earlier. When the fervent reception finally died down and Suzuki took the stage, he provided an important punctuation mark by offering his own endorsement of the Living Building Challenge. For many, including McLennan, receiving Suzuki's very public support in front of the vast majority of the green design community was key to the success of the Standard's launch.

"I was in the audience when Jason launched the Challenge and I was really captivated. Lots of people had been talking about going farther than LEED, but it wasn't clear what path would get us there. There was a bit of awe and excitement as we all wondered what could happen next with this Living Building Challenge idea, which was so inspirational."

AMANDA STURGEON, INTERNATIONAL LIVING FUTURE INSTITUTE

"Jason is such a powerful speaker, and the feeling in the room was just overwhelming excitement and engagement in this idea. It was probably the most inspiring standing ovation I'd ever been a part of. Jason and Bob had asked a question: 'Is this something you want to be a part of?' People weren't just applauding; they were jumping up, saying, 'This is something we really care about.'"

JESSICA HALE WOOLLIAMS, FIRST CASCADIA BRITISH COLUMBIA DIRECTOR

"I was sitting in the front row when Jason announced the Challenge at Greenbuild. I was at a moment in my career where I wanted to reconnect to some of the things that I had read and thought about when I was in school. Then, here comes Jason with this idea and I thought, 'This is the coolest thing ever, it's exactly what we should be doing, it's raising the bar, it's returning us to the roots of ecological design, and it's completely impossible. I'm in.'"

RICHARD GRAVES, UNIVERSITY OF MINNESOTA

"The announcement went exactly as I had pictured it would and we got so much support. It was beautiful; it was goosebumps-inducing; it was magic."

JASON F. MCLENNAN, INTERNATIONAL LIVING FUTURE INSTITUTE

"My personal response was a resounding, 'Yeah, this is exactly where we have to go,' but I would say the general response was all over the map. There were folks who were feeling the same way I was; there were folks who were a little bit confused by it; there were folks for whom it created a lot of anxiety. There was a very broad spectrum of reactions to it."

SANDY WIGGINS, CONSILIENCE

"It was a perfect storm: the collective experience of the people in that room, plus Suzuki bringing his own integrity and clarity to put wind in the sails of this idea. It was meant to be, in many ways."

BOB BERKEBILE, BNIM

"There was an incredible buzz in Denver. I remember talking with several people at Greenbuild about the future of green design; how LEED and the Challenge could really complement each other. The Challenge could go beyond what was practical and explore what was possible."

BETH HEIDER, SKANSKA USA

"It was perfect timing. People were sick and tired of checkmarks and little boxes just to get their rating done. But this was aspirational. It went to the next level."

PLINY FISK III, CENTER FOR MAXIMUM POTENTIAL BUILDING SYSTEMS

> "[By the time the Living Building Challenge was announced] we were eight years into working with the market to create something that was meeting the market's needs as it defined them. Jason and others had a perspective on that work that inspired them to build off of LEED's advance work. They tapped into the subset of the movement who wanted to go further faster than we could, because to do so would have been to abandon the vast majority of the market we were so carefully nurturing."

RICK FEDRIZZI, U.S. GREEN BUILDING COUNCIL

A POLITE USGBC RESPONSE

The USGBC had not been made aware of Cascadia's intention to launch a new standard at Greenbuild, so they first heard of the Living Building Challenge just as everyone else in the room did. This certainly added to the flair of the moment, but did nothing to endear McLennan to certain members of the USGBC leadership team.

Michelle Moore, then a USGBC senior vice president,[54] was busy attending to other con-ference-related responsibilities and did not hear McLennan's announcement in real time.

> "I was a leader at USGBC at the time and I thought, 'Why are our friends from the Cascadia region — one of the birthplaces of green building — gunning for us?' There seemed to be a message coming from within that LEED wasn't good enough anymore, and it came at a time when we really needed all hands on deck to meet the challenges we were facing from conservative organizations in the industry that were attacking green building."

MICHELLE MOORE, GROUNDSWELL

54 Moore served as Senior VP at the USGBC from 2002 to 2007. From there, she began a stint working in President Barack Obama's administration, first as Chief Sustainability Officer and then as a senior advisor in the Director's Office in the White House Office of Management and Budget. Moore was named CEO at Groundswell in 2015. She and McLennan have developed a strong friendship in the years since the launch of the Challenge and she has become very supportive of the program.

When she learned of it soon thereafter, though, she couldn't help wondering why one of the USGBC's most influential chapters — Cascadia — would offer up something that could potentially compete directly with LEED. The timing, she felt, was unfortunate. LEED was already battling resistance from outside entities. Industrial interests were pushing back against the market transformations being driven by LEED, claiming that it raised the bar too high. People were also talking about an article entitled "LEED is Broken — Let's Fix It" that had recently appeared on iGreenBuild.com. There was movement-wide buzz about the building code's very viability, which the USGBC was actively working to combat. Whatever this new Living Building Challenge was, it felt, at least to Moore, like competition coming from inside the USGBC's own community at a time when unity was needed most.

However, when USGBC leaders saw the audience's positive response to the notion of codifying Living Buildings, they chose to officially endorse it. CEO Rick Fedrizzi stood and applauded the idea along with the crowd in a gesture that was both symbolic and unifying.

Within hours, in a move that helped propel the Living Building Challenge beyond Cascadia's borders, the USGBC announced that it would sponsor a Living Building Challenge design competition, the winners of which would be displayed at the following year's Greenbuild event.[55]

"Because of the prior information that had been available about the concept of Living Buildings — like what came out of the Packard Study, and BNIM's involvement, and Berkebile's presence — it was certainly taken seriously. But very quickly I would say that the internal dialogue at USGBC (where I was chair at the time) began to be more anxiety-ridden about it. There was real concern that this would dilute LEED's place in the market; that it would cannibalize LEED."

SANDY WIGGINS, CONSILIENCE

55 That competition did end up being held and two co-winners were announced the following year, first at the debut Living Future unConference in April 2007 and again at Greenbuild that fall. One of the winning projects was submitted by Amanda Sturgeon and a team of her Perkins+Will colleagues. For more information, see Chapter 9.

"The Challenge came at a time when LEED had become such a recognized and respected tool that it served almost as a baseline. So there was almost a yearning for those out on the bleeding edge for something new — something that did zero harm. Jason gave that vision a reality."

DALE MIKKELSEN, SFU COMMUNITY TRUST

"We're always going to be struggling with wanting things to be better because there's always a way to improve things. People who were there for the Denver launch could see the potential of the Challenge. It felt like a vehicle that got the right ideas out there in a way that people could visualize."

DEB GUENTHER, MITHUN

"When Jason announced the Living Building Challenge, it was such a strong statement about where we all needed to be. It was obvious it would be a formidable challenge, but the market wasn't ready for it. Hardly anybody — including me — was comfortable enough with themselves or their role in the design process to say, 'I can do that.' It was scary and still is. But it was bold. And it was out there."

KATH WILLIAMS, KATH WILLIAMS + ASSOCIATES

121

> "The Living Building Challenge was seen by the USGBC as a potential competitor, as if it was an either/or proposition when it never really was. We're past that now, but Greenbuild Denver was where the discussion and debate began. At that point, Jason had only been with Cascadia for a few months and our engagement with the USGBC was already in full swing."

CLARK BROCKMAN, SERA ARCHITECTS

EARLY ACTION

By Saturday, November 18, Greenbuild 2006 had come to an end. But the Living Building Challenge was just getting started. Even as the Cascadia team packed up its buttons and boards, eager architects, engineers, and owners began to approach McLennan with ideas and questions about how to get started registering Challenge projects. Bob Berkebile, too, started fielding queries from BNIM clients interested in moving proposed or underway projects from LEED Platinum to Living Building status. (The highest profile of those was the Omega Center for Sustainable Living in Rhinebeck, New York, which shifted its aspirations to the Challenge and ultimately became one of the first three projects ever to be certified as a Living Building.[56])

> "The launch went just as I wanted it to, but now there was work to do. We clearly had a viable program that people were excited about, but that meant we had to actually do it!"

JASON F. MCLENNAN,
INTERNATIONAL LIVING FUTURE INSTITUTE

Suddenly, from seemingly out of nowhere, the Living Building Challenge went from theory to reality. There was clearly enough demand for a new green building standard so there were numerous details to attend to right away to help bring it to fruition.

The Cascadia staff and board returned to Seattle ready to take on the challenge of the Challenge. In spite of the organization's modest financial and human resources, they felt buoyed by the reception they had received from their peers in Denver. There was undeniable hunger for something that pressed the movement forward; that drove transformational change. Cascadia had just the tool.

56 For more on the Omega Center for Sustainable Living, see Chapter 10.

Opinions differ on whether that day in Denver — with McLennan elbowing his way onto the Greenbuild agenda, launching his manifesto so theatrically, and the community responding so noisily — fundamentally changed the green building game. But few deny that it served as a turning point. Just as LEED had done years earlier, the Living Building Challenge offered an understandably impatient industry a new way of solving urgent environmental problems inherent in the existing paradigm. Whether or not this new standard felt truly attainable, it unquestionably raised the bar. It provided a roadmap for anyone yearning to stretch beyond the limits of LEED Platinum and pursue genuinely sustainable, regenerative design. Plenty of practitioners were thinking about and experimenting with net zero buildings and even zero impact buildings by that point, but the Living Building Challenge codified those — and other — ideals, giving designers something more definitive they could work with.

The seeds had been planted. Now it was up to Cascadia to construct a trellis strong enough to support the weight of its idea.

123 ——

EMPLOYING THE PRECAUTIONARY PRINCIPLE

A LIVING BUILDING BLOCK

The precautionary principle states that no action should be taken that poses a potential risk to environmental or human health, even when definitive scientific evidence does not exist to prove or quantify the extent of that risk. The burden of proof should be on proving something is safe.

The Living Building Challenge is structured around this rule.

Industrialized societies, however, seldom employ the precautionary principle. Products and processes are rarely tested before they are released into the world. Chemicals and technologies are unleashed with little thought to the adverse effects they might have. Unfortunately, the poorest human populations along with vulnerable animal and plant species are often the ones that suffer the unintended consequences.

The Living Building Challenge — specifically in its Materials Petal — calls for an end to these flawed constructs. It pushes the precautionary principle forward as the only responsible way to behave.

The precautionary principle states that no action should be taken that poses a potential risk to environmental or human health, even when definitive scientific evidence does not exist to prove or quantify the extent of that risk. The burden of proof should be on proving something is safe.

09

"Build today, then strong and sure,
With a firm and ample base;
And ascending and secure.
Shall tomorrow find its place."

HENRY WADSWORTH LONGFELLOW

CREATING THE INFRASTRUCTURE

AN ORGANIZATION COMES TOGETHER

The Cascadia Green Building Council team returned from Greenbuild excited to respond to the interest the industry had expressed in the Living Building Challenge. But they were also realistic. The small non-profit needed to seriously bolster its infrastructure if it had any chance of taking the Challenge where it now appeared capable of going. Before adding staff, creating a solid program, building an effective brand, or marketing the Standard, Cascadia needed to ramp up its funding efforts. Quickly.

STRENGTHENING THE FINANCIAL BASE

Jason F. McLennan knew that he could leverage the Greenbuild audience's enthusiasm with existing and potential funders, so he, his staff, and the board mapped out a strategy for a new capital campaign as soon as they returned from Denver. Within days, McLennan was meeting one-on-one with influential grant makers throughout the region.

> "The support we received from the Russell Family Foundation is a good example of how energizing the Living Building Challenge idea was. That foundation has been central to the story of the Challenge."
>
> **DEB GUENTHER, MITHUN**

He knew he could rely on funds from the consistently supportive Russell Family Foundation, which championed the concept from the start. Other repeat and first-time funders stepped up in a steady stream beginning in late 2006, providing Cascadia with an increasingly solid footing. Many donors gradually upped their contributions as they became more familiar with the Challenge and Cascadia's plans for it. The Kendeda Fund, for example, initiated its support in 2007 with a donation that doubled each of the following few years to the point where Kendeda became one of Cascadia's largest funders.[57] The Kresge Foundation and the Bullitt Foundation were among the other funders that lent significant support in the months following Greenbuild, strengthening Cascadia's ability to expand its Living Building Challenge operation.

> "A lot of funders were coming to us rather than the other way around, which is rare in the non-profit world. It was like the universe was coming forward to say, 'Here you go.' It was amazing."
>
> **JASON F. MCLENNAN, INTERNATIONAL LIVING FUTURE INSTITUTE**

THE SILVER BULLITT

The Bullitt Foundation began its now storied relationship with Cascadia in 2007, when McLennan met with then-program officer Amy Solomon to promote Cascadia and the Living Building Challenge as worthy grantees. In the middle of McLennan's presentation, Solomon stopped him abruptly, insisting that she had to bring Denis Hayes into the room to hear about this new building standard. (Hayes initially made a name for himself among environmentalists as the national coordinator of the first Earth Day in 1970 when he was only 25. He has led the Seattle-based Bullitt Foundation since 1992 and has since helped shape its commitment to urban ecology.)

McLennan, of course, was aware of Hayes and his critical role in the larger movement but had never met him personally until that day. So he was thrilled to welcome Hayes into the conversation about Living Buildings. Little did McLennan know, though, that Hayes was

---

57 By 2015, the Kendeda Fund had become such a strong advocate of the Challenge that it gave Georgia Tech a $30 million grant — the largest single gift in its giving history — to develop the Southeast's first major education and research facility registered under the Living Building Challenge Version 3.0.

Denis Hayes and Jason F. McLennan

in the preliminary stage of planning for a dedicated Bullitt Foundation headquarters that he wanted to build to even more stringent standards than LEED Platinum. As McLennan went into further detail about the Living Building Challenge, Hayes and Solomon began to consider that they may have discovered the roadmap that would lead them to their future headquarters.

McLennan left that meeting with far more than a likely investor; he had found a strategic partner and the eventual owner of the Bullitt Center, the world's greenest office building and current home of the Living Building Challenge. (For more on the Bullitt Center, see Chapter 13 or refer to the project's case study book, *The Greenest Building: How the Bullitt Center Changes the Urban Landscape*.)

"I had this magical meeting with Amy Solomon when I first went to the Bullitt Foundation to talk about the Challenge. Suddenly, she said, 'Wait! Denis needs to hear this.' I ended up giving them both my spiel about Living Buildings and the future of architecture and all that. What I didn't know is that he wanted to build a building. They were very interested in what we were doing and they have funded us ever since. Now they are part of us."

JASON F. MCLENNAN, INTERNATIONAL LIVING FUTURE INSTITUTE

THE FREEDOM TO GROW

Several of Cascadia's biggest donors have a history of giving unconditionally, offering Cascadia the flexibility to use the funds in whatever ways best serve the organizational mission in any given fiscal year (which, as Cascadia worked to launch its new Standard, typically meant that most funds applied to Living Building Challenge-related costs). Those donors that did specify how they wanted their grant money to be used during the initial Living Building Challenge appeal often requested that it support the new Standard's efforts.

As funds came in, Cascadia's operating budget gradually expanded to the point where personnel could be added. When McLennan joined in summer 2006, the organization had a full-time staff of three — Marni Evans Kahn (Washington state director), Gina Franzosa (Oregon state director), and Brandon Smith (deputy/interim director whom McLennan later named COO) — along with a dedicated core of on-call volunteers. Still, more minds and bodies would be needed to manage the organization's broadening scope.

To bolster Cascadia's presence in British Columbia, McLennan hired Jessica Hale Woolliams in late 2006 as the first Vancouver-based director. As co-founder (with Helen Goodland) of Light House Sustainable Building Centre, Woolliams had previously partnered with Cascadia on various green building and social entrepreneurship ventures throughout the province. Once she joined Cascadia as a full-time employee, Woolliams was responsible for helping spread awareness of the Living Building Challenge around British Columbia.

"Cascadia was all about where we wanted to go and how to help leaders accelerate. I joined because I really believed in the power of Jason's vision: to create a truly sustainable built form."

JESSICA HALE WOOLLIAMS, FIRST CASCADIA BRITISH COLUMBIA DIRECTOR

A NEW INDEPENDENCE

McLennan also tapped the talents of independent graphic designer Erin Gehle, one of the creative brains behind BNIM's brand and the person responsible for infusing Ecotone's books with visual beauty, to breathe new life into the marketing collateral for both Cascadia and the Living Building Challenge. Working closely with McLennan, Gehle created new logos, revamped an outdated website, and introduced a distinctive look and feel for all online and print materials.

The branding efforts served several purposes: to elevate Cascadia's professional profile, to establish a graphic identity for the Challenge, and to distinguish both the organization and its Standard from the U.S. Green Building Council (USGBC).[58] An overarching goal was to wrap Cascadia in branding beauty that rivaled any design firm's; to weave elegance into its materials and message as a way of demonstrating the type of beauty that a Living built environment could embody.

Although the branding process was one of the first of many moves McLennan and his team would make over the coming years to differentiate the Cascadia chapter and its offerings from the national operation, there were occasional early attempts to combine their strengths. In early 2007, just a few months after Greenbuild, McLennan still envisioned an approach that he felt would serve all parties. He wrote a proposal calling for the USGBC to "buy" the Living Building Challenge for $1 but cede all operational oversight to Cascadia and fully fund its deployment. The USGBC would put its full weight behind the Challenge and offer it as the level above LEED Platinum, while Cascadia would run the program. McLennan's strategic mistake, he realized later, was not taking the idea directly to the USGBC's executive leadership. Instead, he first ran it by board members, floating the concept with them to get their input prior to formally submitting it. But the USGBC passed on the idea. The Living Building Challenge would not be folded into the LEED family of standards.

The Living Building Challenge Versions 1.0 and 1.2

---

58 Since that time, Gehle has continued to design the majority of the organization's materials and most of the titles in the Ecotone Publishing library of books, including this one.

> "The first Living Future was the worst run conference in the world! We slapped it together so fast; it was a complete mess with awful catering disasters. But there was lots of heady stuff happening and people loved it. It had a great spirit and that's all because of Marni and the staff, who made it work. I think everyone was surprised that in such a short amount of time there were so many people pursuing Living Buildings. We were off to the races."
>
> **JASON F. MCLENNAN, INTERNATIONAL LIVING FUTURE INSTITUTE**

A MEETING OF THE MINDS

Meanwhile, plans were already underway for Cascadia's first stand-alone conference. Cascadia board member Peter Dobrovolny, a green building specialist for the City of Seattle, was adamant that the organization hold its own event that could capitalize on the Denver energy and activate people who were ready for a different approach to green building. Besides, he argued, there were few options beyond Greenbuild for individuals interested in serving as true change agents within the movement. Dobrovolny persuaded his board colleagues and McLennan that the idea was worth further stretching their already thin resources, and the team got to work planning the inaugural Living Future meeting for April 2007 — just a few months away.

Staff member Marni Evans Kahn worked closely with McLennan on the logistics, despite the fact that neither had planned a professional gathering anywhere near that size before. Given the extremely tight time frame, they had to prioritize. They locked down the date (April 25-27, 2007), secured a venue (Seattle Center Pavilion), and booked the keynote speaker (Ed Mazria).

Cascadia also joined forces with the American Institute of Architects (AIA) Seattle Committee on the Environment to piggyback onto its well established "What Makes It Green" event, created and run by Amanda Sturgeon. (Sturgeon first met McLennan when she hired Elements on behalf of the City of Seattle, then through her position as a Cascadia board member. By 2007, she was national sustainable design co-director at the Seattle office of Perkins+Will.) Before Living Future came along, What Makes It Green was the only gathering of its kind for the region's green building community. Sturgeon and her AIA Seattle team saw the value in sharing messages and audiences with Cascadia, and the two organizations created a dual event.

> "I do remember that first Living Future to be very chaotic, but there was this very edgy new focus that they brought that made it exciting. It introduced a new way of thinking that was all about Living Buildings. It took the green building conversation to the next place."

AMANDA STURGEON,
INTERNATIONAL LIVING FUTURE INSTITUTE

For their side of things, McLennan and Kahn prioritized their common goal of creating an event that really stood out. In fact, they decided early in the planning process that they sought to offer the *opposite* of what attendees were used to. Kahn suggested they start with the name itself. Instead of a conference, she said, they should deliver to the movement an unConference. McLennan agreed completely.

The agenda included a ceremony naming the winners of the Living Building Challenge design competition McLennan had announced the previous fall at Greenbuild in Denver. Sharing the top honors were two entries, one of which was a project managed by Sturgeon, then at Perkins+Will. Excited by the new Standard and eager to get her firm moving toward Living Buildings, Sturgeon encouraged her team to adapt designs for a new office building on behalf of the Washington State Department of Ecology and submit the entry. The plans accommodated every Petal of the Living Building Challenge, including net zero energy and on-site water treatment strategies.[59] It was Sturgeon's first experience working to satisfy the rigorous requirements of the Challenge, and provided critical insights that later enhanced her ability to work with project teams as an Institute staff member.

The 2007 Living Future unConference will not be remembered for its logistical excellence, nor for its financial success.[60] However, it was wildly successful when it came to connecting the people and ideas already swirling around the Living Building concept. It was where a new brand and a new annual industry event were born. Even McLennan was surprised by the number of project teams in attendance who were engaged in the process just a few months after the launch in Denver. When he asked the assembly, "How many people in this room are working on a Living Building project?" he expected just three or four people to respond out of the nearly 500 in attendance. When approximately 50 hands shot up into the air, he recalls being both ecstatic and terrified.[61]

---

59 The project did not receive the necessary funding to be built.

60 Living Future unConferences continued to lose money in each of the following four years, although attendance numbers grew annually. The event began to be profitable in 2011.

61 McLennan has a history of using colorful language during presentations, which is something that Living Future audiences have come to expect. When he saw the staggering numbers of hands raised by self-described Living Building project team members at the first unConference, he responded with an astonished, "Holy shit!"

133

THE GARDEN OF EDEN

Living Future 2007 also yielded another important asset for the Living Building Challenge: its first director. Even as Cascadia grew its employee roster in the months following McLennan's arrival, it was still a small non-profit where everybody's job descriptions overlapped to some degree. It concerned McLennan that no one person was officially responsible for overseeing either the Challenge or the Pharos Project. So with his board's permission, he initiated a search for the first Challenge/Pharos director by announcing the job opening at Living Future 2007. As it happened, he didn't have to look far.

> "Eden was always the person who was willing to go the extra mile, and she put in a lot of hours. She built much of the original infrastructure that helped us move forward."
>
> **JASON F. MCLENNAN,**
> **INTERNATIONAL LIVING FUTURE INSTITUTE**

Eden Brukman had first heard McLennan speak on November 2, 2006 at a presentation at Portland's Ecotrust Building, where he laid out the Living Building Challenge and Pharos in preparation for Greenbuild later that month. At the time, Brukman was a licensed architect working as sustainability coordinator at SERA Architects, reporting directly to Cascadia board member Clark Brockman. Her life-long passion for green issues, particularly clean materials advocacy, drew her "like a gravitational pull" to the programs McLennan introduced.

Encouraged by Brockman to get more involved with Cascadia, she immediately volunteered her time and expertise to the organization. In addition to supporting the Portland office with technical guidance, she offered to join the contingent scheduled to travel to Denver later that month, where she and other volunteers stealthily scoped out a corner of the Greenbuild convention hall so they could set up a modest booth to promote the Living Building Challenge. Following Greenbuild, Brukman's volunteer commitment increased, as did her belief in Cascadia's game-changing initiatives. She and her SERA colleagues spent the next several months conceptualizing one of the first proposed Living Buildings, the plans for which they would submit to the first Living Building Challenge competition at the first Living Future unConference.

By April 2007, when Brukman sat in the Living Future audience and heard of Cascadia's job opening to create the programmatic infrastructure for the Living Building Challenge and Pharos, she was already fully invested in the organization and the radical change it was capable of. She approached McLennan, essentially telling him that he need look no further for his candidate. After a few formal interviews, she was hired.

Brukman and McLennan both expected the position to require a fairly even split between the two programs, but the Challenge quickly eclipsed Pharos in terms of the amount of

> "While Eden and Thor worked together, they were given a nearly impossible task. Suddenly, we had a program, but we had more work than money. Even with our new funding, it was too much work to do with what we had. It was incredibly exciting, but it was tough."
>
> **JASON F. MCLENNAN, INTERNATIONAL LIVING FUTURE INSTITUTE**

time required. McLennan had also hired Thor Peterson, whom he knew through the City of Seattle Green Building Team, to join forces with Brukman. While Peterson was with Cascadia for less than a year, he and Brukman worked tirelessly in those months to establish the infrastructure for the Living Building Challenge (and, to a lesser extent, Pharos).

After Peterson's departure in 2008, Eden continued to strengthen the Living Building Challenge foundation. She created systems that allowed projects to register and interface with one another, as well as the program's Ambassador and Collaborative networks, all while serving as the primary liaison between Cascadia and the growing list of project teams. (For more on the Ambassador and Collaborative networks, see Chapter 12.) When McLennan was unavailable, Brukman spoke directly with architects, engineers, and builders about the Challenge, answering technical and logistical questions accurately and extensively.

> "Eden's ability to conceptualize and launch the Ambassador and Collaborative programs proved to be an enduring piece of the puzzle. She was always able to represent the Standard as I would. She's one of the smartest people on the planet and technically brilliant."
>
> **JASON F. MCLENNAN, INTERNATIONAL LIVING FUTURE INSTITUTE**

THE USER'S GUIDE THAT WASN'T

As word of the Living Building Challenge spread and more teams stepped up to register projects, it became increasingly obvious that the Standard was missing a key component promised from the beginning in the published Standard: a user's guide. McLennan had inserted the phrase "See User's Guide for more information" throughout the footnotes of Version 1.0 of the Challenge, fully intending to draft such a document when he had time

"Between 2008 and 2010, it was hard for us to keep up with the demand; we didn't have all the tools we needed to help project teams. We were like a start-up, not refined or mature enough yet to provide the best customer service and we got complaints. Luckily, the people pursuing the Challenge were die-hards and passionate and forgiving."

JASON F. MCLENNAN, INTERNATIONAL LIVING FUTURE INSTITUTE

to do so.[62] But his frenzied schedule actually promoting and running the Standard never allowed him the hours required to write out what he knew needed to be an extremely detailed resource guide. Even Brukman and Peterson attempted to take on the task, but had to set it aside when their other duties continued to take precedence.

Frustrated project teams began to voice their concerns — loudly. The Living Building Challenge was very complex, they argued, and they needed written clarification on much of its nuanced content. Nobody had ever done these kinds of projects before and they wanted the roadmap. The Cascadia team agreed completely and assured their "customers" that they were working on a variety of tools that would support Challenge teams. The reality, though, was that they were scrambling just to keep one foot in front of the other. It became an inside joke between McLennan and Brukman that any phone time project representatives could get with one of them was what constituted the User's Guide. Their most common response to queries from the field was, "Figure it out, then share it with the world." In the end, no formal User's Guide ever got published. Instead, project teams now refer to Petal Handbooks as well as the Living Building Challenge Dialogue, an online information sharing resource.[63]

THE COST OF GREEN

Even as more projects registered for the Living Building Challenge, there was a lingering perception that green buildings — and certainly Living Buildings — come at a prohibitive price. Assuaging those cost concerns became part of the work of promoting the Standard.

The 2001/2002 Packard Sustainability Matrix had explored side-by-side cost comparisons of a single structure built to mainstream, LEED, and Living Building standards. But market

62 Here, another example of the three-quarter-baked approach in action: McLennan released the Challenge without a user's guide so that the community's feedback could help flesh it out.

63 For more on the Dialogue, see Chapter 10. For more on Petal Handbooks, see Chapter 14.

dynamics shifted measurably in the years following that report's publication. If the industry were going to embrace the Challenge as a viable alternative, it had to be convinced that it was a fiscally sound approach by using updated numbers.

Not long after the Living Building Challenge was introduced, Cascadia teamed up with SERA Architects, Skanska USA Building, Gerding Edlen Development, New Buildings Institute, and Interface Engineering to update the financial data related to the Standard. Their findings were published in 2009 in "The Living Building Financial Study: The Effects of Climate, Building Type and Incentives on Creating the Buildings of Tomorrow." In it, nine existing LEED Gold buildings were conceptually transformed into Living Buildings, and all associated initial and long-term costs were quantified using simplified lifecycle analysis. The buildings represented a range of typologies and came from four climate zones — temperate, hot/humid, hot/arid, and cool.

THE NINE STRUCTURES INCLUDED:

1. A university classroom

2. A K-8 school

3. A low-rise office building

4. A mid-rise office building

5. A mixed-use renovation

6. A single family residence

7. A multifamily residence

8. A high-rise mixed-use structure

9. A hospital

The peer-reviewed Financial Study revealed that there are, indeed, up-front costs to constructing Living Buildings, but the return on investment comes quickly during the buildings' operational phases. Importantly, the study showed that the ongoing savings have more to do with an absence of power and water bills. It also helped to convince the market that buildings can be used not just as teaching tools but as reflections of developers' and tenants' brands — intangible benefits that can add to a structure's enduring value.

Most teams pondering the Living Building Challenge now refer back to the Financial Study as they explore the fiscal feasibility of their projects. And with every passing year, there are more Living Buildings whose measurable operational data further prove the point: Living Buildings make environmental *and* fiscal sense.

LIVING BUILDING FINANCIAL STUDY
COST COMPARISON MATRIX

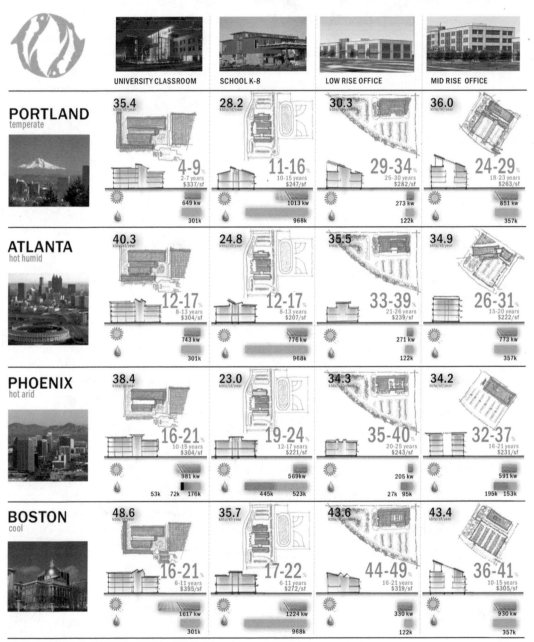

	UNIVERSITY CLASSROOM	SCHOOL K-8	LOW RISE OFFICE	MID RISE OFFICE
PORTLAND temperate	35.4 kbtu/sf/year — 4-9 % 2-7 years $337/sf — 649 kw — 301k	28.2 kbtu/sf/year — 11-16 % 10-15 years $247/sf — 1013 kw — 968k	30.3 kbtu/sf/year — 29-34 % 25-30 years $282/sf — 273 kw — 122k	36.0 kbtu/sf/year — 24-29 % 18-23 years $263/sf — 851 kw — 357k
ATLANTA hot humid	40.3 kbtu/sf/year — 12-17 % 8-13 years $304/sf — 743 kw — 301k	24.8 kbtu/sf/year — 12-17 % 8-13 years $207/sf — 776 kw — 968k	35.5 kbtu/sf/year — 33-39 % 21-26 years $239/sf — 271 kw — 122k	34.9 kbtu/sf/year — 26-31 % 15-20 years $222/sf — 773 kw — 357k
PHOENIX hot arid	38.4 kbtu/sf/year — 16-21 % 10-15 years $304/sf — 981 kw — 53k 72k 176k	23.0 kbtu/sf/year — 19-24 % 12-17 years $221/sf — 569kw — 445k 523k	34.3 kbtu/sf/year — 35-40 % 20-25 years $243/sf — 205 kw — 27k 95k	34.2 kbtu/sf/year — 32-37 % 16-21 years $231/sf — 591 kw — 195k 153k
BOSTON cool	48.6 kbtu/sf/year — 16-21 % 6-11 years $395/sf — 1617 kw — 301k	35.7 kbtu/sf/year — 17-22 % 6-11 years $272/sf — 1224 kw — 968k	43.6 kbtu/sf/year — 44-49 % 16-21 years $319/sf — 330 kw — 122k	43.4 kbtu/sf/year — 36-41 % 10-15 years $305/sf — 930 kw — 357k

138

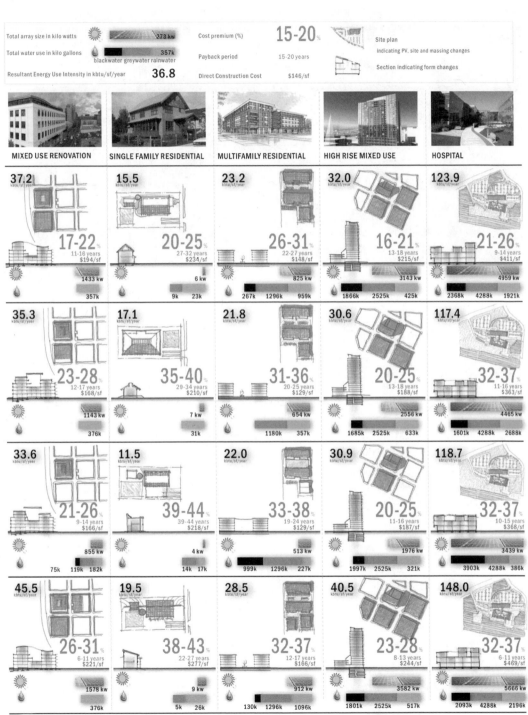

Legend:

Total array size in kilo watts — 273 kw
Total water use in kilo gallons — 357k (blackwater greywater rainwater)
Resultant Energy Use Intensity in kbtu/sf/year — 36.8
Cost premium (%) — 15-20%
Payback period — 15-20 years
Direct Construction Cost — $146/sf
Site plan indicating PV, site and massing changes
Section indicating form changes

MIXED USE RENOVATION	SINGLE FAMILY RESIDENTIAL	MULTIFAMILY RESIDENTIAL	HIGH RISE MIXED USE	HOSPITAL
37.2 kbtu/sf/year; 17-22%; 11-16 years; $194/sf; 1433 kw; 357k	**15.5** kbtu/sf/year; 20-25%; 27-32 years; $234/sf; 6 kw; 9k 23k	**23.2** kbtu/sf/year; 26-31%; 22-27 years; $148/sf; 825 kw; 267k 1296k 959k	**32.0** kbtu/sf/year; 16-21%; 13-18 years; $215/sf; 3143 kw; 1866k 2525k 425k	**123.9** kbtu/sf/year; 21-26%; 9-14 years; $411/sf; 4959 kw; 2368k 4288k 1921k
35.3 kbtu/sf/year; 23-28%; 12-17 years; $168/sf; 1143 kw; 376k	**17.1** kbtu/sf/year; 35-40%; 29-34 years; $210/sf; 7 kw; 31k	**21.8** kbtu/sf/year; 31-36%; 20-25 years; $129/sf; 654 kw; 1180k 357k	**30.6** kbtu/sf/year; 20-25%; 13-18 years; $188/sf; 2556 kw; 1685k 2525k 633k	**117.4** kbtu/sf/year; 32-37%; 11-16 years; $363/sf; 4465 kw; 1601k 4288k 2688k
33.6 kbtu/sf/year; 21-26%; 9-14 years; $166/sf; 855 kw; 75k 119k 182k	**11.5** kbtu/sf/year; 39-44%; 39-44 years; $218/sf; 4 kw; 14k 17k	**22.0** kbtu/sf/year; 33-38%; 19-24 years; $129/sf; 513 kw; 999k 1296k 227k	**30.9** kbtu/sf/year; 20-25%; 11-16 years; $187/sf; 1976 kw; 1997k 2525k 321k	**118.7** kbtu/sf/year; 32-37%; 10-15 years; $368/sf; 3439 kw; 3903k 4288k 386k
45.5 kbtu/sf/year; 26-31%; 6-11 years; $221/sf; 1578 kw; 376k	**19.5** kbtu/sf/year; 38-43%; 22-27 years; $277/sf; 9 kw; 5k 26k	**28.5** kbtu/sf/year; 32-37%; 12-17 years; $166/sf; 912 kw; 130k 1296k 1096k	**40.5** kbtu/sf/year; 23-28%; 8-13 years; $244/sf; 3582 kw; 1801k 2525k 517k	**148.0** kbtu/sf/year; 32-37%; 6-11 years; $469/sf; 5666 kw; 2093k 4288k 2196k

"Living Buildings can be built cost effectively in today's market-driven economy given the rising costs of energy and water. The first-cost premiums for many building types are significantly lower than what many would predict for an energy- and water-independent structure. The degree of cost effectiveness depends on the interplay of four factors: client, climate, scale, and building use — as originally thought by the study team. The study found that two additional factors: 1) the availability of incentives, and 2) the costs of energy and water, can tip the scales for economic competitiveness."

EXCERPT FROM *THE LIVING BUILDING FINANCIAL STUDY*

INSTITUTING CLARITY

— **140** By 2009, the organization also realized it had a branding problem to solve: people were confused about where the lines were drawn between Cascadia and the Living Building Challenge. If the Cascadia Green Building Council was a regional chapter of the USGBC and oversaw green building efforts — including LEED projects — in the Pacific Northwest, were Living Building Challenge teams from elsewhere still supposed to register projects with the Seattle office? If so, were Living Building Challenge projects tied to the USGBC, or just to Cascadia? Would a regional organization be equipped to handle international requests with authority? And why was the USGBC unable to answer questions about the Living Building Challenge?

"Here's what the Financial Study showed clearly: for long-term owners or institutional investors with longer investment horizons, the return on investment could be attractive if you're in a climate where the demand for heating and cooling is really high and the cost of energy is too. Then it makes financial sense to design a building that produces all its own energy and harvests its own rainwater. There's a very strong business case for Living Buildings."

BETH HEIDER, SKANSKA USA

To simplify things and to give the burgeoning Standard a proper home, Cascadia established a separate non-profit entity in April 2009 called the International Living Building Institute (ILBI), whose entire mission was to oversee the Living Building Challenge and its projects. Cascadia continued to operate as a regional USGBC chapter and advocacy group run out of shared offices with the ILBI, with many staff members serving both non-profits.

With dedicated staff and growing awareness, the Living Building Challenge was coming into its own. The project teams that had demonstrated the earliest interest in the program — including those individuals who had been present at Greenbuild in Denver in November 2006 — had travelled far enough down the planning, designing, funding, and building paths that the world's first registered Living Buildings were beginning to take shape by 2009. What once was merely an audacious idea had finally evolved into the structures that aspired to be the greenest on the planet.

"Creating the ILBI as a subservient but separate entity from Cascadia and the USGBC chapter system helped us clarify our intentions that the Challenge wasn't just a little Pacific Northwest initiative. It required a much bigger framework. We deliberately put the word 'international' into the title to reassure people that we were, in fact, international — even though that made the name wordier. We always intended to drop it when it became obvious."

JASON F. MCLENNAN, INTERNATIONAL LIVING FUTURE INSTITUTE

UNCOVERING OBSTACLES IN ORDER TO REMOVE THEM

A LIVING BUILDING BLOCK

Systemic change can only happen when new opportunities for improvement can be identified. Yet it can be difficult to identify all the barriers standing in the way of progress until one really focuses on creating significant change.

The Living Building Challenge was written in a way that encourages – and depends upon — feedback from project teams who are out in the field learning as they go and running into barriers to adoption. Through

transparency and dialogue, the community collaborates on the Standard's evolution and works to remove obstacles that present themselves.

For example, when McLennan first wrote the Standard, he suspected that the Water Petal was illegal in every jurisdiction in the U.S. But it would have been impossible for him to identify the distinct manifestations of water codes in every city, county, and state. As project teams began working with the Challenge, they uncovered the specifics of their local codes and often found ways to overcome them — paving a trail for all other projects to follow. Thanks to the Living Building Challenge, water and waste regulations have been changed all over the continent.

The Living Building Challenge purposely shines bright light onto various aspects of the design-build industry that need to be rethought, reconfigured, and reexamined. Whether it's unwritten inequities now called out through the JUST program or a lack of transparency in materials highlighted by Declare, the program continually works to identify, signal, and remove barriers standing between the present and a truly Living Future.

10

"Faith is taking the first step even when you don't see the whole staircase."

MARTIN LUTHER KING, JR.

COMING TO LIFE
THE FIRST LIVING BUILDINGS

The Living Building Challenge had momentum as soon as it hit the market in November 2006. By 2007, with scores of project teams already planning their own Living Buildings, the Standard was gaining speed. The exhilaration felt by the staff and volunteers at the Cascadia Green Building Council (and, after 2009, the International Living Building Institute) was matched by the determination of a growing list of designers and owners eager to prove that it was possible. Everybody busy planning and fundraising for proposed Living Buildings wanted theirs to be the first structure in the world to receive the coveted certification. The race was friendly, but it was on.

Cascadia began formally registering projects in mid-2007, with Eden Brukman and Thor Peterson overseeing the process. Registrants paid fees according to typology, size, and whether projects aspired to Petal Recognition or full certification. There was no time frame in which project teams were required to complete construction. However, once occupied, every structure needed to undergo a 12-month operational phase during which performance data would be tracked and documented. Only after a successful on-site audit and data review could a project be certified as Living.

Not all aspirational Living Buildings that registered early for the Challenge ended up getting built. Some projects fell away because of the same financial or logistical factors that typically threaten any mainstream design or construction project. Still others were cancelled due to the extremely difficult economic conditions that stretched from late 2007

Cambrian College, Sudbury, ON

and continued all the way into 2011 during the dip now referred to as the Great Recession. As a result, it took some time after it was launched before there was any proof that the greenest standard was doable.

AN EARLY EFFORT LANDS CLOSE TO HOME

Technically, the first project to register for the Living Building Challenge was already in progress when the Standard was introduced in 2006. Near the end of his tenure at BNIM, Jason F. McLennan led design efforts for an energy demonstration project on the campus of Cambrian College in his hometown of Sudbury, Ontario. (This was a particularly poignant effort for McLennan, as Cambrian was located across the road from the high school he attended and his father taught at the college for 31 years.) McLennan used the Cambrian College project as a testing ground for the Living Building concept — before it evolved into a codified standard — and developed architectural and systems designs that would turn the Cambrian structure into the first real-world example using all six of the original performance areas (Site, Energy, Materials, Water, Indoor Quality, and Beauty and Inspiration).

When McLennan transitioned to Cascadia in the summer of 2006, he continued to design on the Cambrian project with Sudbury-based architect Dennis Castellan; when he drafted the first version of the Living Building Challenge, he used the Cambrian plans as a reference point; when the Challenge was finally open to registrants, he ensured that Cambrian College was first on the list.

The Cambrian College project was scheduled to begin construction in 2008, get occupied by 2009, and was expected to be first to achieve Living Building certification approximately 12 months later. While the project was moving ahead at full steam, team leaders John Hood and Les Lisk traveled by train from Sudbury to Seattle in April 2007 for the first Living Future unConference. Along the way, they put on a great show, granting media interviews to raise awareness of the project and proudly boast their plans to "win" the world's first Living Building certification.

Unfortunately, financial and political realities delayed and eventually cancelled the plans for a Living structure on the Cambrian campus. The funds ended up being reallocated for a library addition. (However, Hood and Lisk took it upon themselves to organize their own Sudbury-based Living Future conference that ran for three years.)

"I really thought the Cambrian College project was going to make it, and it would have been poetic for me if the first Living Building had happened in Sudbury. We had a great team and they loved the idea of competing against Americans to become the first certified project, but it didn't happen."

JASON F. MCLENNAN, INTERNATIONAL LIVING FUTURE INSTITUTE

ANOTHER EARLY CONTENDER

Meanwhile, Cascadia board member Clark Brockman and his SERA Architects colleagues[64] were racing against Cambrian College with plans for their own aspirational Living Building in Portland, Oregon. The way key team members characterize the genesis of the idea, the Kenton Living Building was commissioned on the day the Challenge was launched at Greenbuild in 2006. Brockman reports that developer Peter Wilcox of Renewal Associates, an existing SERA client who was also present for the Denver conference, approached him immediately after McLennan's announcement and insisted that they pursue a Living Building project together — something that would offer both societal and environmental advantages. The result was Kenton, a proposed 5,300 square foot mixed-use Living structure to be supported by a Green Investment Fund grant from the City of Portland Office of Sustainable Development.

64 Including Lisa Petterson, who later joined the International Living Future Institute board.

"The Cambrian guys took the train all the way out from Sudbury to Seattle, very happy to show up for our first Living Future in 2007 saying that they were going to beat the American team. Cambrian and Kenton were the first two and one of those was supposed to be the first Living Building."

JASON F. MCLENNAN, INTERNATIONAL LIVING FUTURE INSTITUTE

By Living Future 2007, McLennan wanted to shine light on these two groundbreaking projects as a way of celebrating the teams' ingenuity and promoting their progress to other meeting attendees. At the first unConference in Seattle, he invited members of both project teams to the stage to create a friendly display of competition between Cambrian College and the Kenton Living Building. Which structure would be completed first? Which would enter its certification phase first? Which would reach the Living line first?

Unfortunately, even though the Cambrian and Kenton projects seemed to be the most promising potential Living Building pioneers, both ultimately faced insurmountable economic and political hurdles. They were the first two to register for the Challenge, but neither ended up getting built. Meanwhile, as 2007 turned to 2008 and 2008 to 2009, the list of registered Living Building projects grew. But the question remained: which project, if any, would enter its operational phase first? Of those, which would successfully pass its audit and achieve Living Building certification before all others?

Until there was proof that it could be accomplished from both a performance and an economic perspective, the Living Building Challenge was just another big idea.

THE THREE THAT FIRST EMERGED

Gradually, some of the earliest projects to register began to rise above the rubble of those that had fallen away during the difficult months of the Great Recession. Several buildings had made enough progress to offer the promise of completion. A handful were even beginning to be occupied and had initiated their 12-month operational audit phases. Of those, three were in the lead in the marathon race toward Living Building certification by mid-2010: the Omega Center for Sustainable Living in Rhinebeck, New York; the Tyson Living Learning Center in Eureka, Missouri; and the Eco-Sense Residence in Victoria, British Columbia.

65 http://serapdx.com/projects/kenton-living-building/

> "The Kenton Living Building was a pioneering green investment for Portland [noted] for its extraordinary measures to achieve net zero energy, water, storm water, and waste water usage. The tremendous innovation of the Kenton Living Building is embodied in its attempt at the complete fulfillment of The Living Building Challenge. In doing so, the Kenton Living Building will accelerate the advancement of Portland's green building movement towards full sustainability."
>
> **FROM THE SERA ARCHITECTS WEBSITE**[64]

The ILBI chose not to disclose — to the public or to the three project teams — the leaders' precise status as they all neared the end of their audit phases to avoid elevating the importance of one above the others. Also, the three buildings provided an interesting blend of typologies that would demonstrate the Standard's broad applicability when presented as a trio of projects capable of achieving such a rigorous set of goals. Instead of singling out one project as the first "winner" to reach the Living goal, the Institute decided to approach each project team and float the idea of a three-way tie. They made the case that creating a group victory was more in keeping with the collaborative spirit of the movement in general and the Challenge in particular. All players agreed without hesitation, recognizing what a powerful statement they could help make by sharing the figurative podium with their fellow Living Building champions. All three were certified in the fall of 2010.

STURGEON LENDS HER STRENGTH

Another important development occurred amid the flurry of those first three projects' march toward certification. Thanks to a few successful years of fundraising, the organization had modestly growing budgets with which to expand its staff. Among the new hires in summer 2010 was someone who would prove to be one of the Institute's most valuable and powerful additions: noted Seattle-area architect Amanda Sturgeon, FAIA and LEED Fellow.

In addition to being a founding Cascadia board member, Sturgeon was an active AIA and USGBC volunteer. She was a veteran of the City of Seattle as well as two top-tier green design firms, Mithun and Perkins+Will, where she introduced the Living Building concept

"It was a big deal that we had three projects that were emerging to be certified at about the same time. We knew that the public story would be very much about who won. It was more poetic not to have a single winner but to present the first three together."

JASON F. MCLENNAN, INTERNATIONAL LIVING FUTURE INSTITUTE

"For those early project teams, this was a fledgling program. They didn't have any information about how the rules were clarified or how exactly they would be certified. But they knew it was what they'd been wanting and needing to do with their buildings, and they were determined to show that a Living Future is possible. That's a consistent theme we've seen when people find the Living Building Challenge and get excited by it. It lights up their passion and there's just no stopping them."

AMANDA STURGEON, INTERNATIONAL LIVING FUTURE INSTITUTE

"[USGBC Founder] David Gottfried always said that green building is not about the buildings; it's about the people. Without the visionaries who were willing to give it their all to develop programs and advocate for the work and share their stories all over the world, none of this would be possible — not LEED and not the Living Building Challenge. Then it takes the professionals — architects, engineers, general contractors, electricians, lighting designers, and others — willing to put in the time and energy to drive the ideas forward."

MICHELLE MOORE, GROUNDSWELL

"Coming to the Institute was a pivotal point in my career. I could either keep practicing or I could apply that body of knowledge to the program side and help the entire practitioner movement carry out these ideas. I decided to bring my perspective of having actually worked on Living Buildings to help other architects do the same thing."

AMANDA STURGEON, INTERNATIONAL LIVING FUTURE INSTITUTE

"I came to the organization when the Challenge was still in its release phase. My role has been to help scale it; to help it grow to the next place where it needed to go; to find the pathways to allow people to do it. In those early days, we did that by bringing in some integrity, showing it was possible, and working with teams a bit more closely to help ensure their success."

AMANDA STURGEON, INTERNATIONAL LIVING FUTURE INSTITUTE

to as many clients and projects as possible. An early Ambassador for the Challenge, she led workshops to familiarize project teams with its complexities. She was well-known throughout the regional green design community for her skills and advocacy.

Sturgeon was also an early adopter of LEED. As a project architect, she oversaw sustainability efforts on a LEED pilot project that eventually earned the first LEED Gold certification in the State of Washington.[66] When she joined the Institute, she brought that valuable first-hand experience as a practitioner who understood the rigor of the Living Building Challenge.

Brought on board to deepen the Institute's in-house group devoted to the Living Building Challenge, Sturgeon joined Brukman and others in their efforts to do whatever needed to be done to respond to the growing demand for the Challenge. Having an extra pair of hands made an enormous difference to the still-lean team and Sturgeon's expertise made her contributions even more significant. As she was helping elevate the status and strength of the Living Building Challenge, Sturgeon was also beginning her own dramatic rise within the organization.

Immediately upon her arrival, Sturgeon was asked to help usher the Omega Center for Sustainable Living, the Tyson Living Learning Center, and the Eco-Sense Residence toward Living certification.

66 IslandWood, an outdoor learning facility on Bainbridge Island.

152 THE OMEGA CENTER FOR SUSTAINABLE LIVING

The Omega Institute for Holistic Studies in Rhinebeck, New York was already working with BNIM to sketch plans for a new LEED Platinum structure on its campus when architect Laura Lesniewski threw a curve ball in the direction of Omega CEO Skip Backus. Her friend and former BNIM colleague Jason F. McLennan was putting together a new green building standard called the Living Building Challenge, which BNIM co-founder Bob Berkebile had helped him develop, and the Omega project might be a great testing ground for it. Was Backus interested in shifting gears?

> "The qualifying part of the Challenge was interesting to me. Either you do it or you don't do it. But there was no guiding definition. It was up to us to figure out how to get to where we wanted to go."
>
> **SKIP BACKUS, OMEGA INSTITUTE**

Backus was intrigued. He had never been a fan of LEED's point-accumulation system and he was drawn to the Living Building Challenge's non-prescriptive nature. Besides, the Omega Institute was dedicated to innovation, education, and experimentation. Adding a physical structure to the campus that helped embody those principles seemed like an appropriate way to further its mission.

"The whole idea of doing this project as a Living Building was about putting a stake in the ground and making a leadership statement. If we were going to do this, we figured we may as well step as far forward as we possibly could. That's what the Challenge gave us — that future step."

SKIP BACKUS, OMEGA INSTITUTE

"Omega happened because Skip Backus drove it forward. It took a lot of effort to convince his board but he wouldn't take no for an answer. He was really persistent; he believed that the impossible was possible and wanted to show that to the world."

AMANDA STURGEON, INTERNATIONAL LIVING FUTURE INSTITUTE

"The Omega Living Building has changed that institution — its reach and its breadth — and it has changed the people who work there. They now host a regional conversation in the Hudson River Valley and receive inquiries from all over the planet about the building and the work they do there."

BOB BERKEBILE, BNIM

153

Backus decided to embrace the Living Building Challenge in addition to pursuing LEED Platinum certification for his organization's new endeavor, the Omega Center for Sustainable Living. Running both standards simultaneously meant making a series of big changes to the project's plans and scope. For instance, instead of aiming for a certain number of energy points in LEED, the architects and engineers needed to design an energy strategy that allowed the structure to generate 100 percent of its own power to qualify for the Challenge's Energy Petal. They had to hire additional engineers to create a new concrete formula that would comply with the Materials Red List Imperative. And the original water strategy was expanded to include a fully transparent and aesthetically inviting wastewater treatment demonstration space.

Charting such new territory proved to be extremely difficult and time-consuming for all involved in the Omega project. Even with the direct involvement of Berkebile, who was as familiar with the Living Building concept as anybody, the project's designers, engineers, builders, and vendors all faced daily struggles adhering to the standard's rigorous Imperatives. Still, Backus continued to provide the necessary financial and moral support to keep things moving forward. His compassion and determination, even in the face of confusion, inspired the project's entire team to stay the course.

> "LEED got bureaucratic in its execution; for us, it eventually just became a paper trail. The Living Building Challenge became the journey of a century." SKIP BACKUS, OMEGA INSTITUTE

> "The Living Building Challenge puts you in a system and gives you a way of living as part of that system. It's that level of connectivity that has become a part of Omega — it's in all that we teach, what we program, how we speak publicly, and what positions we take. It has become central to our mission."

SKIP BACKUS, OMEGA INSTITUTE

Looking back, Backus now credits Omega's Living Building with permanently altering the culture of his organization. The process of designing and constructing the Center for Sustainable Living gave everyone on the site a new understanding of how humans and the structures they create can and should interact with the natural environment — specifically how Omega manages the 125 buildings spread across its own 260-acre campus. The building even informs the types of curricula available at Omega, as it has enhanced the educational connections among the various programs and classes now offered. More than 4,500[67] visitors tour the Omega Center for Sustainable Living each year.

67 www.eomega.org/omega-in-action/key-initiatives/omega-center-for-sustainable-living/visit-the-ocsl

The Tyson Living Learning Center, Eureka, MO
PHOTO: JOE ANGELES / COURTESY OF HELLMUTH+BICKNESE ARCHITECTS

THE TYSON LIVING LEARNING CENTER

The Tyson Living Learning Center is on the site of Tyson Research Center, a 2,000-acre environmental field station affiliated with Washington University. The Tyson facilities are located in Eureka, Missouri, approximately 20 miles from the university's main St. Louis campus.

Shortly after winning the contract, the Tyson Living Learning Center's designers at Hellmuth + Bicknese Architects began to ponder whether it might be a good fit for a new green building standard they had recently heard about. Firm Principal Dan Hellmuth had attended Greenbuild 2006 and was present for McLennan's launch of the Living Building Challenge, and was eagerly looking for the right project with which to apply some or all of the new approaches. Tyson seemed the ideal candidate. The building was intended to be a deep green research station and its construction would be overseen by environmental scientists, biologists, and sustainability directors from the university. The project's pre-design programming and charrette phase began in June 2008, at which point

"During our first charrette, we introduced the Living Building Challenge as a possibility. The project's stakeholders looked into it and never looked back. As biologists and environmental scientists, they really got the biological analogy."

DANIEL F. HELLMUTH,
HELLMUTH + BICKNESE ARCHITECTS

> "After presenting the conceptual design, we asked the code reviewers to help us accomplish these goals rather than tell us why we couldn't. They actually got really excited and were quickly fully on board."

DANIEL F. HELLMUTH,
HELLMUTH + BICKNESE ARCHITECTS

the architects proposed the Living Building Challenge idea. In August, they received the notice to proceed on the design phase.

Bolstered by the university's support, the project team took its first steps toward planning a Living Building. Since the Tyson campus is in an unincorporated section of St. Louis County, they rightly assumed that gaining regulatory approvals for their proposed systems would be among the most difficult aspects of the process. When Hellmuth and his colleagues first approached the county with rough plans for a building that would generate its own energy, collect its own water, and treat its own waste, they were met with firm and fast refusals. But they returned with a delegation that included university representatives, this time meeting with the highest level zoning and coding officials in the county, and received a more encouraging response. The difference, reports Hellmuth, was asking the county to participate in the problem-solving rather than submitting specific plans that were so radical that they would be deemed undoable. By involving them in the systems designs, the team turned the county regulators into champions of the project.

> "The Tyson team did a lot of work to get the rainwater-to-potable-water use approved as an alternative compliance path. That took a lot of meetings and time because they were told yes, and no, and yes again. They were also Red List pioneers because no manufacturers had ever been asked about their product configurations before, so they couldn't get straight answers from anyone. They had a lot to overcome ... and they did it."

AMANDA STURGEON, INTERNATIONAL LIVING FUTURE INSTITUTE

The Tyson project's construction phase proceeded at lightning speed, completed in only six months between December 2008 and May 2009. During that hectic period, the team interacted constantly with Cascadia/ILBI representatives, usually Brukman. Both efforts — the building and the Standard — were in their infancy and both were evolving as a result of the other's discoveries.

Following a year of occupancy, the building was nearly ... but not quite ... eligible for Living Building certification. Energy data showed that the structure was drawing slightly more power than it was producing, so the decision was made to add to the existing photovoltaic array while making minor envelope adjustments. A follow-up audit revealed that the building met all of the

> "There was absolutely no precedent for what we were doing, so none of us knew what the boundaries were. The ILBI had an extremely strong concept with the Living Building Challenge, but the procedural part of it was still being invented even as we were designing and building."
>
> **DANIEL F. HELLMUTH, HELLMUTH + BICKNESE ARCHITECTS**

Imperatives of the Living Building Challenge version 1.3. The Tyson Living Learning Center was officially certified as a Living Building in autumn 2010 and hosted a formal certification award celebration in February 2011.

Hellmuth was driving to his farm in the Ozarks when he got a call informing him that the building was eligible for certification. He describes it as "one of those nice, euphoric moments that you rarely get as an architect but that you live for." It was a culmination of intense effort on the part of everyone involved — the designers, engineers, owners, investors, and regulators.

> "None of the technology or systems in this building is rocket science. It's just a matter of assembling it all together in one structure and getting everything to do what it needs to do so that systems work together."
>
> **DANIEL F. HELLMUTH,**
> **HELLMUTH + BICKNESE ARCHITECTS**

Since it opened its doors, the Tyson Living Learning Center has become of one the jewels in the Washington University crown. Even as other capital projects were frozen during the recession, this one was allowed to push forward. It was a small enough investment and promised a large enough pedagogical return that it always retained sufficient backing among key university leaders.

Visitors continue to stream through the Tyson campus, even given its remote location, mostly to see and study the Living Learning Center. Even the building's furnishings became an educational opportunity, with approximately half of the furniture built from FSC-certified wood by university students studying everything from forestry to industrial design. The building is more than a research center; it is a 3,000 square foot sustainability demonstration piece.

> "This project allowed us to bring architecture back to where it should be. We catalyze the Living Building Challenge as an educational framework, creating a much more inclusive, creative process. The educational benefit of this one building goes far beyond the cost per square footage." **DANIEL F. HELLMUTH, HELLMUTH + BICKNESE ARCHITECTS**

THE ECO-SENSE RESIDENCE

Ann and Gord Baird had successfully built a cob woodworking shop (made from load-bearing clay, sand, and straw) on their property in Victoria, BC and had already poured the foundation for a cob residential structure when they attended a local sustainability education program in early 2007. The speaker was Cascadia's Vancouver-based director, Jessica Hale Woolliams, who was touring British Columbia to introduce the concept of the Living Building Challenge to the region.

During the presentation, the Bairds had the sense that Woolliams was speaking directly to them; everything she described about the Challenge precisely matched their environmental and philosophical goals for the multi-generational home they were beginning to build. They decided that very evening to register their project for the Challenge.

> "Our goal was to build a home that functioned as an extension of the living ecosystem, where Mother Nature was the architect of our structure. So we had a lot of the same values as the Living Building Challenge."
>
> **ANN BAIRD, ECO-SENSE RESIDENCE**

The Bairds were drawn to the Challenge because it echoed so many of their own convictions about humans' responsibility to create a sustainable built environment. Further, it supported their commitment to earthen architecture in ways that avoided the "counterculture" stigma they felt was often associated with such approaches. They wanted to bridge those gaps and construct a home that proved the utility and value of natural building materials. The Living Building Challenge helped legitimize their efforts in the broader design-build community.

"Had the Challenge not been so inclusive, we wouldn't have been able to do what we did. What's considered right in one culture or climate or according to one person's individual tastes are all going to be different from what's right elsewhere. So to have a prescriptive type of green building platform is ludicrous. That's where the Challenge really fit our values." **ANN BAIRD, ECO-SENSE RESIDENCE**

They were also intrigued by the non-prescriptive nature of the standard. Unlike LEED, the Living Building Challenge mapped out performance targets without specifying how each structure needed to reach its goals. The Bairds were scientists, not architects or engineers, and their project was self-financed. So it was never going to be accomplished using traditional methods. They appreciated the procedural freedom the Challenge provided them.

"The Eco-Sense project had a lot of regulatory barriers, but Ann
and Gord ended up taking a great approach. They helped educate
the building inspector about the systems they wanted to use.
Even though they had to start with flush toilets in order to get
permitted, they educated the inspector about how composting
toilets can connect to on-site constructed wetlands. Now, their
composting toilets are a big feature in every tour they give of
their building."

AMANDA STURGEON, INTERNATIONAL LIVING FUTURE INSTITUTE

"Eco-Sense is an amazing project ecologically. The fact that it was
only certified for four of the six Petals does not at all mean that
it was any less green than the other early projects. It was just a
reflection of the way Ann and Gord's plans had already unfolded
prior to their embrace of the Challenge."

JASON F. MCLENNAN, INTERNATIONAL LIVING FUTURE INSTITUTE

"Pursuing the Living Building Challenge with our project really
showed that you could build a comfortable, beautiful single family
home that met these environmental criteria. It really opened doors
with the mainstream, proving that the Challenge could be applied
to a broader set of projects."

GORD BAIRD, ECO-SENSE RESIDENCE

The Eco-Sense Residence, Victoria, BC
PHOTO: ANN BAIRD

160

As soon as they registered for the Challenge, the Bairds knew it would be difficult for them to achieve the Energy and Materials Petals because of certain decisions they were too far down the path to change. Specifically, their energy strategy required combustion (strictly forbidden in early versions of the Challenge) and their source list included Chinese bamboo that exceeded the maximum sourcing radius requirements. But modifying such key aspects of their plan late in the process was logistically and financially unrealistic.

As such, Eco-Sense house was Petal-certified for Site, Water, Indoor Quality, and Beauty and Inspiration. Perhaps more significantly, it earned the distinction as the first legal load-bearing cob residence in North America. Overcoming such substantial regulatory hurdles — and potentially effecting permanent changes to the British Columbia building codes — is arguably the much more important accomplishment.

The Bairds now serve as passionate ambassadors for the Challenge and all forms of environmental design, giving tours of their cob structures and advocating for the use of nature as architect.

> "A common thread woven through those first three projects was passion. These groups found ways to create Living Buildings despite modest budgets and the very real fact that there had never been one before."
>
> **JASON F. MCLENNAN, INTERNATIONAL LIVING FUTURE INSTITUTE**

A POWERFUL NEXT SET

While Omega, Tyson, and Eco-Sense were the first three projects to earn certification bragging rights, several other structures followed close behind and were equally ... if not more ... important in proving what was possible within the program. (For more on the second wave of aspirational Living Buildings, see Chapter 13.)

As more projects registered for the Challenge, Institute staff needed to discern which would be most likely to meet all of the program's Imperatives and accomplish full certification, and which would be better suited to Petal certification. The trick was to encourage all efforts without compromising the integrity of the program by easing up on its rigorous requirements.

Eden Brukman fielded most calls from project representatives eager to inquire about possible exemptions that would allow them to bypass certain Imperatives. It was up to her to cheer on frustrated team members, maintain the Standard's high bar, and offer technical assistance when needed — all at the same time. It was also her responsibility to remind people that the Challenge was designed as a tool to guide the movement toward better design-build solutions, but it wasn't ever intended to be the only end goal. When teams lobbied aggressively for exemptions simply so that they could earn Living certification, it was Brukman's job to gently remind them that the Challenge, just like LEED before it, was part of a larger vision. It was a way to help architects, engineers, builders, and owners contribute to the process of restoring a healthy relationship between the built and natural environments. Earning individual Petal certification rather than full Living status was worthy of celebration, as was making any attempt to strengthen a structure's green profile even if it did not lead to a plaque on the wall. What mattered most was contributing to the larger goal of changing the industry.

The Omega Center for Sustainable Living, Rhinebeck, NY
PHOTO: COPYRIGHT ASSASSI / COURTESY BNIM

A BUILDING DISCUSSION

In an effort to share some of the valuable discoveries early project teams were making about how to meet Living Building Challenge Imperatives, Brukman began to post information to an online forum hosted by the organization. Initially structured more like a blog, the forum provided open-source information for anyone curious about strategies that were working for their counterparts on other Living Building projects. The forum proved equally useful to Institute staffers who used the information to hone subsequent versions of the Challenge itself.

The forum evolved into the Living Building Challenge Dialogue, a portal where registered project teams may post questions, read answers to other inquiries, and seek clarification on technical aspects of Imperatives. The Dialogue was the answer to the missing User's Guide. In addition, it was an important example of the programmatic commitment to transparency. Hundreds of project team members now visit the Dialogue on an annual basis.

> "Those first few projects were historic. They were small, but they showed what could be done."
>
> **JASON F. MCLENNAN,**
> **INTERNATIONAL LIVING**
> **FUTURE INSTITUTE**

The Tyson Living Learning Center, Eureka, MO
COURTESY OF HELLMUTH+BICKNESE ARCHITECTS

THE REAL DEAL

As the once-modest list of registered Living Building Challenge projects lengthened, eventually yielding a small but growing number of structures ultimately certified as the world's first Living Buildings, the Standard's impact was becoming undeniable. Each individual who participated in the bold experiment helped validate and grow the program. What had begun as a singularly daring idea had evolved into a game-changing and broadly respected concept that was creating real and measurable change in the built environment. It was now bigger than McLennan; it was bigger than his staff; it was bigger than any one project. The Living Building Challenge was demonstrably helping to reinvent a movement.

"The spirit of the people working on those early projects was just amazing. They've had a huge influence on the change that's now happening in the movement. It continues to be a whole stream of people, but it always takes someone to jump in. Without them, the Challenge may not have rolled out as it did."

AMANDA STURGEON, INTERNATIONAL LIVING FUTURE INSTITUTE

USING A "HALO" EFFECT TO DRIVE CHANGE

A LIVING BUILDING BLOCK

In the product arena, Apple® may be the most-studied example of companies whose products are so desirable that they inspire fierce brand loyalty among customers. But Apple's success is owed as much to its strategy of building a "halo" than to its products' quality and ease of use.

When Steve Jobs started rebuilding Apple after rejoining as its CEO, he worked to build an ecosystem of products that linked together to create an overall seamless experience. The Mac already had software that was perfectly compatible with its operating system (as opposed to PC platforms where multiple companies create different experiences), but as Jobs developed further related products (such as the iPod, iPhone, and iPad), they all worked together as an overall ecosystem. Each pulled in new customers and drove demand for the other products within the halo. The company had one successful product launch after another.

Operating on a dramatically different economic scale, the International Living Future Institute purposefully emulated this approach with its own halo of offerings, providing multiple entry points through which practitioners can enter a deeper environment of change. Each program, conference, or tool links together within the larger Living vision.

The Institute's core offering is the Living Building Challenge, designed to invite architects, engineers, builders, owners, and all affiliated professionals into the world of Living Buildings. The Institute's additional programs broaden the appeal and reinforce the message. Declare, JUST, Petal Certification, the Living Community Challenge, Net Zero Energy Building Certification, the Living Community Challenge, Reveal, and other innovations pull people and market segments into the Living framework even when they are not able to commit to a full Living Building Challenge project. Meanwhile, *Trim Tab* magazine and Ecotone Publishing's growing library of books communicate the mission and Living Future unConferences create educational and networking opportunities for those who seek them. In the Living ecosystem, all programs are designed to stand alone and reinforce one another, educating people on the Living principles regardless of whether they participate in a Living Building Challenge project.

This programmatic breadth diversifies the Institute's revenues and market reach — a tactic that allowed it to survive even the leanest years of the Great Recession and to keep growing despite how difficult it is to comply with its programs.

One way of expanding impact is to lower the bar, but the International Living Future Institute has broadened its scope while holding the bar where it should be. As a result, the Institute has something to offer virtually any practitioner or organization. And once people enter the Living realm, they are more likely to stay.

11

"The rung of a ladder was never meant to rest upon but only to hold a man's foot long enough to enable him to put the other somewhat higher."

THOMAS HENRY HUXLEY

THE NEXT BIG THING

A BOLDER, BETTER CHALLENGE MAKES ITS DEBUT

A modest Living garden was beginning to bloom by 2009 as the first Living Building Challenge projects finished construction and entered their occupancy phases. During the year-plus when those projects were tracking their performance in preparation for their official certification audits, the International Living Building Institute was making improvements to its own eponymous offering.

As the Standard's debut crop moved from theory to reality, several critical pieces of information were revealed. First, proof now existed that the Living Building Challenge, for the most part, did actually work and Living Buildings were possible. Second, the completed structures yielded data about how the concept could be improved. Analyzing the feedback they gathered from project teams allowed the Challenge team to identify and address the strengths and gaps in Versions 1.2 and 1.3 (released in April 2007 and August 2009 respectively).

Thanks to courageous pioneers such as those from Omega, Tyson, and Eco-Sense, Jason F. McLennan and his staff had enough hard evidence (even as much as a year before those projects were certified) to finesse the Challenge's next major release.

McLennan, Eden Brukman, and their colleagues (Amanda Sturgeon had not yet joined the staff) took a fresh look at the Living Building Challenge in the months

> "The Standard has always evolved through relevant feedback we get from project teams via the Dialogue. When it was new, we really focused on what we heard because we wanted to know what did and did not work. Version 2.0 emerged when it was apparent that we did not have it quite right yet; we needed to make some big changes."
>
> **JASON F. MCLENNAN, INTERNATIONAL LIVING FUTURE INSTITUTE**

leading up to Greenbuild 2009, to be held in Phoenix in November of that year. Their goal was to assess the Standard from top to bottom, evaluating it more holistically than they had ever done before. There had been modifications previously made to the Challenge to move it from Version 1.2 to Version 1.3, but they were minor and considered "point" updates. This time, McLennan and Brukman sought to implement the first set of changes significant enough to warrant a new number in the sequence of Living Building Challenge releases.

The Living Building Challenge Version 2.0 was officially unveiled at Greenbuild 2009. McLennan explained to those in attendance that Version 2.0 reflected an important set of changes that, together, contributed to a fundamental shift in the Standard. The update contained these key modifications:

- An expanding scale

- A renamed Petal

- A new seventh Petal

- "Prerequisites" reclassified as "Imperatives"

- Remapped and enhanced Imperatives

> "There are more and more buildings that are finding success meeting the Challenge, especially in terms of cost effectiveness, by using the Scale Jumping component. That has really opened up everyone's eyes to neighborhood infrastructure. To me, that's the future of sustainable building construction and design."
>
> **DALE MIKKELSEN, SFU COMMUNITY TRUST**

LIVING
BUILDING
CHALLENGE™
2.0

A Visionary Path to a Restorative Future

INTERNATIONAL
LIVING BUILDING
INSTITUTE™

November 2009

AN EXPANDING SCALE

From its earliest iteration, the Living Building Challenge was designed to accommodate any building typology because of its performance-based framework. In Version 2.0, that philosophy was broadened to reach beyond the single-building scale into neighborhoods and eco-districts through a more generous approach to Scale Jumping.

Scale Jumping had been mentioned briefly in the context of the Water Petal in earlier versions of the Standard, but it was more thoroughly fleshed out in Version 2.0. Also, Cascadia had briefly experimented with a separate Living Site Challenge, which had gained very little traction, so the decision was made to fold that effort's intentions into the more successful Living Building Challenge. As a result of the new allowances, virtually any project could aspire to Living certification — whether it was a modest structure or a masterplanned development.

Text of Version 2.0 clarified the scale expansion two ways:

"All potential types of construction in the built environment are addressed, working across various scales of development and settings, from partial building renovations to entire struc-

> "A lot of what we were advocating with water and energy systems actually worked better at the larger scale than they did on the single building scale, so it made sense to us to allow for Scale Jumping as we were writing Version 2.0."

JASON F. MCLENNAN, INTERNATIONAL LIVING FUTURE INSTITUTE

tures, and from individual landscape and infrastructure projects to whole communities." (from "What is Different About Version 2.0")

"Living Building Challenge projects have their own 'utility,' generating their own energy and processing their own waste. They more appropriately match scale to technology and end use, and result in greater self-sufficiency and security. Yet, the ideal scale for solutions is not always within a project's property boundary. Depending on the technology, the optimal scale can vary when considering environmental impact, first cost, and operating costs. To address these realities, the Living Building Challenge has inserted the concept of Scale Jumping to allow multiple buildings or projects to operate in a cooperative state — sharing green infrastructure as appropriate and allowing for Living Building, Site or Community sta-tus to be achieved as elegantly and efficiently as possible (from "How the Living Building Challenge Works")

A RENAMED PETAL

What was once called the Indoor Quality Petal was rechristened as the Health Petal in Version 2.0. The new name better de-scribed the true intent of the Petal, which reached well beyond the perceived limits of what most industry professionals referred to as IEQ — or indoor environmental quality. McLennan and Brukman wanted the Petal to help designers, engineers, and builders envision a more holistically positive interior

> "Indoor Quality was just an inadequate name because the Petal — now the Health Petal — is about so much more than that. The language was limiting and needed to be reset."
>
> **JASON F. MCLENNAN,**
> **INTERNATIONAL LIVING FUTURE INSTITUTE**

experience for the occupants and visitors of Living Buildings. They hoped to guide project teams toward structures that protect — and even enhance — the physical and emotional health of the people who come in contact with the built environment.

> "I had been wanting to address equity in the Challenge, but I did not have my arms around it enough in the first version. But as the program got off the ground, it became clear that we had to add it in because you cannot have true regenerative design if the design is inequitable. So we decided to take the lead and get it started. We thought of it as Version 1.0 of the Equity Petal, even though it was Version 2.0 of the Challenge."
>
> **JASON F. MCLENNAN, INTERNATIONAL LIVING FUTURE INSTITUTE**

A NEW SEVENTH PETAL

It had always bothered McLennan that he and other well-meaning members of the green building industry talked a lot about the concept of equity but did very little about it through their design work. There were no codified tools that supported the efforts of architects and engineers interested in incorporating universal access and social justness into the built environment. Version 2.0 of the Living Building Challenge offered an opportunity to change that.

Equity appeared sixth in the newly expanded list of seven Petals in the updated Standard. McLennan and Brukman knew that it might be deemed a radical addition to the more objectively measurable performance areas such as Energy and Water, but considered it a logical counterpart to the Beauty Petal — another seemingly immeasurable characteristic unapologetically but successfully incorporated into the Challenge.

The Equity Petal did not attempt to tackle all the world's inequities. It did, however, aim to address equity relative to individual buildings. It sought to ensure that all occupants of Living Buildings have equal access to nature, regardless of physical ability or professional status. It also prohibited Living Buildings from blocking any neighboring structures' access to nature, whether it is to be used for biophilic or performance purposes.

Unlike any standard before it, the Living Building Challenge intended to prevent the practice of "externalizing the negative environmental impacts of our actions onto others." Through its Equity Petal, the Challenge prohibited builders with money and power from taking more than their projects' fair share of clean air, water, and soil.

The Equity Petal was a slightly risky new addition to the Standard's text, and had the potential to confuse project teams. But McLennan felt strongly that it reflected the larger vision of the Challenge and he was willing to test it with users. If it needed correcting, he knew they would help get it where it needed to be. It would evolve along with the Challenge.

"PREREQUISITES" RECLASSIFIED AS "IMPERATIVES"

In a subtle departure from the language of LEED, the Living Building Challenge stopped using the phrase "Prerequisites" beginning with Version 2.0. Instead, the requirements embedded within each performance area Petal began to be called "Imperatives." Not only did this help to further distinguish one standard from the other, but it better described the non-prescriptive nature of the Challenge. The term "imperative" conveyed more of a call to action than a strictly defined rule, which more poetically echoed the Living Building philosophy. There was no one way to accomplish any of the Imperatives; there was simply one list of goals to meet.

"Switching from Prerequisites to Imperatives was yet another way for us to stop existing in LEED's shadow. We had no interest in putting down LEED to make ourselves look better, but it was time to stop drawing that comparison."

JASON F. MCLENNAN, INTERNATIONAL LIVING FUTURE INSTITUTE

REMAPPED AND ENHANCED IMPERATIVES

Using knowledge collected from project teams using Versions 1.2 and 1.3, McLennan and Brukman carefully reworked the Standard's list of Imperatives. Some existing Imperatives were consolidated while others were renamed and redefined. Six brand new Imperatives were debuted and distributed among three Petals. By the time it was launched, Version 2.0 contained a grand total of 20 Imperatives across seven performance area Petals.

The six newly added Imperatives were:

URBAN AGRICULTURE (SITE PETAL): This Imperative addressed the need to reintroduce a "culture of food" into the built environment wherever possible, aiming to reconnect people with the food they consume and the plantable land they might occupy. It took the bold and unprecedented step of tying a project's floor area ratio (FAR) to urban agriculture goals. The authors anticipated — and were pleased to eventually see — a wide variety of creative solutions to this requirement, including on-site vegetable gardens, orchards, chicken coops, and rooftop beehives.

CAR FREE LIVING (SITE PETAL): Discouraging motor vehicles on or around Living Building sites was not such a stretch, but it was an important addition to include in the next version of the Standard. It distanced projects from fossil fuels while encouraging pedestrian-friendly development.

"The Urban Agriculture Imperative was never about generating a lot of food on a project site; it's more about putting people back in touch with their food supplies. Attaching a food requirement to a project's FAR acknowledges that you cannot grow much if you are in a dense urban environment. But if you are in the suburbs, suddenly you have fruit trees and gardens. It doesn't make up for sprawl but it pushes back against it."

JASON F. MCLENNAN, INTERNATIONAL LIVING FUTURE INSTITUTE

BIOPHILIA (HEALTH PETAL): The philosophy of biophilia — the psychologically beneficial impact of natural systems — was woven through all earlier versions of the Challenge, but it was clearly defined and expected for the first time in Version 2.0. Although it was added as a specific Imperative within the Health Petal, the notion of biophilia is implicit in numerous other performance areas (such as Beauty and Equity). Incorporating it formally was further evidence of the holistic nature of Version 2.0.

HUMAN SCALE AND HUMANE PLACES (EQUITY PETAL): This new Imperative sought to manage the types of projects eligible for Living Building certification. According to the text of Version 2.0, designing and building projects to a scale that complemented humans rather than automobiles was a way of "bringing out the best in humanity and promoting culture and interaction."

"As we thought about the Human Scale and Human Places Imperative, we took a look at all the awful places in the built environment and made sure they couldn't get certified as Living Buildings. We did not want to come across a big box retail store with a huge parking lot in front that destroyed urban life and urban scale and have to give a plaque to it and certify it as Living because it was built without Red List chemicals and it harvested its own water and energy. That's not the future we want. Living Buildings need to make our communities better and that includes dealing with issues of scale and urban form."

JASON F. MCLENNAN, INTERNATIONAL LIVING FUTURE INSTITUTE

DEMOCRACY AND SOCIAL JUSTICE (EQUITY PETAL): This Imperative started where Americans with Disabilities Act (ADA) accessibility guidelines left off, codifying the need to treat all occupants, visitors, and even passersby fairly and equally. The thinking was to broaden the accessibility discussion beyond American borders and into the international arena, given that there were Living Building Challenge projects registering all over the world. This new Imperative called for all externally focused elements of Living Buildings to be accessible to all members of the public, regardless of their relationship to the structure itself.

RIGHTS TO NATURE (EQUITY PETAL): Thanks to this third Imperative in the new Equity Petal, no Living Building could restrict or diminish the quality of any individual's access to nature. It included specific guidelines related to fresh air, sunlight, and natural waterways.

A RESPECTFUL DISTANCE

Updating the Standard was necessary from strategic, programmatic, and branding perspectives. It also helped further distinguish the Living Building Challenge from LEED, both in language and philosophy. Still, McLennan and his staff were committed to the idea that the two building standards could co-exist within the market; both had their rightful places.

A piece published in *BuildingGreen* in March 2009 helped bring the industry up to date on the Challenge and its relationship to LEED. The article also got to the heart of why Cascadia (and, later, the Institute) has always described it as a philosophy first, an advocacy tool second, and a certification program third.

> "With Version 2.0, we set the program on its own feet."
>
> **JASON F. MCLENNAN, INTERNATIONAL LIVING FUTURE INSTITUTE**

In "Aiming for the Stars: A Manifesto in the Guise of a Standard Raises the Bar," *BuildingGreen* President Nadav Malin wrote:

LEED has been accused — or credited, depending on your perspective — of being a Trojan horse — drawing people in with a checklist that looks at first to be straightforward, only to unleash a litany of detailed requirements that are not as simple as they first appeared. The Living Building Challenge takes an opposite approach, coming on with an idealistic vision of buildings that do right by nature in every way, but then introducing compromises in the form of "temporary exceptions" to account for marketplace limitations. Somewhere on a spectrum between LEED Platinum and Living Building status (which has yet to be achieved), the two systems meet.

"I think the Living Building Challenge is a great complement to LEED. From the beginning, I was a huge advocate for LEED and worked on one of the first LEED pilot projects. But I could see that it just wasn't going far enough. There was momentum among people who had been using LEED who realized we needed to look more comprehensively into ecological and social systems. LEED services a group of people and a collection of projects that are just entering the green building arena. Once they have completed a LEED project or two, they start to see that they can do more. The Living Building Challenge offers a vision of what that might look like."

AMANDA STURGEON, INTERNATIONAL LIVING FUTURE INSTITUTE

"This so-called 'rivalry' between the Living Building Challenge and LEED is actually productive for the industry. The Challenge team always looks for ways to fit the programs together and make them complementary. Unfortunately, the USGBC sometimes assumes it's a competition and has put up a few roadblocks, but I think that has hurt them more than anything else. Their resistance to it actually gave the Living Building Challenge more street cred; it made people view it like a rebel."

RICHARD GRAVES, UNIVERSITY OF MINNESOTA

"We're not even two decades in to creating a market that simply didn't exist and now is about $1 trillion globally. All of us working together with the integrity of third-party validation and working jointly towards a holistic view of assessment is what got us here. LEED and the Living Building Challenge have different roles but we make joint progress."

RICK FEDRIZZI, U.S. GREEN BUILDING COUNCIL

For the right client, LBC provides a much more compelling vision of sustainability, untainted by the market-savvy compromises of LEED. Designers who have worked with it find that, even if LBC proves too demanding for a project, using it as a framework for discussion raises everyone's expectations — taking projects that might have targeted LEED Silver up a few notches. "It's amazing when [LEED] Platinum becomes the fallback position," notes McLennan.

MATURATION

The introduction of Living Building Challenge Version 2.0 did more than polish the Standard. It also helped solidify the operational objectives of an entire organization. First Cascadia, and now the International Living Building Institute (ILBI) was gaining measurable traction with the professions it sought to influence as well as the funders it sought to attract. Launching Version 2.0 meant the Living Building idea had legs. And forming the Institute meant the market was ready for more. Buildings would eventually lead to communities, products, and more.

In spite of the difficult economic climate that lingered in the months following the formation of the ILBI and the debut of Version 2.0, the Standard and the organization that ran it were gradually garnering the world's attention. Projects located all around the planet began to register for the Challenge and global advocacy groups started to publicly acknowledge the change-making nature of McLennan, his big ideas, and the talented people who brought them to bear. The Living Building Challenge was growing up.

THINKING HOLISTICALLY

A LIVING BUILDING BLOCK

The moment we categorize something, we take a reductionist approach, which can lead to seeking solutions in isolation. Unfortunately, this is the precise method that has resulted in many unintended consequences in modern society. Yet categorization is a useful tool to help people understand complex topics in order to break them down into manageable chunks. This tension is what the Living Building Challenge theory of change tries to harness.

As with other green building programs, the Challenge is sorted into separate categories (Petals) that makes the program look, at first blush, just similar and relatable enough to different disciplines that people can grasp it. But this is where the program operates as a bit of a Trojan horse. It looks enough like a reductionist tool not to overwhelm people and pull them

178

in, but any attempt to meet all the requirements means solving them in a holistic, integrated fashion and requires abandoning a reductionist approach to problem-solving. Indeed, optimizing in isolation leads to failure with the Living Building Challenge.

The Challenge encourages teams to *begin* by thinking holistically to find solutions that tackle multiple issues at once.

The Challenge encourages teams to *begin* by thinking holistically to find solutions that tackle multiple issues at once. There is never one way for a structure to achieve Living status, but the best set of solutions are those that reach across the Petals. A water system's power needs must be factored into the energy budget; materials must be non-toxic and aesthetically pleasing to satisfy both Materials and Beauty demands; floorplans must provide all occupants with access to amenities to adhere to equity requirements, to name a few.

Systems are linked; solutions are nested; answers are integrated. Holistic problem-solving naturally ties a project's various performance areas together, resulting in a more elegant and united Living structure.

12

"This world is but a canvas for our imagination."

HENRY DAVID THOREAU

A GLOBAL CAMPAIGN

THE CHALLENGE SPREADS ITS WINGS

The Living Building Challenge entered its global phase following the launch of Version 2.0. Interest in the Standard started to spread beyond North America and eager advocates began to organize and align their efforts. The difficult economic landscape created by the Great Recession continued to slow the pace of many projects for several years after it officially ended in 2009, but interest rippled outward from each new Living Building that registered. Even amidst extremely pinched worldwide financial conditions, any structure that aspired to the greenest standard generated attention among professional and lay audiences.

It was particularly exciting to the Living Building Challenge team when international projects emerged beyond the United States and Canada. The earliest of these cropped up in Mexico, Australia, and New Zealand.

MEXICO

The Challenge first moved south of the American border as a result of a friendship that emerged between Jason F. McLennan and Carolyn Aguilar-Dubose, director of the architecture department at the Universidad Iberoamericana in Mexico City. Having used McLennan's *Philosophy of Sustainable Design* as a core text in the university's sustainable design and construction diploma course for several terms, Mtra. Aguilar-Dubose met the author in person at the 2006 Greenbuild conference — the same meeting where he formally introduced the Living Building Challenge. When she heard that pivotal presentation in Denver, Aguilar-Dubose was duly impressed by the concept of codifying the idea McLennan addresses in the book. They exchanged stories about the work their respective teams were doing and began talking about how to introduce the Challenge to the Mexican design-build audience.

"LEED is a more common building certification program in Mexico than the Living Building Challenge, partly because the Challenge is so much more demanding. We're doing a lot of work with net zero water and energy, but we have great difficulty with the Materials Petal. Mexican companies don't usually specify what their products contain, so it's very difficult to choose non-toxic materials. But we have a lot of interested designers and there are a few projects that are in progress that are going for Petal recognition or for the complete certification."

CAROLYN AGUILAR-DUBOSE, UNIVERSIDAD IBEROAMERICANA

In 2008, McLennan made the first of many trips to Universidad Iberoamericana, where he shared the Living Building idea with students and professionals. Aguilar-Dubose enthusiastically promoted his visits, generating increasingly large crowds at each of his lectures. She quickly became the Living Building Challenge's biggest cheerleader in Latin America, even attempting to form a dedicated Mexican entity tied to the Cascadia Green Building Council (neither the International Living Building Institute nor the International Living Future Institute existed yet) that could oversee its implementation in that country. The legal hurdles became too difficult, so Aguilar-Dubose and several of her department's faculty members became some of the program's earliest Ambassadors, incorporating the Challenge agenda into their curricula. In addition, she volunteered to produce the first official translation of the Standard and in January 2011, Version 2.0 was released in Spanish. She did the same for Version 3.0 in 2015. (Translations have also since been done in French and Mandarin.) In 2013, Aguilar-Dubose joined the board of what by then had become the International Living Future Institute (ILFI).

Sustainable Buildings Research Centre (SBRC), University of Wollongong
PHOTO: MARK NEWSHAM PHOTOGRAPHY

AUSTRALIA

The Challenge spread to the Southern Hemisphere with a burst of activity beginning in 2011. In Australia, the University of Wollongong was actively planning its Sustainable Buildings Research Centre (SBRC) — intended from the start to serve as a living laboratory for sustainable building — when designers learned of the Living Building Challenge. The project was slated to meet the most rigorous Six Star level of Australia's Green Star Design rating, but when project leaders heard McLennan speak in Sydney while he was on a global speaking tour that year, they knew their building should aim for both standards.

Meanwhile, the University of Queensland in Brisbane was putting plans in place for a Living Building of its own. Architects at HASSELL, led by Principal Mark Roehrs, designed the Global Change Institute to meet the Challenge as well as the Six Star Green Star rating.

The timing was right for the Living Building Challenge to take root in that part of the world. The small, tight-knit Australian green design community had grown somewhat frustrated with the pace with which their modest movement was able to make change. The Challenge was just the type of new initiative they had been waiting to rally around.

The SBRC team soon formally registered as an aspirational Living Building and its core team, led by Lance Jeffery, became enthusiastic local evangelists for the Standard. The Living Future Institute Australia was formally established in 2012, the Global Change Institute opened its doors in 2013, and the SBRC opened in 2014.

"The green building industry across Australia is a pretty well-connected community of practice, and together we've made strong strides in improving the performance of our building stock and making green a baseline expectation instead of a fringe thing. With that being established in the market, a few of us had started asking, 'Where's the next horizon? What's the next hurdle?' Jason's talk in Sydney really resonated with us. It got us thinking in the same sort of direction — a new approach and a new baseline to strive for, and it gave us something to come together around."

MARY CASEY, LIVING FUTURE INSTITUTE AUSTRALIA

NEW ZEALAND

Meanwhile, neighboring New Zealand was busy with its own debut Living Building project. The Tūhoe people, a Maori tribe, initiated their quest for a new tribal structure well before McLennan arrived in the region in late 2011. But when project leaders heard his presentation, they shifted their priorities and decided to do what was necessary to design and build their structure as an aspirational Living Building.

Architect Jerome Partington drove the effort. He first heard of the Challenge in 2009 and was intrigued enough by the idea to make the trip to Vancouver, BC for Living Future in

"The Living Building Challenge carries a powerful message of vision and hope that we can all share. It asks, 'What does our sustainable future look like?' It has a foundation in nature and natural systems; it paints a picture that people resonate with and are desperate to see."

JEROME PARTINGTON, JASMAX

"The Tūhoe tribal leaders decided to build this building because they saw it as an opportunity to redirect the future for their people in a positive way. They recognized that creating a Living Building is not just about the finished building but about the process of building it, creating jobs, building pride, and supporting the re-emergence and celebration of a profound culture. They have a vision to transform their community that will take several generations to achieve."

AMANDA STURGEON, INTERNATIONAL LIVING FUTURE INSTITUTE

"The Tūhoe building is radical — a game-changer — that shows what's possible when we have nature and people front of mind and firmly in our value system."

JEROME PARTINGTON, JASMAX

2011. There, he met McLennan and enrolled in Ambassador training so that he would be thoroughly qualified to take the concept back to New Zealand. Partington was instrumental in bringing McLennan to Auckland that November.

Partington's campaign to elevate the project's sustainability goals was a success. With the blessing of tribal leaders as well as lead architect Ivan Mercep, the team accepted the Challenge. In March 2014, Te Uru Taumatua — the Tūhoe headquarters' formal name — welcomed visitors to its opening celebration. The building reflects the Moari worldview that life is one continuous whole; that there is no disconnection between humans and the rivers, mountains, and soil that surrounds them.

The project is also the subject of a documentary, *Ever the Land*, which explores the building's evolution as well as the political, historical, and cultural realities that informed the process.

KUDOS

As awareness of the Living Building Challenge grew among the professions, the Standard and its author also began to attract attention from the broader international audience. (Trade publications had written about McLennan and the Challenge from the beginning, but now the publicity net was being cast more broadly.) The Institute's own quarterly magazine, *Trim Tab*, began to shine bright green light on the movement's transformational designs, people, and thoughts as of its debut issue in January 2009.[68]

Along with increased local, national, and international media coverage, McLennan and the Challenge received recognition and awards from ever more prestigious organizations.

CLINTON GLOBAL INITIATIVE

In 2010, the Clinton Global Initiative (CGI) granted McLennan and the Living Building Challenge the Commitment Maker designation, which included the first of many invitations for McLennan to participate at the CGI's annual meeting. It gave McLennan his first opportunity to interact directly with heads of state, chief executive officers, non-profit leaders, and other visionaries, as the four-day annual meeting is designed to bring change agents together to explore solutions to the world's most pressing issues. For McLennan, being placed in such company meant that he and his Standard were being taken extremely seriously.

"Getting the attention of the Clinton Global Initiative helped to legitimize the program. It moved us from 'Those guys are just the radical fringe' to 'They may be on to something.'"

JASON F. MCLENNAN, INTERNATIONAL LIVING FUTURE INSTITUTE

ASHOKA FELLOWSHIP

In 2012, McLennan was named a Fellow by Ashoka USA, a non-profit entity committed to building networks of "pattern-changing social innovators." The Fellowship gives him ongoing access to a growing community of entrepreneurs tied by their common dedication to addressing the world's most serious social challenges, in addition to support and collaboration opportunities.

---

68 With steadily increasing circulation numbers, *Trim Tab* has since continued to share the Living story with an ever-widening readership.

CLINTON GLOBAL INITIATIVE

Commitment to Action

WE COMMIT TO TAKE ACTION

TO ADDRESS A SPECIFIC GLOBAL CHALLENGE. THROUGH THIS COMMITMENT WE ARE JOINING THE GROWING CGI COMMUNITY, WHICH SEEKS TO IMPLEMENT INNOVATIVE SOLUTIONS DESIGNED TO PRODUCE TANGIBLE RESULTS THAT WILL POSITIVELY CHANGE LIVES.

September 30, 20

Bill Clinton

William Jefferson Clinton

Former President Bill Clinton and Jason F. McLennan

12: A GLOBAL CAMPAIGN

"Winning the Buckminster Fuller Challenge was magical because of the lineage. I don't think about awards very much but that one means everything to me, since my mentor Bob Berkebile was Bucky's student. It's a very strong, very personal fit."

JASON F. MCLENNAN, INTERNATIONAL LIVING FUTURE INSTITUTE

"In the spirit of Fuller's life and work, we're looking for strategies that allow human beings to be regenerative collaborators within the planetary biosphere. The Living Building Challenge really encapsulates that idea."

DAVID MCCONVILLE, BUCKMINSTER FULLER INSTITUTE

Jason F. McLennan and Eden Brukman at the 2012 Buckminster Fuller Challenge award ceremonies

"There is definite alignment between the Buckminster Fuller Challenge and the Living Building Challenge. Talking to people in the regenerative design movement has opened my eyes to the resonances between the architecture world and what we try to do. It's all about understanding the deeper connections between traditions and legacies and how we're changing our thinking about the design of civilization."

DAVID MCCONVILLE, BUCKMINSTER FULLER INSTITUTE

BUCKMINSTER FULLER CHALLENGE

The Living Building Challenge received its most poetic recognition to date when it won the Buckminster Fuller Challenge in 2012. After being named as a finalist in 2010, the Standard rose to the top of the list of nominees two years hence. McLennan considers it one of the high points in his career, given his nearly familial connection to Fuller. (McLennan's mentor, Bob Berkebile, studied under Fuller while at the University of Kansas in the 1950s, so McLennan traces many of his foundational ideas back through this professional family tree.)

The Buckminster Fuller Challenge shines lights on innovations from all over the world that strive to address "humanity's most pressing problems." It named its first winner in 2008, making the Living Building Challenge only the fifth concept to earn the coveted prize. In its summary remarks about the 2012 winner, the Buckminster Fuller Challenge jury noted that, "The Living Building Challenge successfully shows how humans and their built environment can be harmoniously, benignly integrated within ecosystems. Above all, its rigorous standards and daringly innovative, revolutionary approach to building are already having a considerable impact on the thinking of designers and architects around the world, influencing all levels of design and technological approaches, radically pushing forward the field."

ENR AWARD OF EXCELLENCE

In April 2016, McLennan received the prestigious Award of Excellence from *Engineering News-Record (ENR)*. Each year, ENR honors 25 individuals whose contributions to the global construction industry are particularly noteworthy, then singles out one of the honorees as worthy of special recognition. McLennan (and, by association, the Living Building Challenge) earned the 2016 Award of Excellence for deep and lasting efforts to make the world a better place through more sustainable built environments.

AMBASSADORS, COLLABORATIVES, CONGRESSES

Slowly but surely, people throughout the green design world were taking notice of the Living Building Challenge as it entered its third, fourth, and fifth years. Even those who were not formally associated with aspirational Living Building projects wanted to get involved; to learn; to participate. In response, the International Living Building Institute (ILBI) created the Ambassador Network.

Developed by Eden Brukman in 2008 and significantly expanded by Institute staff in the years since, the Ambassador program is intended to utilize the enthusiasm of professionals who are interested in the principles of the Challenge and use that energy to expand the Standard's reach.

Anyone in any part of the world may become an Ambassador. All it takes is a passion for a Living built environment, a commitment to undergo formal training administered by Institute representatives, and a willingness to take the message back into the community. If one looks at a global map of registered and certified Living Buildings overlaid onto a map of Ambassadors, they are nearly identical. Wherever there are like-minded volunteers advocating for and exchanging ideas about the Challenge, there is a greater likelihood of aspirational Living Buildings in some stage of development.

Once there are sufficient Ambassadors in any city or region, they form a Collaborative. Collaboratives are informal groups (not legal entities) that operate much like loosely formed chapters; their "members" meet to share strategies and push the agenda forward.

The Ambassador and Collaborative programs proved successful in bringing together the individual professionals who lend their expertise to the movement, so the Institute turned next to the industry's thought leaders. In 2014, it introduced Living Future Congresses as a way of organizing the change agents capable of moving policy in a more sustainable direction. These volunteers are senior-level professionals who seek to influence larger ge-

> "Our Ambassadors are people who feel really passionate about their communities. They look at the Living Building Challenge and they see what they want the world to look like when their children are having children. It's not about having a project to add to their resume. They get involved because they really want to work on something that increases livability and brings the world to a better place."
>
> **HILARY LAROSE, INTERNATIONAL LIVING FUTURE INSTITUTE**

ographies. They interact with political leaders on key leverage points that are likely to have ripple effects — such as municipal Living Building pilot programs, statewide laws governing net zero water, etcetera. The underlying goal of the Congresses is to remove regulatory barriers that make Living Buildings more difficult to pursue by "greening up" public policy.

"The Congresses are really all about turning public policy into Living Policy. They help challenge our cultural expectations around the kinds of systems required by Living Buildings. The technologies are there, but society needs to become more comfortable with the idea. Our job is to push that; to send the market signal that this is the new normal."

STACIA MILLER, INTERNATIONAL LIVING FUTURE INSTITUTE

MATERIAL CONCERNS

Other interesting programmatic developments occurred during this era, including two noteworthy material-specific examples.

The first was an innovative new Institute offering called Declare, which McLennan announced via a soft launch at Living Future 2010 in Vancouver. Presented much like a food nutrition label, Declare was designed to promote full transparency in the manufacturing realm. A product's Declare Label clearly states its full ingredient list, region of origin, and end-of-life options, simplifying the process of searching for Red List-compliant supplies for Living Building projects. The industry responded positively to the idea of Declare and interest began to grow following its 2010 soft launch. By the time a more comprehensive Declare program emerged in 2012, sufficient demand existed to support dedicated Institute staff. (For more on Declare, see Chapter 14.)

Meanwhile, a global brand embraced the wisdom of the Red List. Google announced in 2010 that it would rely on the Living Building Challenge Red List when specifying materials for any of its building projects in North America as a way of providing healthy workplaces for its employees. The company also asked suppliers to meet the transparency requirements of the Pharos Project.[69] The move put manufacturers on notice that material transparency was a real and growing concern and established Google as an environmentally forward-thinking corporation. In addition, it demonstrated one of the many ways in which the Living Building Challenge was beginning to shape other ideas within the green building realm.

69 www2.buildinggreen.com/article/peek-inside-googles-healthy-materials-program-0

THE INSTITUTE TAKES ON THE FUTURE

On the administrative side of the house, the organization that oversaw the Challenge was keeping up with its growth. After creating the ILBI in 2009 as a dedicated non-profit entity responsible for overseeing its namesake Standard, McLennan and his staff soon realized the group's name did not fully reflect its mission. Their work was devoted to far more than individual structures; they were out to do nothing less than change the future of the built environment. The organization's unConference — Living Future — did a better job of describing its purpose than its own legal name did. So in early 2011, the International Living Building Institute (ILBI) was rebranded as the International Living Future Institute (ILFI). The Cascadia Green Building Council would operate side-by-side with the ILFI and share office and personnel resources but the two would exist as separate non-governmental organizations. Cascadia became a program of the Institute, not the other way around. The change shifted the infrastructure on its head.

Amid these structural adjustments came personnel changes as well. In mid-2012, Eden Brukman decided to offer her expertise in socially and environmentally responsible human habitats to a broader palette of clients. She left ILFI to open her own consultancy, Concenter Solutions. Amanda Sturgeon was then named ILFI vice president, taking on the day-to-day oversight of all Living Building Challenge efforts at the Institute.

McLennan, meanwhile, who had been at the helm — first at Cascadia, then at the ILBI, then at the ILFI — scaled back his executive duties during the same time period. His full-time CEO responsibilities were reduced by half in the summer of 2012, which allowed the organization to bring in its first executive director, Richard Graves.

> "When we formed the ILBI in 2009, Cascadia was like the parent organization. When we shifted to the ILFI in 2011, we flipped it so Cascadia became like the child. It was all part of us beginning to grow up and get our own identity; it was about organizing ourselves so we could become who we needed to be."
>
> **JASON F. MCLENNAN,**
> **INTERNATIONAL LIVING FUTURE INSTITUTE**

Graves brought an ideal blend of design, administrative, and advocacy experience to the job. A veteran of Perkins+Will's sustainability practice and a former member of both USGBC's board and its senior staff, Graves came to his ILFI position eager to lead and equipped to manage. Having overseen large departments at Perkins+Will as well as USGBC's chapter infrastructure, Graves knew how to scale an operation to accommodate growth.

McLennan still devoted enormous time and energy to the organization but was able to pursue independent projects outside of the Institute to reinvigorate and connect him back to

"Running the organization during those lean years wasn't very fun. Ironically, the concept of the Living Building Challenge was taking off but it wasn't translating into much money. I was having to hustle and work crazy hours just to keep the ship going and I got very burnt out. I never lost any affection for the mission of the Challenge, but the job was killing me."

JASON F. MCLENNAN, INTERNATIONAL LIVING FUTURE INSTITUTE

the industry he was helping lead. The transition gave him a bit of relief from the extremely taxing job of keeping the Challenge, Cascadia, and the ILBI/ILFI alive during the worst economic downfall in 80 years — a period marked by diminished donor funding, reduced conference attendance, staff-wide pay cuts, and hiring freezes. When Graves came along, he introduced new business practices and helped diversify funding streams that were more appropriate for an organization that had grown in just a few short years from a three-person operation to one that employed nearly 30 people.

It felt like the right time to bring in fresh perspectives. McLennan wanted to remain active but not carry the entire administrative load for the organization or its building standard. Letting Sturgeon take the lead on the Challenge and Graves on the ILFI meant McLennan would still have an influence but his would not be the only voice speaking on behalf of the Institute or the Challenge.

The reorganization rejuvenated McLennan, creating some much-needed emotional space in which to operate. In the period that followed, he introduced several new Institute initiatives — Declare, JUST, Reveal, Net Positive, the Living Product Challenge, the Living Community Challenge, and others. With Graves responsible for senior executive leadership, McLennan was free to do what he did best: innovate.

His new role also allowed McLennan greater flexibility to tour and support the growing number of Living Buildings that were taking shape by that time. With each physical wall that went up, another perceived barrier came down. Living Buildings were real; they were performing; they were proving what was possible. All over the planet, the built environment was taking on a dramatically new shade of green.

13

"That some achieve great success is proof
to all that others can achieve it as well."

ABRAHAM LINCOLN

BRANCHING OUT
PROJECTS THAT CHANGED THE GAME

The first three certified Living Building projects — Omega, Tyson, and Eco-Sense — validated the concept of the Challenge. One might say, though, that the projects that followed in their wake were even more crucial, as they helped move the Standard out of the shadows and closer to the heart of the green design movement.

The second wave of aspirational Living Buildings was a more diverse lot; various typologies in a range of sizes from different climate zones representing an assortment of ownership models all stepped up to register. Gradually, because of these innovative projects, the list of unanswered questions about how to create a Living Building was shrinking. One by one, Living Buildings were changing designs, systems, processes, rules, and municipal codes.

> "The Living Building Challenge has changed the objective, from doing less bad to doing more good. It has shifted the paradigm."
>
> **BETH HEIDER, SKANSKA USA**

The Hawaii Preparatory Academy Energy Lab, Kamuela, HI
PHOTO: MATTHEW MILLMAN COURTESY OF FLANSBURG ARCHITECTS

HAWAII PREPARATORY ACADEMY

The Hawaii Preparatory Academy Energy Lab on the Big Island came right on the heels of the noted "first three." From its earliest planning meetings in 2006, the 6,100 square foot structure was intended to be designed and built with green features that would help educate the K-12 school's students and faculty on the merits of sustainable practices, particularly related to energy strategies. But when project stakeholders, led by the lab's director, Dr. Bill Wiecking, began to discuss the possibility of pursuing the greenest of all standards — the new Living Building Challenge — it deepened the potential impact and importance of the project.

With the support of school administrators and a generous individual donor, the project formally registered as an aspirational Living Building. Construction began in September 2008, with staff and students first occupying the building in January 2010. Following a successful audit, the Hawaii Preparatory Academy Energy Lab received its Living Building certification in April 2011 — the fourth structure and the first school in the world to earn Living status.

"Achieving LEED Platinum would have been fine. But the Living Building Challenge really demonstrates the ethos of always trying to do more than what you already know you can do. It allowed us to set these outrageous goals and see how close we could get to them."

DR. BILL WIECKING, HAWAII PREPARATORY ACADEMY

"Bill Wiecking is an incredible visionary who wants to engage kids in hands-on learning about energy use in the built environment. He's taken the spirit of the Living Building Challenge and put it into the everyday life of those kids so they can be educated to play a key role in transforming the way we think about energy in buildings. Anyone who goes there and sees the students in action can't help but be transformed by the strength of Bill's vision."

AMANDA STURGEON, INTERNATIONAL LIVING FUTURE INSTITUTE

"The Hawaii Prep project really helped elevate the program in the eyes of the architectural community because it is such a beautiful building."

JASON F. MCLENNAN, INTERNATIONAL LIVING FUTURE INSTITUTE

"As a teacher, you can influence maybe a few thousand people in your career. But this building is a place where people can come after I'm long gone; it gives us a chance to influence many more thousands of people who will come through here and learn from this building."

DR. BILL WIECKING, HAWAII PREPARATORY ACADEMY

McLennan was on-site to help award the school its certification. Prior to the ceremony, he took a solo walk around the building and crossed paths with a 15-year-old student who was on hand to help set up for the presentation. Recognizing him as a visitor, she asked him if he would like a tour of her school's new energy lab. In the minutes that followed, she provided a detailed and technically accurate explanation of all of the building's systems, enhancing her descriptions with the philosophical context of each performance area. She told her guest how proud she was to be part of such an exciting project and how thrilling it was for her to have learned so much about building design, engineering strategies, and sustainability.

McLennan was struck by his guide's poise, and the ease with which she summarized and even operated such complex aspects of the building — in a way that even seasoned professionals are sometimes unable to do. When they reached the end of the impromptu tour, the student turned to McLennan and asked, "So have you ever heard of the Living Building Challenge?"

"Having that young girl walk me around the HPA project showed me that there was a new normal being created. That building was taking on a life of its own and becoming part of the educational offerings at the school, teaching children about systems and connections and energy, water, and waste. It was a powerful moment."

198

JASON F. MCLENNAN, INTERNATIONAL LIVING FUTURE INSTITUTE

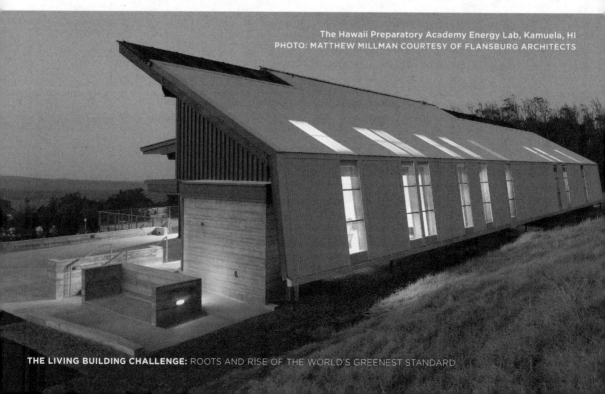

The Hawaii Preparatory Academy Energy Lab, Kamuela, HI
PHOTO: MATTHEW MILLMAN COURTESY OF FLANSBURG ARCHITECTS

"By the time I heard Jason speak about the Challenge, we were already primed to hear his message. It was a profound enough concept that it prompted us to shift gears on the final phase of our expansion plan."

RICHARD V. PIACENTINI, PHIPPS CONSERVATORY AND BOTANICAL GARDENS

THE CENTER FOR SUSTAINABLE LANDSCAPES

A similarly inspirational project was simultaneously underway in Pittsburgh, Pennsylvania on the grounds of Phipps Conservatory and Botanical Gardens. The organization's executive director, Richard V. Piacentini, was mapping out the final phase of a three-part expansion effort, sketching out ideas for an office and classroom structure that would meet its own water and energy needs and feature integrated operational systems, when he heard McLennan speak at Greenbuild in November 2006. Excited by the promise of the Living Building Challenge, Piacentini returned to Pittsburgh and floated the idea with his board, along with his architecture and engineering team, of accepting the Challenge. With full support of the necessary stakeholders, he led efforts to design and build Phipps' Center for Sustainable Landscapes.

The project registered with the International Living Building Institute in early 2007, and began its intense integrated design process that fall. The economic downturn of 2008-2009 slowed fundraising efforts, delaying construction until late 2010. But two years later, the Center for Sustainable Landscapes welcomed occupants. The project was Energy Petal certified as a net zero structure in February 2014 and received its full Living certification in March 2015.

"The Living Building Challenge has helped us connect everything: people, plants, health, planet, and beauty. The Challenge recognizes that everything operates within a connected system, which is how nature works."

RICHARD V. PIACENTINI, PHIPPS CONSERVATORY AND BOTANICAL GARDENS

UniverCity Childcare Centre, Burnaby, BC
PHOTO: MARTIN TESSLER

UniverCity Childcare Centre, Burnaby, BC
PHOTO: PHIL WYATT / COURTESY SPACE2PLACE

200

"Our goal was to use the entire Standard to get full certification, but we believed that a Petal-awarded Living Building would still be more meaningful in exploring the future of green building than a LEED Platinum building. We felt comfort and solace knowing that even if we didn't achieve full Living status, we'd still be delivering an exceptional building."

DALE MIKKELSEN, SFU COMMUNITY TRUST

UNIVERCITY CHILDCARE CENTRE

At the top of British Columbia's Burnaby Mountain adjacent to Simon Fraser University (SFU) sits the sustainably designed community known as UniverCity. A planned residential and commercial district developed by the SFU Community Trust, UniverCity is framed by four cornerstones: environment, equity, education, and economy. The 200-acre project got underway in 2003, with a masterplan that included a town center, parks, housing, schools, and other community amenities.

The crowning green jewel at UniverCity is its Childcare Centre. Though it was originally intended to continue the "LEED theme" of the rest of the development, the school's project team (led by Dale Mikkelsen, who began serving on the Cascadia board of directors in 2003 and was part of the committee that hired McLennan in 2006) decided to raise the sustainable bar. The Childcare Centre would aim for the Living Building Challenge, hoping to earn Canada's first certification — if not for the whole building, then via individual Petal performance areas.

The UniverCity Childcare Centre registered as a Living Building Challenge project in May 2008 and officially opened its doors in April 2012. The project has since been Petal-certified for all but one performance area (Energy). An energy system upgrade is expected to help the Childcare Centre meet the remaining Imperative — net zero energy — so that it can be certified as a Living Building in 2017.

VanDusen Botanical Garden Visitor Centre, Vancouver, BC
PHOTO: NIC LEHOUX / COURTESY: PERKINS+WILL

VANDUSEN BOTANICAL GARDEN VISITOR CENTRE

VanDusen Botanical Garden is located just 16 miles west of UniverCity, in the heart of Van-couver, British Columbia. The 55-acre garden first opened in 1975 and needed a new built entry point for visitors by the early 2000s. Vancouver's Board of Parks and Recreation gave the designers at Busby Perkins+Will the proverbial green light to create something that

"In terms of sustainable buildings and how they might change over time, we now have access to a variety of sustainable design standards, all of which are influencing design decisions and having a dramatic impact on architecture. Today, we are diving deeper into the tenets of regenerative design in an attempt to make what was once a strictly academic concept into something that is usable and practical, linking human (construction) activity with the natural world on which our survival depends."

PETER BUSBY, PERKINS+WILL

tested architectural and sustainability boundaries. The result is the dramatic orchid-shaped Visitor Centre, whose very form connotes the Petals of the Living Building Challenge.

Designed in 2007-2008 and opened in 2011, the VanDusen project is one of the planet's most elegant examples of regenerative design. With an undulating roofline emanating from a central solar chimney "stem," the building appears and performs much like a flower. The Visitor Centre is designed to meet human needs within the context of a thriving natural environment, and is supported by systems that adhere to all performance areas written into the Living Building Challenge.

As of early 2016, the VanDusen Botanical Garden Visitor Centre was in its Living Building Challenge audit phase.

BERTSCHI SCHOOL SCIENCE WING

The Bertschi School project stands out not only because it was a pioneering effort within the context of the Living Building Challenge but because it grew out of sheer enthusiasm and grit, the product of professional selflessness and dogged determination.

Chris Hellstern and Stacy Smedley were young associates in the Seattle office of KMD Architects when their firm sent them to Portland to attend the 2009 unConference. There, they first heard of the Challenge during McLennan's animated, impassioned keynote address. The presentation touched such a nerve that they spent the return trip to Seattle strategizing how to identify and embark on a project where they could test this intriguing new Standard.

"When it came to designing the Bertschi project, we started with the students. We used the flower metaphor, which made sense to them, and asked them what that might mean in a classroom. We let them think like kids and be creative in ways we couldn't let ourselves be, then took their ideas and turned them into solutions. The Challenge is perfect for that kind of approach." STACY SMEDLEY, SKANSKA USA

They found it at Bertschi School in Seattle, an existing KMD client whose leaders had also just learned of the Challenge through their own research and were considering it for the final, as-yet-unannounced project in their masterplan. The small K-5 private school was known for its commitment to green design and construction, having built the first LEED Gold structure on any independent school campus in the Northwest. Perhaps its new building could become a Living laboratory where children could be surrounded by the sustainability concepts they studied.

"To promote restorative buildings and make significant change with our work, we wanted to do something more than just create another research study or white paper. We wanted to build an actual building that would teach us as we designed it and teach others for years to come. We believed it was time for a built case study to serve as an example to show that restorative buildings are possible; to reach for what seems impossible." CHRIS HELLSTERN, THE MILLER HULL PARTNERSHIP

Hellstern and Smedley assembled a group of like-minded practitioners who were equally drawn to the concept, equally excited about involving children in the creative process, and equally realistic about how much of their time would need to be donated to the cause. (The slow state of the market at the time meant that many firms were looking to keep their best people busy, so a pro-bono effort such as this was well-timed.) They effectively harnessed the talents of eager professionals and persuaded their employer to grant them the necessary time to plan, design, and build what would become the Bertschi School Science Wing.

The project registered as an aspirational Challenge project in September 2009, construction began in June 2010, and the building opened in February 2011 — a mere seven-and-a-half months after ground was broken. When it received its Living Building certification in April 2013, the Bertschi School Science Wing was only the fourth commercial building in the world to reach this goal and the first of any typology to do so under Version 2.0 of the Living Building Challenge.

Bertschi School Science Wing, Seattle, WA
PHOTO: DEREK REEVES

THE BULLITT CENTER

Of all the early Living Building Challenge projects that made it through the planning, funding, and regulatory obstacle course and actually got built, one stands out as the biggest all-around game-changer: The Bullitt Center. This now-iconic 52,000 square foot, six-story commercial office building overlooks downtown Seattle, proudly representing what is possible in the built environment.

> "When I first saw the Bullitt Center and spent some time there with Denis Hayes, I was in tears. They were tears of happiness."
>
> **SIM VAN DER RYN,**
> **ECOLOGICAL DESIGN COLLABORATIVE**

Denis Hayes, a longtime environmental advocate popularly recognized for his efforts coordinating the first Earth Day in 1970, took the helm of the Seattle-based Bullitt Foundation in 1992. When the Foundation sought new headquarters in 2008, Hayes and the board made two critical decisions that would prove to forever alter the urban landscape: it would build a new structure, and that structure would aspire to be the largest-ever Living Building.

Hayes worked with the developers at Point 32 to assemble the project's core team: The Miller Hull Partnership (architects), PAE (engineers), and Schuchart (builders). With impressive portfolios of local green projects and a demonstrated willingness to explore uncharted territory, the team topped what eventually became a lengthy list of individuals, firms, government officials, advocates, educators, students, and neighbors who contributed their time and expertise to the effort.

"The first time I visited the Bullitt Center and saw that incredible Living Building in Seattle with its glorious solar roof and composting toilets and the micro park in the front of the building, it was just extraordinary. It demonstrates that a building can be completely net zero and function effectively within the fabric of the downtown environment." MICHELLE MOORE, GROUNDSWELL

The Bullitt Center, Seattle, WA
PHOTO: NIC LEHOUX

Planning began in June 2009, the project registered as an aspirational Living Building in March 2010, ground was broken in August 2011, and the Bullitt Center officially opened on Earth Day in April 2013. The opening day ceremony celebrated what the project set out to prove: that a built environment — even an urban one — can sustain itself using Living systems.

Tour guides took visitors through the building, pointing out just a few of the features of the Bullitt Center that help it comply with the Living Building Challenge:

SITE: The central location in close proximity to public transportation, residential neighborhoods, and community amenities

WATER: The rainwater harvesting system that meets all the building's potable and greywater needs

ENERGY: The solar array that generates more energy than the building consumes

HEALTH: The interior spaces that are bathed with daylight and ventilated by fresh air

MATERIALS: The majestic heavy timber FSC-certified beams that provide a non-toxic framework

EQUITY: The open-layout office spaces that allow a fair distribution of interior amenities to all occupants

BEAUTY: The sweeping views of Seattle's skyline, Puget Sound, and the 100-year-old trees salvaged as part of the rejuvenation of adjacent McGilvra Place Park

When the Bullitt Center received its official certification as a Living Building in April 2015, it was considered a profound accomplishment — not only for the individual structure, but for the Standard to which it adhered.

"By proving that Living Buildings can be comfortable, productive, and affordable — while achieving performance levels that many considered impossible — we hoped the Bullitt Center would help make Living Buildings the 'new normal.' We weren't just trying to build a structure; we were trying to spark a revolution. The sooner people stop viewing the Bullitt Center as extraordinary, the happier we will be. I get sick to my stomach every time I walk past a construction crane assembling a structure that will be wasting energy every day for the next century."

DENIS HAYES, BULLITT FOUNDATION

SEEDclassrooms

After co-leading the Bertschi School effort, architect Stacy Smedley decided that the project owed its success to its most important team members: children. Never before had she incorporated kids' ideas into a project's plans nor observed students learning in and from a Living Building, and never before had she felt more proud of her work. Then, when a fifth-grader from Bertschi wondered aloud why all buildings aren't Living Buildings, it reminded Smedley why she pursued green design in the first place. If a single classroom could inspire just one child so profoundly, what effect might a collection of sustainable classrooms have on generations of kids? With that, Smedley decided to do something to allow a broader swath of children the opportunity to learn from the Living.

> "The SEED idea is all about how much positive effect one person can have on the earth and the built environment. As an architect, I can go out and have an impact on a handful of buildings in my lifetime. But if I can create a Living classroom for a tribe of eight year olds who are so influenced by it that they grow up and take that message out into the world, that's what it's all about."
>
> **STACY SMEDLEY, SKANSKA USA**

In 2012, Smedley paired up with fellow Bertschi School team member Ric Cochrane to create a non-profit called SEED (Sustainable Education Every Day). SEED designs and manufactures freestanding classrooms for schools and other organizations. The ideal is for each SEEDclassroom to operate as a Living Building, with similar systems to those used in Bertschi's Science Wing but proportionally reduced to match the size of a traditional school portable.

Smedley and Cochrane began their collaboration in 2012 and a SEEDclassroom prototype was exhibited at Living Future 2013. Its composting toilet, rainwater collection system, water treatment system, photovoltaic panels, and Red List-friendly materials helped it meet all Imperatives of the Challenge. Richard V. Piacentini from Phipps Conservatory and Botanical Gardens was so inspired by the concept that he commissioned a fully Living SEEDclassroom to be placed adjacent to the Center for Sustainable Landscapes. (The SEEDclassroom prototype that had been on display was later purchased by The Perkins School in Seattle.) Orders then began to trickle in from around the country.

To be available to public school districts, not all SEEDclassrooms can attain Living status due to certain cost and code constraints. In some of the early cases, the structures aspire to meet at least one Petal. But with SEEDclassrooms sprinkled around the U.S. and paid for using a variety of funding approaches, Smedley and Cochrane consider that viable proof of the SEED concept.

SEEDclassroom at the Center for Sustainable Landscapes, Pittsburgh, PA PHOTO, TOP: BANKO MEDIA, BOTTOM: LAUREL MCCONNELL

14

"No man ever wetted clay and then left it, as if there would be bricks by chance and fortune."

PLUTARCH

RIPPLING OUTWARD

A FRAMEWORK FOR REMAKING EVERYTHING

It did not take long for Jason F. McLennan and his colleagues at the International Living Future Institute (ILFI) to realize that the philosophy that drove the Living Building Challenge had the potential to change far more than just the built environment. Within only a few years of its official introduction in 2006, the Challenge had garnered passionate support from architects, engineers, builders, and owners around the world and had managed to shift huge market segments in sustainable directions. If it was capable of effecting such dramatic change in the design-build industry, the ILFI had ideas about how to expand the Living boundaries.

The Challenge's Materials Petal, with its Red List of chemicals banned from any Living Building, had compelled manufacturers to develop non-toxic alternatives, so why not create a dedicated standard devoted exclusively to Living Products? The idea of Scale Jumping had been woven into several Petals of the Challenge beginning with Version 2.0, so why not apply the same Living concepts to entire communities? The Equity Petal had successfully codified social justness within structures, so why not ask that of companies as well?

It was the next logical strategic and programmatic step for the Institute: apply the proven Living philosophy to initiatives that move people, organizations, communities, and resources forward. Enabling a Living Future meant d*esigning a framework for remaking everything.*

VERSION 3.0

First, the core offering got an overhaul. In May 2014, the Institute released its most polished refinement of the Living Building Challenge yet: Version 3.0. It was the first issue of the Standard to fully reflect Amanda Sturgeon's influence on the ILFI, as well as include ideological contributions from the now robust roster of professionals who worked at the Institute.

Version 3.0 factored in the critical data culled from every effort that came before. Through the end of 2014, 233 projects registered for the Living Building Challenge and 20 accomplished either Net Zero Energy (9), Petal (4), or full Living Building (7) certification. Every one of those projects yielded valuable information that helped improve the Standard and clear some of the procedural clutter for future teams. Since Sturgeon spent her first four years with the Institute overseeing project teams' efforts, she was intimately familiar with those features of the Standard that tended to slow down the process.

"Version 3.0 definitely reflects how I see my role at the Institute, which is to listen to our stakeholders so we can really understand how they use our programs to make change. When Jason and I wrote 3.0, we incorporated changes based on what we'd heard from project teams about the difficulties they faced. It was a turning point in terms of being able to update the Challenge in ways that would help create impact and change."

AMANDA STURGEON,
INTERNATIONAL LIVING FUTURE INSTITUTE

For Version 3.0, McLennan and Sturgeon modified the elements that were deemed too onerous to achieve. The Living target remained the same, but the rewrite gave teams a clearer, more relevant sense of how to accomplish the specified performance goals.

Arguably more important than the content updates contained in the new draft was its more powerful underlying intent. Version 3.0 reached well beyond the goal of doing no harm; it aimed for nothing less than resilience, equality, and regeneration in the built environment. It was about being net positive, literally and figuratively.

LIVING
BUILDING
CHALLENGE℠
3.0

A Visionary Path to a
Regenerative Future

INTERNATIONAL
LIVING FUTURE
INSTITUTE™

CHANGES

New features of Version 3.0 included:

A SINGLE-BUILDING FOCUS: It was clear to McLennan and Sturgeon as they approached the update that they needed to address the question of scale. Previous versions of the Living Building Challenge had accommodated neighborhood and community scales, but the few projects that had attempted them within the construct of that Standard had faltered. So, as of Version 3.0, the Neighborhood Typology was removed from the Living Building Challenge and found its way into a dedicated new framework: the Living Community

"Version 1.0 of the Living Building Challenge was this audacious thing that nobody thought was achievable and Version 2.0 was when we started to broaden the innovation. But Version 3.0 was the beginning of the maturity — of the Challenge and of the organization behind it."

JASON F. MCLENNAN, INTERNATIONAL LIVING FUTURE INSTITUTE

Challenge. (More on the Living Community Challenge appears later in this chapter.) Scale Jumping was still allowed in Version 3.0, but several other Imperatives specifically related to larger-scale projects were taken out. Refocusing the Standard on individual buildings strengthened the potential impact of single structures, which would, in turn, have ripple effects on surrounding communities.

A RENAMED PETAL: The Site Petal was renamed to the Place Petal, acknowledging the unique aspects of each project location. The new moniker better emphasized the concept of placemaking — the human connection to landscape — and the philosophy that any place was always more than a "site" waiting to be developed.

A NOD TO RESILIENCY: Resiliency had risen high on the industry's list of critical topics in the years since Version 2.0 emerged, so McLennan and Sturgeon wrote some important resilience strategies into Version 3.0. Although any Living Building is inherently resilient — with its own energy supplies and water treatment systems, for example, it is typically tied to the grid and still susceptible to disruption. As such, the updated language called out specific requirements to ensure each structure's ability to withstand uncertainty. With emergency reserves, Living Buildings can stand as beacons of stability, retreat, and safety.

> "Adding resiliency to Version 3.0 was very much in keeping with Jason's approach of releasing Version 1.0 of a new idea to get the conversation started. It wasn't intended to be the one and only solution to these issues, but it acknowledges the importance of the idea, encourages discussion, and begins to reveal some answers. In that way, we achieved what we set out to do."

AMANDA STURGEON, INTERNATIONAL LIVING FUTURE INSTITUTE

A POSITIVE MOVE: New language in Version 3.0 clarified that Living Buildings are meant to be net positive, not net neutral. By 2014, there were numerous certified Living projects that were not only meeting their energy and water performance goals but exceeding them. Those "over-producing" buildings, combined with ever-improving technologies that streamlined building systems, made the shift to net positive an easy one for McLennan and Sturgeon to justify. It also reinforced the concept of resiliency, as excess energy and water stores may be drawn on in emergencies.

A DEEPER COMMITMENT TO EQUITY: Building out the Equity Petal was an enormous priority to McLennan and Sturgeon as they finessed Version 3.0, and allowed other Institute initiatives to be woven into the Standard's framework. With the rewrite, the Equity Petal became more robust and specific. Project teams were now asked to incorporate the JUST Label to ensure organizations involved in creating Living Buildings operated in a fair

"Strengthening Equity was a really big piece of 3.0. JUST was a fabulous addition to help companies think about their organizational habits, and the offset Imperative required teams to submit payments to charities of their choice. It was a way to strengthen some pilot Imperatives that we had in Version 2.0 that weren't quite being adopted in the ways we had hoped."

AMANDA STURGEON, INTERNATIONAL LIVING FUTURE INSTITUTE

and equitable manner. (More information about JUST may be found later in this chapter.) Further, an Equity offset Imperative required that charitable donations be folded into any project budget.

A FRESH TAKE ON MATERIALS: The Materials Petal offered a richer set of resources in Version 3.0, giving project teams access to a broadened database of Red List-compliant products. The Responsible Industry Imperative incorporated Declare, a type of ingredient label for manufactured goods. (See the next section for more information on Declare.) Aspirational Living Buildings were required to use at least one Declare-labeled product for every 500 square meters of project area and to send Declare information to at least ten manufacturers not currently using it. As the Declare database grew, it provided a much more useable list of approved materials suitable for Living Buildings. The Materials Petal also expanded in Version 3.0 to include furniture systems.

215

"The Materials Petal has always been the hardest to achieve and project teams had so many questions about how to track it. The more information we gave, the more questions they would ask. We knew there was a different way to get at the intent so we gave it an overhaul in Version 3.0. We embedded Declare, which made a lot of sense and made it easier for people to follow."

AMANDA STURGEON, INTERNATIONAL LIVING FUTURE INSTITUTE

A NEW SET OF OFFSET OPPORTUNITIES: Three new Living Future Exchange offset programs were added and/or modified in Version 3.0. Habitat and carbon exchanges, which had appeared previously, were enhanced, simplifying the process for project teams to allocate funds to worthwhile causes as a way of extending the global benefit of their Living Buildings. The Equitable Investment Imperative was a new addition to the Equity Petal, giving project teams the choice between donating .5 percent of total project costs to their preferred charities or contributing the same amount to an ILFI fund that supports renewable infrastructure for charitable enterprises.

AN UPDATED LIST OF EXCEPTIONS: McLennan and Sturgeon took a close look at all Living Building Challenge exceptions and released a new set with Version 3.0 that accommodated changing industry realities. They analyzed each existing exception according to how well it applied to current technologies and whether it was still a necessary component of the Standard. (For example, fluorescent lighting was banned with very few exceptions, given the broad availability of greener alternatives.)

PETAL HANDBOOKS

The new version of the Living Building Challenge also came with a full collection of something project teams had been clamoring for: Petal Handbooks. An initial wave of three Handbooks — to accompany the Energy, Water, and Materials Petals — had been released alongside Version 2.0. But with the more robust Version 3.0, a complete set was made available for the first time.

"Having a Handbook for each Petal brings a certain logic to how to explain things, which is something I'd been wanting to do since I joined the Institute. It extracts all the valuable information we'd gathered from teams and posted on the Dialogue and presents it. logically. It's brilliant how it helped to scale the program."

AMANDA STURGEON, INTERNATIONAL LIVING FUTURE INSTITUTE

The Handbooks essentially serve as Petal-specific User's Guides, which never ended up getting produced in writing in spite of the organization's genuine intention to do so. (When the Institute released Version 2.1 in 2012, it finally eliminated all references to the User's Guide in the text of the Challenge.) Sturgeon drove the effort to complete the Handbook library, receiving significant support from fellow staffers Allison Capen and James Connelly.

Sturgeon knew how valuable the Petal Handbooks would be to project teams, having been on the industry side herself as a practicing architect and then guiding many teams through their own efforts as the programmatic liaison after she joined the Institute.

Petal Handbooks

"The Living Building Challenge had some momentum, which the ILFI wanted to use to pull along ancillary programs in the interest of sailing a bigger ship. The point was never to sail a small ship. They just had to be careful to find a balance; not to let the coattails effect create a drag on the primary program."

NADAV MALIN, BUILDINGGREEN

SPINOFFS

Between 2012 and 2014, the ILFI leadership team — McLennan, Amanda Sturgeon, and Richard Graves — conducted several off-site brainstorming sessions to toss around ideas about how to broaden the reach of the Living philosophy. There was unmistakable momentum building around the Challenge, and they wanted to take advantage of what seemed like the ideal opportunity to extend the brand. The worst of the Great Recession was over, the first Living Buildings had been certified, a growing list of registered projects were under construction around the world, and people were suddenly paying very close attention.

McLennan had studied how the "halo effect" benefited Apple® products, and he wanted nothing less for the Living doctrine. (For more on the halo effect, refer to its Living Building Block description.) He and his Institute colleagues envisioned a family of Living initiatives, all interconnected and mutually complementary. The ideal looked something like this: Living Buildings, constructed of Living Products and Declare-labeled goods, would crop up in Living Communities, which would thrive in economies supported by JUST businesses. It called upon consumers, designers, engineers, builders, manufacturers, and the companies that employed them to accept a theoretical Living Future Challenge.

The first steps toward this environmentalist's utopia began with a call for transparency among manufacturers.

DECLARE

Declare is similar to a food nutrition label, but applied to manufactured products. Introduced by the ILFI via a soft launch in 2010 and then more comprehensively in 2012, its goal is to create full ingredient transparency in the materials economy. It emerged from the realization that of the three most difficult requirements of the Living Building Challenge — net zero energy, net zero water, and non-toxic materials — the first two are solvable via technological insight. In other words, innovative engineering systems are capable of helping a project reach its net zero goals. But to construct a Red List-friendly building

"Declare helped solve a specific problem that was limiting the uptake of the Living Building Challenge: that it was nearly impossible for early project teams to identify Red List-compliant products. That process used to take a huge amount of time and effort, so we recognized it as a key area where transformation was needed."

JAMES CONNELLY, INTERNATIONAL LIVING FUTURE INSTITUTE

"The thing about manufactured materials is that their formulas change all the time, so information about Red List-compliant products that work for one project can be out of date very quickly, which means it doesn't apply to the next project. A Declare label has a one-year license, so people know that any product that's Declare-registered is currently on the market. Project teams can refer to the Declare database to find what they need to use right now. Declare is the key to making the Materials Petal possible and has spurred faster marketplace changes."

AMANDA STURGEON, INTERNATIONAL LIVING FUTURE INSTITUTE

"Jason likes to talk about how one of our roles at the ILFI is to shine a light on problematic business practices and provide a new way forward. The Living Building Challenge did it for the building industry and Declare does it for green product labeling."

JAMES CONNELLY, INTERNATIONAL LIVING FUTURE INSTITUTE

"It's so exciting to watch as Declare continues to gain traction because it really accentuates how we've always looked at transparency as a catalyst for change. It's a very powerful idea that creates very fast change."

AMANDA STURGEON, INTERNATIONAL LIVING FUTURE INSTITUTE

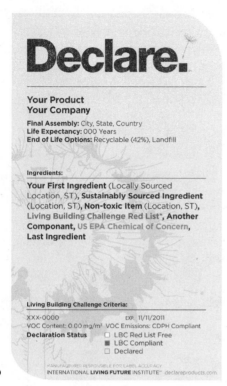

Declare.

Your Product
Your Company

Final Assembly: City, State, Country
Life Expectancy: 000 Years
End of Life Options: Recyclable (42%), Landfill

Ingredients:

Your First Ingredient (Locally Sourced Location, ST), **Sustainably Sourced Ingredient** (Location, ST), **Non-toxic Item** (Location, ST), Living Building Challenge Red List*, **Another Componant,** US EPA Chemical of Concern, **Last Ingredient**

Living Building Challenge Criteria:

XXX-0000   EXP. 11/11/2011
VOC Content: 0.00 mg/m³ VOC Emissions: CDPH Compliant
Declaration Status   ☐ LBC Red List Free
                          ■ LBC Compliant
                          ☐ Declared

MANUFACTURER RESPONSIBLE FOR LABEL ACCURACY
INTERNATIONAL **LIVING FUTURE** INSTITUTE™ declareproducts.com

"The growth of the Declare program has become exponential. With each product that gets added to the database, the cost of doing a Living Building product falls. The goal is for architects to be able to just pick from a pre-approved list of products."

JAMES CONNELLY,
INTERNATIONAL LIVING FUTURE INSTITUTE

requires a broad assortment of non-toxic products. Living Building Challenge teams have struggled since the launch of the Standard to identify suitable supplies and materials that will meet quality and toxicity standards while also adhering to the Red List Imperative.

The Declare Label complements the ILFI's belief in transparency as a catalyst for change, providing the transparency project teams had been looking for in the product realm. It lists all ingredients contained in a product, estimates its life expectancy, identifies its region of origin, and clarifies its end-of-life options (salvageable, reusable, recyclable, etcetera). In short, it takes much of the guesswork out of the specification process for Living Building Project teams seeking Red List-compliant products and it does so via an easy-to-read, visually appealing format.[70]

Declare found its way into the text of the Living Building Standard as of Version 3.0 (introduced in May 2014), embedded into Imperative 12 within the Materials Petal. From that point forward, each Challenge project has been required to use at least one Declare product for every 500 square meters of project area and to send Declare program information to at least 10 manufacturers not currently using Declare. The goal with this nested approach is to create an exponential number of products suitable for Living Buildings. With each new aspirational Living Building, several products will potentially be added to the open-source database of items from which designers and builders can choose.

---

70 McLennan had previously played with the idea of a product ingredient list when he created Pharos while still at Elements in the early 2000s (as described in Chapter 5). The Pharos Project, overseen by the Healthy Building Network, provides a consumer-driven vision of truly green building products, while Declare relies on manufacturers' self-declarations of their products' chemical compositions.

When the USGBC included Declare in the LEED credit system, it demonstrated the need for and the potential reach of the idea. But Declare does not cater only to the Living Building Challenge and LEED community. It is available to any manufacturer of any product serving any industry. All it requires is a commitment to transparency by both sides of the supplier-consumer transactional marketplace. By early 2016, the Institute had issued Declare Labels for 400 products manufactured by approximately 80 different companies.

JUST

The JUST protocol emerged from the tenets of the Living Building Challenge Equity Petal. While the Challenge calls for democracy and fairness to be designed into the built environment, JUST calls on companies to document their organizational commitment to social justice.

JUST could be described as an "ingredients label" for companies. Its purpose is to promote transparency with regard to diversity, equity, safety, worker benefits, local benefits, and stewardship. Organizations register as JUST operations, then begin the process of examining their internal policies according to JUST categories. Policy statements are uploaded to an online portal.

Like most ILFI initiatives, JUST got its start in McLennan's head. He first batted around the idea in 2011, but there were simply not enough resources at the Institute to cover the necessary personnel hours to properly explore the concept's commercial viability. So McLennan did what he had done several times before: he called on his father for help.

"JUST helps companies put their organizational values and principles into words — something that many companies have never done before. It helps them be more intentional about policies related to social justice, equity, and diversity."

FRANCIS JANES,
INTERNATIONAL LIVING FUTURE INSTITUTE

Just.

Organization Name: Super Paint Corp.
Organization Type: LLC
Headquarters: Amherst, NJ
Satellite Facilities: Portland OR, Houston TX, Montreal CAN
Number of Employees: 3,220

Social Justice and Equity Indicators:

Diversity
■□□ Non-Discrimination
■■□ Gender Diversity
■□□ Ethnic Diversity

Equity
■■■ Full Time Employment
■□□ Pay-Scale Equity
■■□ Union Friendly
■■□ Living Wage
■□□ Gender Pay Equity
■□□ Family Friendly

Safety
■□□ Occupational Safety
■□□ Hazardous Chemicals

Worker Benefit
■□□ Worker Happiness
■■□ Employee Health Care
■□□ Continuing Education

Local Benefit
■■□ Local Control
■■■ Local Sourcing

Stewardship
■□□ Responsible Investing
■■□ Community Volunteering
■□□ Positive Products
■■■ Charitable Giving
■□□ Animal Welfare

THE SOCIAL JUSTICE LABEL
INTERNATIONAL **LIVING FUTURE** INSTITUTE

After Frederick McLennan, Ph.D. retired from a 44-year career as a professor and college administrator, he often made himself available to the Institute as a volunteer.[71] His professional experience and his passion for the cause combined to make him well suited for the work. So, at his son's request, the elder McLennan began to research the elements, the metrics, and the industry segments that might be incorporated into the JUST program. Meanwhile, longtime Institute designer Erin Gehle sketched out some preliminary graphic possibilities for a label that would complement the look of Declare.

"The mission of the Institute is to help lead the transformation toward communities that are socially just, culturally rich, and ecologically restorative. The Institute's strong interest in human rights and worker rights is manifested in our social justice program — JUST. When organizations adopt the JUST program and principles, diversity improves, employees feel more engaged, and organizations strengthen ties to their communities."

FRANCIS JANES, INTERNATIONAL LIVING FUTURE INSTITUTE

A pilot program was announced via a soft launch at Living Future 2013 and the complete JUST program was officially introduced at Living Future 2014. By 2015, it was robust enough to support the ILFI program staff assigned to oversee it.

"All of those programs — the Living Building Challenge, JUST, etcetera — help people organize their thinking and help them see the potential of what's already there within their communities. You start with teasing out a city's or neighborhood's needs, fears, goals, and aspirations until you identify what they want to achieve, change, or create anew. Once you've done that, all those resources are available to them. If you can meet communities where they are and build a relationship with them that allows them to know that you're there to help them improve their world, then all of these tools become really powerful."

BOB BERKEBILE, BNIM

71 He also serves as the unpaid editor for Ecotone Publishing titles.

Also similar to Declare, JUST found its way into the text of Version 3.0 of the Living Building Challenge. A new dedicated Imperative within the Equity Petal requires that at least one of the key team members on each Living Building project has a JUST Label for its organization. However, also similar to Declare, JUST is not limited to the Living Building Challenge community. Any company from any industry in any region may apply for a JUST Label.

LIVING PRODUCT CHALLENGE

The Living Product Challenge was the Institute's follow-up innovation addressing the manufacturing realm. It was the next logical step to expand on the success of Declare and to broaden the positive impact the ILFI was having on the material economy. Just as the Living Community Challenge upscales the Living concept to neighborhoods, the Living Product Challenge downscales it to the level of individual goods.

The Living Product Challenge integrates and expands on Declare, calling for a more comprehensive approach to product sustainability. While Declare looks specifically at individual products' ingredient transparency, toxicity, and lifecycle, the Living Product Challenge is an integrated framework that guides manufacturers toward processes that mimic those in the natural world. It is a fully codified standard fashioned much like the Living Building Challenge, complete with performance area Petals. Manufacturers register items as aspirational Living Products, then submit documentation to show how they have adhered to each of the twenty Imperatives. Only after a successful audit by independent auditors do products achieve Living Product certification.

"The Living Building Challenge showed us how an aspirational standard can change the conversation in the marketplace. All of a sudden, things people used to say were impossible in the built environment are now realistic. With Declare, same thing — people never thought companies would disclose their ingredients and now they do. So we know we can do the same thing with the Living Product Challenge. We can help manufacturers create products that actually have a positive impact on society."

JAMES CONNELLY, INTERNATIONAL LIVING FUTURE INSTITUTE

> "Living Products are informed by biomimicry and biophilia; manufactured by processes powered only by renewable energy and within the water balance of the places they are made. Living Products improve our quality of life and bring joy through their beauty and functionality. Imagine a Living Product whose very existence builds soil; creates habitat; nourishes the human spirit; and provides inspiration for personal, political and economic change."
>
> **FROM THE LIVING PRODUCT CHALLENGE VERSION 1.0**

Key to the Living Product Challenge framework is the concept of "environmental hand-printing," the brainchild of Harvard-based lifecycle assessment expert Greg Norris, Ph.D., who joined the ILFI in 2014 as Chief Scientist.[72] Among Norris' first assignments was to help infuse the handprinting idea into the Living Product Challenge.

While an environmental footprint measures negative impacts, an environmental hand-print does the opposite: it quantifies benefits. Norris' work focuses on the fact that every product and service we use to survive carries with it some degree of footprint, which is undesirable but unavoidable. So it is incumbent upon us, he argues, to create an environmental benefit with an equal or greater effect. Handprinting is less about justifying the burden we create on the planet; it is about prioritizing what Norris refers to as "regenerativeness." Norris worked with McLennan and ILFI staff to build the Living Product Challenge upward from this net positive foundation.

The Living Product Challenge was launched in 2015 — a time when the green product

> "Our footprints are unintended and regrettable, but also inevitable. You just can't be alive without causing harm in the world; nobody's carbon footprint can ever get to zero. We started asking from an LCA perspective, 'What can we do about that?' It starts with reducing harm but goes so much farther than just compensating for being a burden on the planet. Handprinting is about being net positive — giving more to the environment than we take."
>
> **GREG NORRIS, PH.D., INTERNATIONAL LIVING FUTURE INSTITUTE, HARVARD UNIVERSITY**

228

72 McLennan first met Norris in Bozeman in the 1990s, when they both worked on the EPICenter project.

"The concepts of handprinting and net positive are incredibly potent, and their relationship with ILFI is symbiotic. They provide a beautiful frame for living and action in sustainability and beyond. Handprinting and the Institute meet each other; they help each other; they're co-evolving."

GREG NORRIS, PH.D., INTERNATIONAL LIVING FUTURE INSTITUTE, HARVARD UNIVERSITY

realm was disorganized in much the same way the green design movement was in the early 2000s. There was a demonstrated interest in sustainable manufacturing processes, but no roadmap that led companies in a common direction. This standard was released as *a* way forward — not necessarily *the* way forward. Its first iteration, Version 1.0, was released in an unapologetically unfinished form, expected to evolve and mature in the same way the Living Building Challenge did in its early years. As more manufacturers take it on, the database of solutions will grow and facilitate the process for the next wave of companies. Eight companies participated in the pilot program, registering ten manufactured goods as aspirational Living Products.

NET ZERO ENERGY BUILDING CERTIFICATION

As the price of solar technologies has continued to drop, a growing number of buildings around the world aspire to energy independence. The Institute recognized an opportunity to celebrate projects that accomplish true net zero energy (including those energy-independent structures that originally aspired to Living Building status but for any number of reasons could not achieve all performance area Petal Imperatives) when it created its Net Zero Energy Building Certification program in 2013. The initiative allows projects that can document their superior energy performance to receive certification that is comparable to Living Building Challenge Energy Petal certification.

"Before the Net Zero Energy Building Certification program came along, the general concept of net zero was gaining traction in the industry but there wasn't a lot of cohesive leadership around the idea. Now, this program is a logical expansion of the Living Building Challenge brand that allows us to start conversations with project teams that want a less intense option. It's a world-class entry into the ecosystem of the Challenge."

BRAD LILJEQUIST, INTERNATIONAL LIVING FUTURE INSTITUTE

> "The Net Zero Energy program is a great way to get people engaged in the conversation about what is possible. When they succeed with this, maybe they try another couple of Petals. Or maybe they register as a JUST organization. It's a way to show teams that they can go a little farther than they've ever gone before. Anything can be a pathway to a Living Building."
>
> **AMANDA STURGEON, INTERNATIONAL LIVING FUTURE INSTITUTE**

The Institute crafted the program to ensure that eligible projects also incorporated other important aspects of the Living philosophy. To achieve certification, a building must meet its own energy needs via on-site renewables on an annualized net zero basis while also meeting three additional Imperatives from the Living Building Challenge:

• Imperative One / Limits to Growth (appropriate site selection)

• Imperative Nineteen / Beauty and Spirit (aesthetic value)

• Imperative Twenty / Inspiration and Education (sharing the success story)

It is an important extension of the Institute's vision, as it is available to both new and existing buildings that can demonstrate energy self-sufficiency. Achieving Net Zero Energy certification can be a stand-alone goal, or it can serve as a first step for projects that aspire to full Living Building status at some point down the road. Either way, it brings more structures and practitioners to the Living party.

To leverage the interest in the Net Zero Energy initiative and its counterpart, net zero water, the ILFI organized an annual conference focusing on both. The Net Positive Energy and Water Conference, first held in 2014, allows professionals to learn, network, and brainstorm. The event attracts many of the same audience members as Living Future, but appeals particularly to those dedicated to the design and engineering of energy and water systems.

The Net Zero Energy Building Certification program has been a huge factor in the Institute's growth, with registered Net Zero Energy projects now outnumbering aspirational Living Building projects. It has proven so successful that the organization hired a full-time staff member in 2015 to oversee its implementation.

"Reveal lets project teams that have done great things with energy efficiency get a touch and a taste of the Institute without having to commit to the entire Living Building Challenge. It helps us articulate a narrative of efficiency that turns the conversation in the right direction."

BRAD LILJEQUIST, INTERNATIONAL LIVING FUTURE INSTITUTE

REVEAL

Products have Declare, companies have JUST, and energy efficient buildings have Reveal. The goal of this program, launched by the Institute in 2015, is to disclose any existing structure's quantifiable energy performance. A building's Reveal Label lists its energy data based on energy intensity index (EUI), its percentage energy reduction over ASHRAE[73] standards, and its percentage of net positive energy. Each Label is valid for two years.

Reveal emerged from the mind of Denis Hayes — solar pioneer, Bullitt Center visionary, and ILFI board member — who came up with the idea at a board meeting. He asserted that the organization needed to do more to celebrate the built environment's most energy efficient structures. McLennan quickly took to this idea and drew up the sketch that would become the label shortly thereafter. The initiative got off the ground thanks to funding from the Northwest Energy Efficiency Alliance.

Here, too, the Institute was intentionally inclusive in its approach. The Reveal program is available to any building, whether it is associated with the Living Building Challenge, LEED, another certification system, or no green building standard at all. It is intended to showcase energy efficiency as a means of promoting the concept, however it is applied.

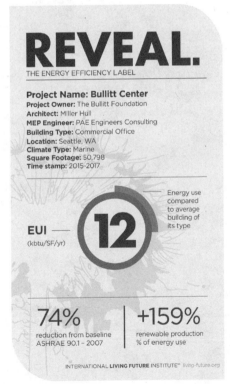

REVEAL.

THE ENERGY EFFICIENCY LABEL

Project Name: Bullitt Center
Project Owner: The Bullitt Foundation
Architect: Miller Hull
MEP Engineer: PAE Engineers Consulting
Building Type: Commercial Office
Location: Seattle, WA
Climate Type: Marine
Square Footage: 50,798
Time stamp: 2015-2017

EUI **12**
(kbtu/SF/yr)

Energy use compared to average building of its type

74%
reduction from baseline
ASHRAE 90.1 - 2007

+159%
renewable production
% of energy use

INTERNATIONAL **LIVING FUTURE** INSTITUTE™ living-future.org

73 The American Society of Heating, Refrigerating, and Air-Conditioning Engineers

"Even though the Living Building Challenge had the community scale in it, we learned that the planning community needed its own framework and language. The Living Community Challenge, like anything that operates at that scale, is very difficult to implement. But we got off the ground with some great pilot projects that helped show that it can work."

JASON F. MCLENNAN, INTERNATIONAL LIVING FUTURE INSTITUTE

"When Jason first started talking about the Living Community Challenge, it struck me as both incredibly profound and incredibly difficult to realize. It's one of those concepts that is philosophically very interesting and practically really challenging."

NADAV MALIN, BUILDINGGREEN

"High-rise projects make efficient use of city infrastructure investments, but the energy intensity use drives past the footprint. That's why the Living Building Challenge applied on the district scale is so important. Compact, multi-modal neighborhoods start to work in a sustainable footprint."

DEB GUENTHER, MITHUN

"I'm excited to see multiple threads of our work come together to drive quantum improvement in how we aggregate sustainable behaviors at the city scale. I think the movement has laid the groundwork for a process that has ignited the curiosity of the business sector and led to some exceptional innovations in products, materials, and protocols. But I think that process is only getting started."

RICK FEDRIZZI, U.S. GREEN BUILDING COUNCIL

"The Net Zero Energy program, along with all the other initiatives that came before and after, helps us gradually broaden the impact of the Living Building Challenge by pulling out sub-programs that drive people toward the full vision. They all point to how the Challenge uses the issues within it to push change in different areas of the industry."

JASON F. MCLENNAN, INTERNATIONAL LIVING FUTURE INSTITUTE

LIVING COMMUNITY CHALLENGE

Scalability was first written into the Living Building Challenge as of Version 2.0, when certain Imperatives allowed solutions that extend beyond a designated project area. Still, the important concept of Scale Jumping got somewhat lost within the context of the mostly single-building-specific Challenge. So the Institute decided to extract it and give it its own standard. Hence, the Living Community Challenge, introduced in 2014, is designed for Living blocks, corridors, neighborhoods, or campuses. It is designed to catalyze change on a grander scale, altering the way designers and planners approach bigger-picture efforts.

Unlike its predecessor, the Living Community Challenge does not require a constructed project to aspire to certification. Instead, planners and developers may submit masterplans for consideration even if their community project is not yet built. Rather than measuring the performance of completed buildings, this Challenge is capable of looking at the projected performance of actual *or conceptual* communities. Auditors evaluate either plans or completed communities, according to slight variations of the same seven performance area Petals found in the Living Building Challenge.

"All of these spin-off initiatives meld beautifully with where the world needs to go — toward robust local economies with sustainably oriented, locally owned businesses. All of these efforts can help move the needle in the right direction."

SANDY WIGGINS, CONSILIENCE

In the program's first year, five projects registered for the Living Community Challenge.

"The Living Building Challenge has opened us up to an aspirational depiction of what the future could look like, mapping a path forward. The Living Future concept has created an important space for changing the discussion from doing less bad to doing more good. It has inspired owners and project teams to take action and ask, 'What does it take to deliver a Living Building; to explore all dimensions of sustainability's triple bottom line, creating integrated teams, disrupting the supply chain, and challenging tenants to be aware of the impact of their behavior on building performance?'"

BETH HEIDER, SKANSKA USA

A GROWING INSTITUTE INFRASTRUCTURE

The ILFI's operational framework grew alongside its list of programmatic offerings. After Institute leadership brainstormed and conceptualized each new initiative, existing staff administered a soft launch to test the waters. This strategy aligned with McLennan's preferred "three-quarter-baked" approach, as it allowed the industry to help fully form these ideas via experimentation and feedback. It also helped protect the non-profit's precious resources by minimizing staff expenditures until a program was deemed viable.

If industry response was positive and an initiative promised to pencil out, then the Institute would gradually add staff to oversee it. Following this launch pattern put temporary pressure on existing personnel each time they were asked to support the early efforts of a new idea, but it kept the organization nimble. There was no hire-and-fire cycle tied to program development. Instead, employees were added only when there was sufficient programmatic income to compensate them.

The underlying strategy was two-pronged: diversify the certification paths that bring people in, and strengthen the tools that support those efforts. The Institute backed its

"Like most start-ups, we reached that pivotal point where we had to figure out how to grow the ideas or risk going under. We realized we needed to diversify to give people more traction. One of the reasons Jason and I have made such a good team is because his strengths are in the big ideas and mine are seeing those visions then figuring out what we need to do to make them work."

**AMANDA STURGEON,
INTERNATIONAL LIVING FUTURE INSTITUTE**

newly robust suite of programs with a deepened commitment to education, training, and accessibility. Whatever route practitioners chose as their entrée to the Living realm, resources and staff were available to guide them through. As a result, more individuals and firms got involved, which created a wider, more sustainable revenue stream for the Institute.

It was the right way to go. The organization steadily but carefully grew, even surviving the extremely lean years of the Great Recession without having to lay off staff. When McLennan joined Cascadia in 2006, he had a staff of three people. Ten years later, the organization he led had matured into a multi-program Institute backed by a team of 35 now led by Sturgeon. Passionate professionals nurtured the Living Building Challenge and the many programs it inspired, guiding project teams from all over the world toward their own Living goals. The Institute was running smoothly, performing well, and changing the course of the movement.

The radical experiment was working.

15

"We are made wise not by the recollection of our past but by the responsibility for our future."

GEORGE BERNARD SHAW

TOWARDS A
LIVING FUTURE
MOVING FORWARD

When Jason F. McLennan joined the Cascadia Green Building Council in 2006, he began sticking individual Post-It notes to the wall of his home office. On each, he wrote a specific goal he had for the organization. Within a very short time, the wall was a colorful mosaic of ambition.

"Launch the world's most stringent green building program to reframe what was possible," one note said. On another: "Elevate the discussion around beauty and good design alongside measurable energy and water performance." Others proclaimed, "Push the subject of equity and social justice more prominently into green building" and "Kickstart a new era of corporate transparency in the materials realm" and "Take the Living Building Challenge to the community scale."

However daring the objective, he wrote and displayed it on a vertical surface that only he scrutinized. His plan was to remove each Post-It as its stated goal was met. That wall served as McLennan's barometer of success — for himself and for the organization he led.

Slowly but surely, the wall that was once covered in a solid blanket of paper began to look more like a checkerboard. One by one, the notes came down. Cascadia, then the International Living Building Institute, then the International Living Future Institute met each goal — gradually but consistently; creatively but sufficiently; lovingly but boldly.

Nearly ten years later, that home office wall was exquisitely unadorned.

GETTING THERE

McLennan and the organization had spent the better part of a decade achieving an impressive set of intentions together. More than 10 million square feet of Living Building Challenge projects had cropped up all over the world, many of which have truly transformed the built environment. State, county, and city regulations had been rewritten to accommodate and encourage Living systems. Manufacturers had reformulated products and responded to the demand for ingredient transparency in building materials. Ecotone Publishing and *Trim Tab* magazine had distributed the green gospel and shared Living Building case studies with the world. The Living Community Challenge had inspired designers and developers to envision the beauty of green cities. There was money in the bank, a steady stream of project teams registering for the Challenge, and a healthy pipeline of innovations.

The beautifully blank wall was a joyful call for change. McLennan knew it was time for the next wave of innovators to take the lead of both the Living Building Challenge and the International Living Future Institute.

Amanda Sturgeon, who stepped into the executive director role in 2014 when Richard Graves returned to academia, had proven herself to be a worthy steward of the Standard and an adept leader of the Institute. Her strategic instincts helped bolster the organization's revenues and infrastructure during its critical transition out of the start-up phase; her hands-on experience as an architect allowed her to see things from the practitioner's point of view; her previous responsibilities as vice president of the Living Building Challenge meant she knew the Standard inside and out. In short, she possessed a valuable combination of business, creative, and programmatic skills that would serve the Institute well.

> "I realized that I was nearing the end of what I had personally hoped to accomplish as the Institute's CEO. As the last Post-It notes came down, I began to hire and promote a new senior class of leaders capable of running the organization without me. There is still so much to achieve at the Institute and under Amanda's leadership I am confident that the organization will continue to grow and thrive."
>
> **JASON F. MCLENNAN,**
> **INTERNATIONAL LIVING FUTURE INSTITUTE**

234

Sturgeon was surrounded by a talented team of fellow advocates at every ILFI office, including a senior team featuring Thomas Bland, Kathleen Smith, Brad Liljequist, James Connelly, Allison Capen, and Greg Norris, Ph.D. McLennan felt confident leaving his beloved organization in these very capable hands.

The Living Building Challenge had grown up and out. It no longer belonged just to McLennan; it belonged to the entire movement. Like a proud parent, he knew he needed to release it in order to help it find its rightful way.

"It's no good to create something only to have it wither the moment you walk away. The Living Building Challenge philosophies have become embedded in lots of people's thinking. The Challenge and the Institute will always have my DNA, but it's time for new blood and new ideas. Amanda is the perfect choice to move them forward because she's tough, she has integrity, and she'll continue to push for excellence. Now is the time for me to find other ways to be a trim tab."

JASON F. MCLENNAN, INTERNATIONAL LIVING FUTURE INSTITUTE

"We've been really good at preaching to the choir and convincing our very strong network of champions about the Living Building Challenge. But now is when we need to take our message outside of that network. Anyone involved in environmental issues should have heard of us. I want it to be thought of as inclusive and not at all elitist. A Living Future isn't possible unless it's possible for everyone."

AMANDA STURGEON, INTERNATIONAL LIVING FUTURE INSTITUTE

So McLennan passed the green baton. In January 2016, he stepped away from his executive duties at ILFI, transitioning to board chair and freeing up time to broaden the reach of his creative interests. He opened the doors of McLennan Design, where he could add his own projects to the ever-growing list of Living Buildings. Designing a Living home for his family — dubbed Heron Hall — was one of his first self-assigned tasks.

NEW LEADERSHIP

When Sturgeon took over as CEO in January 2016, the organization had traction. She had played a key role in helping McLennan (and Richard Graves, during his tenure as executive director) grow the ILFI between 2010 and 2015, strengthening its financial and organizational health so that the programs could mature and become established. In addition, she had helped finesse the Living Building Challenge so that it was even more relevant to the industry. Both the Challenge and the non-profit that runs it had become well established, well respected, and well run due in large part to her co-leadership. The industry regarded the Standard as a credible, powerful tool for change pulling the top end of the market toward more innovative and regenerative solutions.

Having collaborated with McLennan to establish a solid organization and programs, Sturgeon intends to broaden that impact and make the programs more widespread from her position as CEO. She seeks to diversify the ways in which the Living Building Challenge takes root through a wider variety of project types, climate zones, and — perhaps most profoundly — cost ranges. She wants to enable a Living Future for everyone, regardless of income, race, or gender. She envisions Living Hospitals, affordable housing, and entire neighborhoods that generate their own energy and harvest their own water.

This sweeping vision is consistent with Sturgeon's passion for equity and beauty in the built environment. Not only is she committed to forging deep connections between people and nature, but she is committed to ensuring that everyone has access to those same biophilic advantages. To her, the Living Building Challenge is a pathway to social justice.

237 —

Members of the International Living Future Institute staff

"Beauty and access to nature is a fundamental human right; we need to make sure it's front and center in our work. I want to make sure we are creating a Living Future for all, and not just for those who can afford it. We are trying to do things that can give people hope and inspire them about what's to come. That's the big picture of where I want to take the Living Building Challenge."

AMANDA STURGEON, INTERNATIONAL LIVING FUTURE INSTITUTE

She plans to lead the program in a way that widens the circle, broadens the message, and deeply transforms our way of life. Sturgeon's vision of a Living Future is spectacularly all-encompassing.

THE ROAD AHEAD

With Sturgeon at the helm of the organization and McLennan overseeing its trustees, the Institute is prepared to face the Living Building Challenge's second decade. It will continue to expand on the foundational Living concept, spreading the regenerative message ever outward. Its goal, as always, is to work toward a Living Future — one in which humans, their creations, and the natural environment are mutually restorative.

"We all want to meet people where they are, but the Living Building Challenge deliberately sets a high bar because we want to engage people in that really challenging space that's often full of conflict. Because that's where we get new ideas and brilliance; that's the point where change happens."

**AMANDA STURGEON,
INTERNATIONAL LIVING FUTURE INSTITUTE**

Mimicking the process of any healthy organism, the Living Building Challenge matures and changes according to the feedback and support it receives from the surrounding environment. Its seeds were planted in the woods of Northern Ontario, where a young boy found all he needed in and around a rustic self-sustaining cabin. It sprouted at a conference in Denver, where a nurturing industry began to tend to it with care and curiosity. In the years since, each project team adds conviction and ingenuity to strengthen the soil and broaden the canopy. The Living Building Challenge, like the built environment it aims to reinvent and the future it hopes to cultivate, is meant to grow — naturally, beautifully, and harmoniously.

16

"I alone cannot change the world,
but I can cast a stone across the
waters to create many ripples."

MOTHER TERESA

THE VOICES OF GREEN
FURTHER THOUGHTS ON CHANGE

Members of the green building community will always be the stewards of the Living Building Challenge. In the following pages, we hear more from various individuals who have nurtured it through its early years and plan to help usher it into its second decade. Among them are some of the movement's visionaries, the Standard's caregivers, the project pioneers, and the Living philosophy's standard bearers. They are best at telling the once and future story of the Living Building Challenge.

IN WHAT WAYS HAS THE LIVING BUILDING CHALLENGE CHANGED THE GREEN BUILDING MOVEMENT?

"The Living Building Challenge has transformed people to think about systems; to really question what our future will look like. Other green building approaches before this really looked at doing things a little better, and everybody jumped on board because it was easy to do. But now we're saying we need to completely change how we are making our buildings, our products, our communities. And change how we relate to our places. If we don't, we may not have a Living future. The Living Building Challenge has pushed people not just to think about making our buildings better, but to think about our entire relationship with the planet — how we do things, and how we can do all of this better. It's had a huge influence."

AMANDA STURGEON, INTERNATIONAL LIVING FUTURE INSTITUTE

"It continues to inspire people. Nobody debates how inspirational it is; they just debate whether they can achieve it or not. Still, it's giving the market hope. It feeds hope to the movement at a really important time."

RICHARD GRAVES, UNIVERSITY OF MINNESOTA

"It has been critical as the carrot to keep moving people toward that next goal."

DEB GUENTHER, MITHUN

"The Living Building Challenge gave the green building movement a first response to the question, 'What's next, after LEED Platinum?' It also started to formulate the answer to the question, 'Where are we going and where are we going to end up?' Given the Challenge's framework, it can keep getting more and more stringent as we move more toward regenerative, restorative buildings and communities instead of just buildings that are aspiring to true sustainability."

CLARK BROCKMAN, SERA ARCHITECTS

"The Living Building Challenge is enabling incredibly powerful change and having a huge effect on the people and industries involved — like suppliers. In many respects, this is exactly what happened when LEED was introduced in 2000 to the marketplace. People said, 'It's too expensive, it's too hard, you'll never do it, you're out of your mind.' Now, on an order of magnitude, the Challenge is more difficult but having the same kind of impact on people. As more Living Building projects get out in the marketplace successfully and people are able to kick the tires, the pace of adoption will pick up."

SANDY WIGGINS, CONSILIENCE

"The thing that's most important and significant about the Living Building Challenge is that it is a performance-based standard and that it's helping us transition away from a prescriptive and predictive approach to green building certification. It doesn't tie the hands of creative professionals with a bunch of rules and requirements, but sets a high bar that lets the designers reach — or even improve — that performance standard."

ROBERT PEÑA, UNIVERSITY OF WASHINGTON

"The Living Building Challenge is the game changer. If anything is going to change the movement, it will. It speaks to the heart and it speaks to creativity."

SIM VAN DER RYN, ECOLOGICAL DESIGN COLLABORATIVE

"The Living Building Challenge has never been a mainstream thing; it's always been an aspirational approach. What I always say about these leading-edge projects is, 'That which exists must be possible.' When the Challenge was brand new, there were so many naysayers. But now you can point to these completed, certified projects and say, 'They did it so it's not impossible.' That inspires the next wave of people, and it gains traction."

MARK FRANKEL, NEW BUILDINGS INSTITUTE

"It's pushed the needle past doing less harm to doing more good. It's shifted thinking from how does a building use less, to how can a building actually restore a place (its site, its community, etcetera). It's showed that buildings are more than just spaces; they are teaching tools and sources of inspiration and beauty."

STACY SMEDLEY, SKANSKA USA

"It has changed the movement by putting transparency and people in the center."

PAOLA MOSCHINI, MACRO DESIGN STUDIO

"The Living Building Challenge has shown that this type of building is possible. It has made net positive energy, net positive water, and materials transparency regularly-used terms and common aspirational goals."

CHRIS HELLSTERN, THE MILLER HULL PARTNERSHIP

"It has set a new paradigm for what we're all aiming for, particularly with materials transparency. The Living Building Challenge set the groundwork for all that work to move forward."

SUNSHINE MATHON, FOUNDATION COMMUNITIES

"It is helping designers understand that there is more to green buildings than chasing points on a scorecard. It's helping educate them to understand how true net zero energy and water buildings should be designed from the beginning. That the architecture itself, when properly designed to work with the climate, sun, wind, topography, and water, can be a building that actually helps regenerate the environment. Neutral is good but having a positive impact is far better. The fact that there are projects getting certified and many of them perform above expectations and at market rate with little to no 'green' premiums for construction costs are compelling arguments."

GERARD LEE, HMC ARCHITECTS

"The Living Building Challenge has changed the green building movement by changing the vocabulary and dialogue. The topics of health, wellness, community, connections, learning from other systems, and social justice have been incorporated into the discussions of 'regular' planners, architects, scientists, engineers, and others when working on designs. Issues such as material health and concerns about environmental impact are not ignored, and the fiscal impact is being better understood and appreciated."

LORRAINE DOO, DOO CONSULTING

"The Living Building Challenge inspires us to do things that were once considered virtually impossible. Even on projects that don't pursue full Living certification, the Challenge is emboldening project teams to go beyond market convention and do it at near market rate. The Living Building Challenge is enriching the discourse and demonstrating what's possible."

BETH HEIDER, SKANSKA USA

"It is unwaveringly setting the ideal in terms of energy and water performance. We're not just incrementally improving; you always know how far away from a net zero goal you are. Also, the influence on health and materials throughout the industry is obvious."

DREW WENZEL, GOOGLE

"The Living Building Challenge is all about resetting what's possible; creating a framework for a bunch of really motivated people to show how far they can go. It really does pull the entire industry along. The more examples of buildings that exist at that level, the less tenable it is to say, 'Twenty percent improvement is as far we can go.'"

NADAV MALIN, BUILDINGGREEN

"People who engage in business tend to be innovators and entrepreneurs more than systems thinkers. Architects, by the nature of their craft, have to think about systems. The architects involved in the Living Building Challenge are leading-edge systems thinkers; they live and breathe systems. They work primarily with the design of mechanical systems, but recognize that these systems must work with the living systems into which they are introduced and that the living systems have to be primary. When they succeed in connecting them in ways that recognize the primacy of nature, you see the beauty of the human mind at its best — thinking in connected ways."

DAVID KORTEN, AUTHOR, ACTIVIST

"The Living Building Challenge has propelled the green building movement to new heights and is pushing industries to achieve more."

TARA BARAUSKAS, A COMMUNITY OF FRIENDS

"It has provided vision, inspiration, and a roadmap for how to make a difference — an improvement — to provide balance in our natural world."

MARY TOD WINCHESTER, CHESAPEAKE BAY FOUNDATION

"A fundamental characteristic of the green building movement is that there is an element of personal competition; a drive to demonstrate how much one individual can do. In the years since the Living Building Challenge was first introduced, I've come to appreciate that it provides an incredibly important aspirational goal for the marketplace that's continuing to push the leadership edge in terms of technical transformation."

MICHELLE MOORE, GROUNDSWELL

"Together, [LEED and the Living Building Challenge] have challenged the entire continuum of the market. The Cascadia chapter of the USGBC is where the Living Building Challenge originated, so we are rightly proud of what they've accomplished."

245 —

RICK FEDRIZZI, U.S. GREEN BUILDING COUNCIL

"The Living Building Challenge takes the green building movement to the next step and gives it a different framework — something you'd grow into and aspire to. It offers an umbrella framework that represents all the good things you're looking for — the future we all want to live in. It's a framework that pulls good design towards it. I love the fact that it celebrates place in a grounded way by encouraging a nature-inspired design response."

JANINE BENYUS, BIOMIMICRY 3.8

HOW DO YOU ENVISION THE LIVING BUILDING CHALLENGE EVOLVING?

"I think the Living Building Challenge is a very key element to the future of the green movement because of what it's leading to. It's about creating a new approach to living and community, and attached to that are things like new economic systems and new social management systems — some of which the Institute is already making happen, like the Equity Petal. The Living Building Challenge will evolve as a natural organism. There are so many opportunities for transformation. We need to seek them out so that every city has its own rich story."

BOB BERKEBILE, BNIM

"I'm watching Living Buildings move from mission zero to what I call mission generous: this idea that you don't just meet your own needs on the site. Now we're moving into giving the surplus goodness away, which is what ecosystems do."

JANINE BENYUS, BIOMIMICRY 3.8

"I think folks will keep moving toward the Living Building goal until that becomes the norm. When LEED Silver was introduced, we thought of it as such an amazing accomplishment and now we talk about how LEED Gold and even LEED Platinum are doable for many projects. The norm changes as we shift through time."

DEB GUENTHER, MITHUN

"The Challenge will continue to grow organically, which is due to the willingness and acceptance of the Institute to continue pioneering its own program rather than locking in and saying, 'We have a finished product.' They listen and learn and continue to realize that green buildings and neighborhoods will continue to evolve by taking the best knowledge we have and keeping it relevant and scalable. It's a program designed to be updated when it's necessary to embrace change or growth. That's what's compelling."

DALE MIKKELSEN, SFU COMMUNITY TRUST

"I think we're already seeing a shift from static rating systems that assess performance at a moment in time, to tools that help owners and managers assess performance constantly in real time. The market still wants an objective benchmark to measure against, and certification helps validate whether you are above or below a benchmark. But the fact of the benchmark is rapidly giving way to the act of ongoing performance improvement. That's a big step."

RICK FEDRIZZI, U.S. GREEN BUILDING COUNCIL

HOW DO THE LIVING BUILDING CHALLENGE AND LEED COMPLEMENT ONE ANOTHER?

"LEED came first and defined the process and methodology for how buildings could be rated. LEED is now in its fourth version, and with each version the bar has been raised. We've been intentional about how we advance practice, not going so far that we leave the market behind, but rather taking a big enough step so that the market had to stretch. The Living Building Challenge has taken a different approach — rather than trying to get the vast majority of the market to do better, it has worked to pioneer the bleeding edge. It's a kind of laboratory approach that fills a critical role in the market, working with those project teams that want to go as far as possible, leading by example of what could be. The Living Building Challenge has been successful at exploring the 'what ifs.' LEED has been successful at delivering the 'how far,' at scale. Both roles are critically important if we are to achieve the market transformation we both envision."

RICK FEDRIZZI, U.S. GREEN BUILDING COUNCIL

"From the very beginning, it was clear to those of us in the thick of it that the Living Building Challenge was not harmful to LEED and in fact has been beneficial. I think it gives our movement — the same movement that created LEED — a raison d'être, even though it really is a challenge to get there."

CLARK BROCKMAN, SERA ARCHITECTS

"People who have been passionate about sustainability for a long time or are in the green movement because that's where their heart is are completely inspired by the vision of the Living Building Challenge. That was true in 2006 and it's still true today. LEED, meanwhile, supports a large group of users who use it because it makes business sense and because they like the idea of being on the right side of environmental and health issues. LEED is intentionally calibrated to be out in front of mainstream practice — but not too far out there — while the Challenge is calibrated very differently. There is a place in the industry for both, because some LEED users wouldn't know what to make of the Living Building Challenge."

NADAV MALIN, BUILDINGGREEN

"LEED and the Living Building Challenge are definitely cousins. They have a relationship in the market. The best thing LEED did was open the door to make the Challenge possible; it made it imaginable."

JASON F. MCLENNAN, INTERNATIONAL LIVING FUTURE INSTITUTE

"Both of the systems are really important. LEED influences at scale and the Challenge breaks new ground in a way that is potentially disruptive. At the end of the day, they both serve the family of professionals committed to building better buildings. LEED and the Living Building Challenge are mutually reinforcing. They've both evolved in their own way and attracted different players. I see them as essential parts of a shared ecosystem."

BETH HEIDER, SKANSKA USA

"LEED has transformed not just the United States but also the global marketplaces for green building and will continue to do so. The Living Building Challenge is critical to help drive far-forward innovation in sustainable building practices. They co-exist beautifully by creating incredible opportunities for the market to continue to drive itself forward."

MICHELLE MOORE, GROUNDSWELL

HOW HAS THE LIVING BUILDING CHALLENGE INFLUENCED YOUR PROFESSIONAL PRACTICE?

"We're in a co-creating relationship; we help each other evolve. The Living Building Challenge was the first thing to ask us to mature enough to meet our own needs on a site. Where biomimicry comes in is bringing the biological intelligence and wisdom that takes it beyond the metaphor. The closer we get to functioning like a biological system, we need biological literacy. That's where our work meets the ILFI's. That methodology of biomimicry is one of the things that brings you to meet the Challenge. Now that the Living framework is being applied to product design, we're thrilled. We tell our clients to sign up for the Living Product Challenge. Let's try to be as close to biomimetic as we can be — in outcome and in method — in how we create that goodness."

JANINE BENYUS, BIOMIMICRY 3.8

"It has influenced many of the projects I've worked on to strive for the highest level of sustainable design."

LISA PETTERSON, SRG PARTNERSHIP

"The Living Building Challenge framework has been our go-to reference for each and every project we undertake, even though we are not planning for certification. It has set a very high and inspirational bar which we try to reach, whether on architectural or urban projects. It has also helped us bring these issues to light in our part of the world and discuss them with partners and clients, based on concrete case studies and evidence."

ADIB DADA, THEOTHERDADA

"It has influenced me immensely. It helped focus my sustainability passion into a tangible, measurable building. It supports my vision of sustainability and equity in architecture. I'm continually educated by and inspired by the entire community that works for a Living Future."

CHRIS HELLSTERN, THE MILLER HULL PARTNERSHIP

"In school, I was heavily influenced by many of the design lecturers who were designing and building passive solar buildings and exploring alternative construction methods with straw bale and Trombe walls. Sun, earth, wind, and water were elements to be treated with respect and weaved within the fabric of design to create sustainable buildings. I have carried that passion they instilled in me for sustainable design through my career. When the Living Building Challenge emerged, I felt encouraged that there was an organization that would help educate and transform our profession. It pushes the boundaries and encourages all of us to continually improve. Being able to work with ILFI on the West Berkeley Public Library was a truly enjoyable experience and to be able to have it certified by ILFI as a Net Zero Energy Building was extremely satisfying. The Living Building Challenge has inspired and reinvigorated me."

GERARD LEE, HMC ARCHITECTS

"Being part of the Living Building Challenge community has enabled me to push the envelope with everyone whom I engage on the subject of sustainability — whether it be related to buildings or creating a sustainability plan for a community. The basics of energy and water are a given, and now discussions of equity (JUST) and biomimicry are a standard part of the conversation as well."

LORRAINE DOO, DOO CONSULTING

"It has reoriented my understanding of what a green building should be."

BRAD KAHN, GROUNDWORK STRATEGIES

"It's definitely changed the path of my career. At Mithun, it has helped us articulate and define what the range of options are for our clients. It gives us the language, the tools, and the metrics to be able to help clients understand what they might be able to do on a project. It also helps us focus on priorities around things like the Red List, which gives us a way to understand the complexity of the materials question. That's driven a lot of our educational efforts and changed the way we prioritize things in our office. These conversations move along at a much faster clip because the Challenge is out there."

DEB GUENTHER, MITHUN

"It has allowed the students and teachers of our academic programs to be in touch with the vanguard of sustainable building and urban design."

CAROLYN AGUILAR-DUBOSE, UNIVERSIDAD IBEROAMERICANA

"It has given me a new standard toward which to strive both in my design practice and in advocating for change in my community."

JONATHAN BURGESS, THE SPINNAKER GROUP

"My work has centered on the idea that we need to model our economic systems on healthy living systems that organize to optimize conditions essential to life's healthful existence rather than to maximize financial gain. I call them living economies. The Living Building Challenge deals with the other piece of the puzzle — the built environment, which also must be designed to work in a co-productive partnership with nature's living systems. Life can only exist in community — communities of organisms that self-organize to create and maintain the conditions essential to life. The further you get into that, the more extraordinary are the ways in which life works with the physical systems of earth to continuously capture and share and recycle energy, purify water, maintain healthy soils, maintain climate stability, and everything else that's essential to our existence. Unlike money, which is just an accounting token; a made-up number with no intrinsic value, healthy living systems should come to be recognized in true economic terms as the ultimate wealth."

DAVID KORTEN, AUTHOR, ACTIVIST

HOW HAS THE LIVING BUILDING CHALLENGE AFFECTED THE UNDERLYING PHILOSOPHY OF THE GREEN BUILDING MOVEMENT?

"We talk all the time about how the Living Building Challenge is a Trojan horse. Project teams often call in a panic when they're at a particular place: they're going into construction docs, they worry that they haven't started early enough to ask all the questions they should about Red List ingredients; they've promised the client they can do this. We hear them say, 'Tell us what to do!' But we can't do that. What we can do is remind them of the mission of what they're doing. It's not about whether or not you make the Materials Petal; it's about the change that you make that ripples out as a result of you asking the question. When they are reminded of the mission, they get back on track and keep on going."

AMANDA STURGEON, INTERNATIONAL LIVING FUTURE INSTITUTE

"For me, what's most important about the Challenge is the fact that it's based on pure metaphor. You can't help but be inspired by the petals of a flower. Not everyone can do everything, and that's the beauty of it. Even if you use it as a framework for what you do, it's a rich, holistic framework that covers things far beyond what other certification programs cover."

STACY SMEDLEY, SKANSKA USA

"It's stretched the way people in all walks of life think about buildings and infrastructure — from artifacts to extensions of natural systems. It's pushed project teams to think only in systemic and integrated ways, including intentional design for many elements that have historically been left out of consideration like equity, biophilia, and beauty. It has paved the way for leadership projects that are proving the impossible possible, breaking down traditional barriers and thereby inspiring more people every day to reach for the impossible."

SANDY WIGGINS, CONSILIENCE

"The Living Building Challenge has created a new road that seemed unthinkable a few years ago. Now zero-impact buildings are possible."

PAOLA MOSCHINI, MACRO DESIGN STUDIO

"The Living Building Challenge led the way in eliminating toxicity in our building projects and has provided a foundation whereby actual building performance becomes the measuring stick instead of predicted performance."

LISA PETTERSON, SRG PARTNERSHIP

"I believe the green building movement has always been evolving towards what we see manifested in the Living Building Challenge. Initially, it was to minimize our impact on the environment, and then to get to a neutral state and now it's about handprints and giving back to the environment with regenerative buildings. It's helping passive and biophilic design responses become more mainstream and in many ways help set the tone for social justice. By decreasing our demand for fossil fuels and looking at smarter ways of utilizing water and other resources, we can help restore the planet and eventually reduce the negative impact we have on many developing nations."

GERARD LEE, HMC ARCHITECTS

"It has increased the emphasis on actual rather than predicted performance."

AMY JARVIS, ZGF ARCHITECTS

"The underlying philosophy of the green building movement is going through a metamorphosis. It may be subtle, but it is growing substantially. Designers are excited about the health aspects. Engineers and architects understand the fiscal benefits. Developers are beginning, just beginning, to get the potential and fighting less. The green building movement won't need to remain a 'green building movement' because it can become simply the way buildings are built ... it will become the natural way of all building, and will not require a label."

LORRAINE DOO, DOO CONSULTING

"One of the beautiful things about the designs of Living Buildings is how they make visible the integral relationship between humans and nature. These designs make concrete what otherwise may appear abstract."

DAVID KORTEN, AUTHOR, ACTIVIST

"The Living Building Challenge helps us set our aspirational goals high enough and keep them locally appropriate. The ultimate goal is that our human artifacts are functionally indistinguishable from the native ecosystems in which they're embedded; they become a welcome species in that place. The difference between an invasive species and a species from somewhere else that gets established and then naturalized is that the naturalized one gives back. It actually ends up benefitting the ecosystem it's in. That's the pathway to being naturalized rather than being invasive. And that's what we're trying to do with Living Buildings: figure out how to inhabit a place we've become native to. When we do, we're home."

JANINE BENYUS, BIOMIMICRY 3.8

"The Living
Building Challenge
is a breakthrough.
It's another way
of relating to
this complicated
living world."

SIM VAN DER RYN, ECOLOGICAL DESIGN COLLABORATIVE

PROJECT DISTRIBUTION

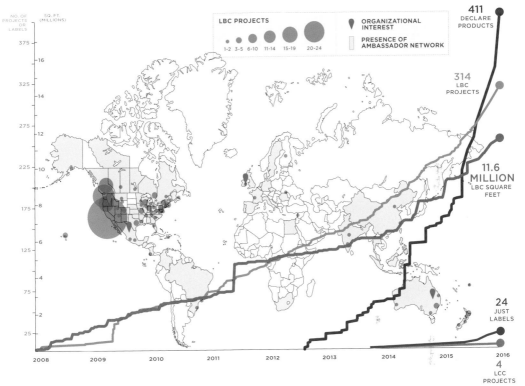

NO. OF PROJECTS OR LABELS
375
325
275
225
175
125
75
25

SQ. FT. (MILLIONS)
16
14
12
10
8
6
4
2

LBC PROJECTS
1-2 3-5 6-10 11-14 15-19 20-24

ORGANIZATIONAL INTEREST

PRESENCE OF AMBASSADOR NETWORK

411 DECLARE PRODUCTS

314 LBC PROJECTS

11.6 MILLION LBC SQUARE FEET

24 JUST LABELS

255

4 LCC PROJECTS

2008   2009   2010   2011   2012   2013   2014   2015   2016

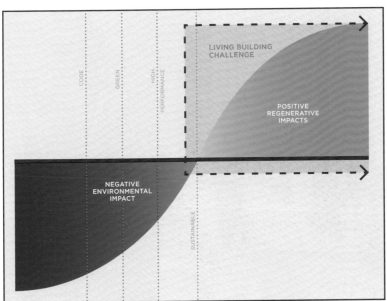

CODE

GREEN

HIGH PERFORMANCE

LIVING BUILDING CHALLENGE

POSITIVE REGENERATIVE IMPACTS

NEGATIVE ENVIRONMENTAL IMPACT

SUSTAINABLE

SETTING THE IDEAL AS THE INDICATOR OF SUCCESS

The Living Building Challenge is a philosophy, certification, and advocacy tool for projects to move beyond merely being less bad and to become truly regenerative.

LIVING BUILDING PROJECTS

**FULL
CERTIFICATION**

OMEGA CENTER
FOR SUSTAINABLE
LIVING
Rhinebeck, NY

PHOTO: FARSHID ASSASSI
COURTESY OF BNIM ARCHITECTS

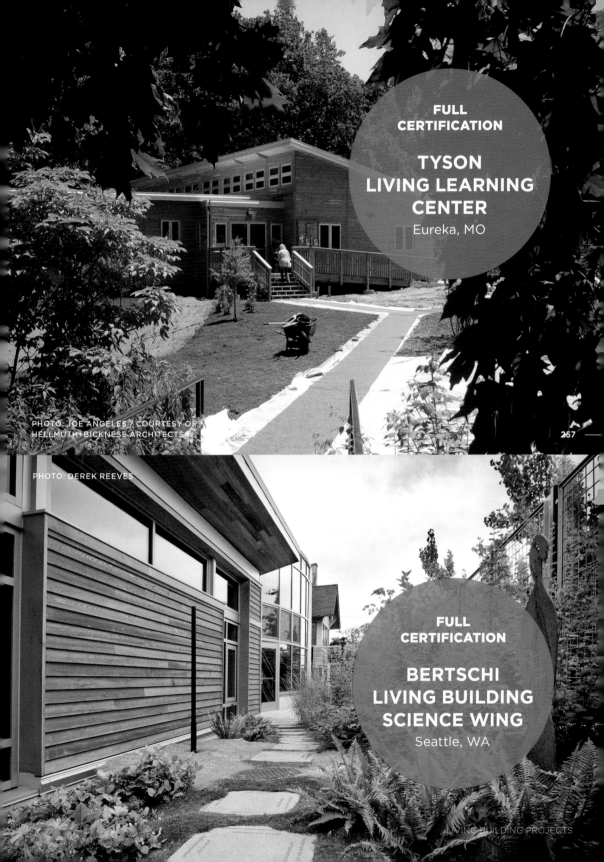

FULL
CERTIFICATION

**TYSON
LIVING LEARNING
CENTER**
Eureka, MO

PHOTO: JOE ANGELES / COURTESY OF
HELLMUTH+BICKNESE ARCHITECTS

257

PHOTO: DEREK REEVES

FULL
CERTIFICATION

**BERTSCHI
LIVING BUILDING
SCIENCE WING**
Seattle, WA

LIVING BUILDING PROJECTS

FULL CERTIFICATION

SMITH COLLEGE BECHTEL ENVIRONMENTAL CLASSROOM

Whately, MA

PHOTO: ETHAN DRINKER
COURTESY OF COLDHAM & HARTMAN ARCHITECTS

258

FULL CERTIFICATION

BROCK ENVIRONMENTAL CENTER

Virginia Beach, VA

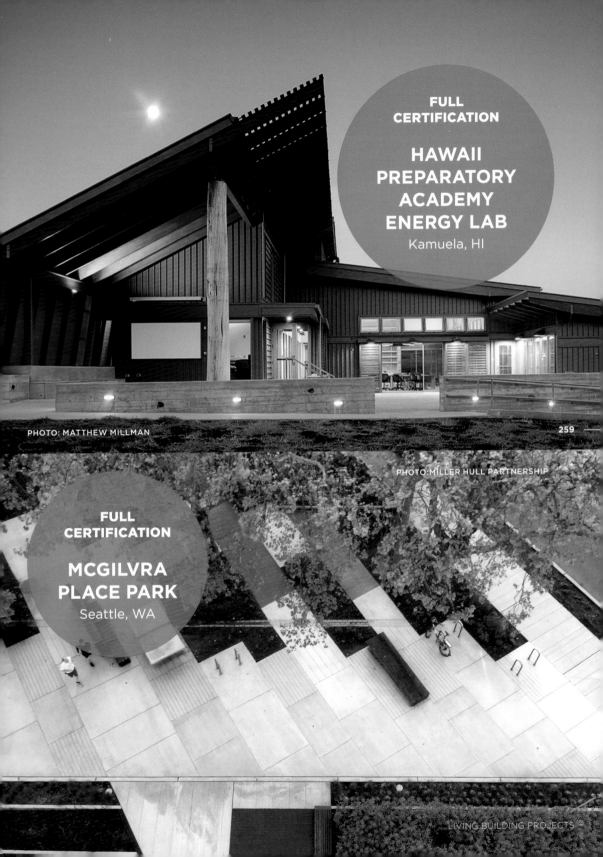

FULL
CERTIFICATION

HAWAII PREPARATORY ACADEMY ENERGY LAB

Kamuela, HI

PHOTO: MATTHEW MILLMAN

PHOTO:MILLER HULL PARTNERSHIP

FULL
CERTIFICATION

MCGILVRA PLACE PARK

Seattle, WA

LIVING BUILDING PROJECTS

FULL
CERTIFICATION

BULLITT
CENTER
Seattle, WA

PHOTO: NIC LEHOUX

FULL CERTIFICATION

PHIPPS CENTER FOR SUSTAINABLE LANDSCAPES

Pittsburgh, PA

NRDC MIDWEST OFFICE
Chicago, IL

PHOTO: M.MOSER

262

PHOTO: KATIE BROWN

PAINTERS HALL
Salem, OR

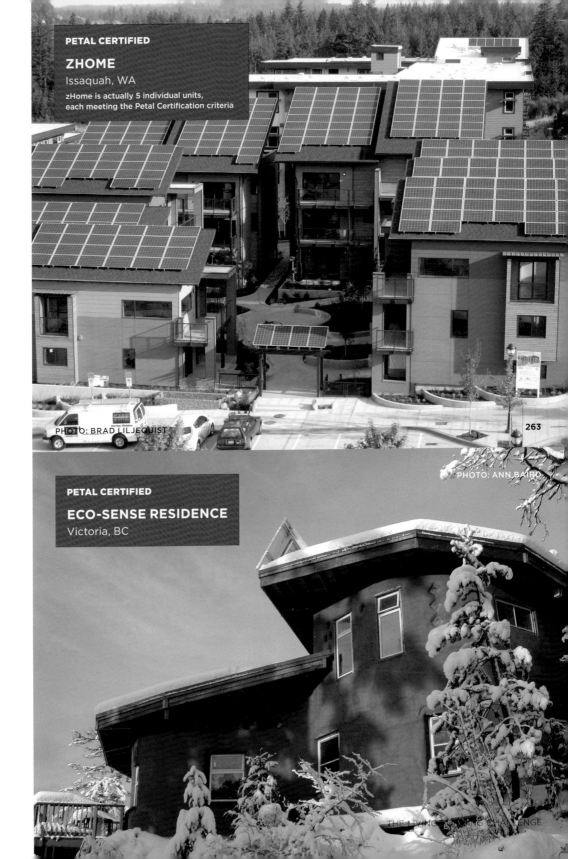

THE LIVING BUILDING CHALLENGE

PHOTO: DAVID WAKELEY / COURTESY OF INTEGRAL GROUP.

PHOTO: MATTHEW MILLMAN
COURTESY OF DAVID BAKER ARCHITECTS

NZEB CERTIFICATION

ZERO COTTAGE
San Francisco, CA

THE LIVING BUILDING CHALLENGE: ROOTS AND RISE OF THE WORLD'S GREENEST STANDARD

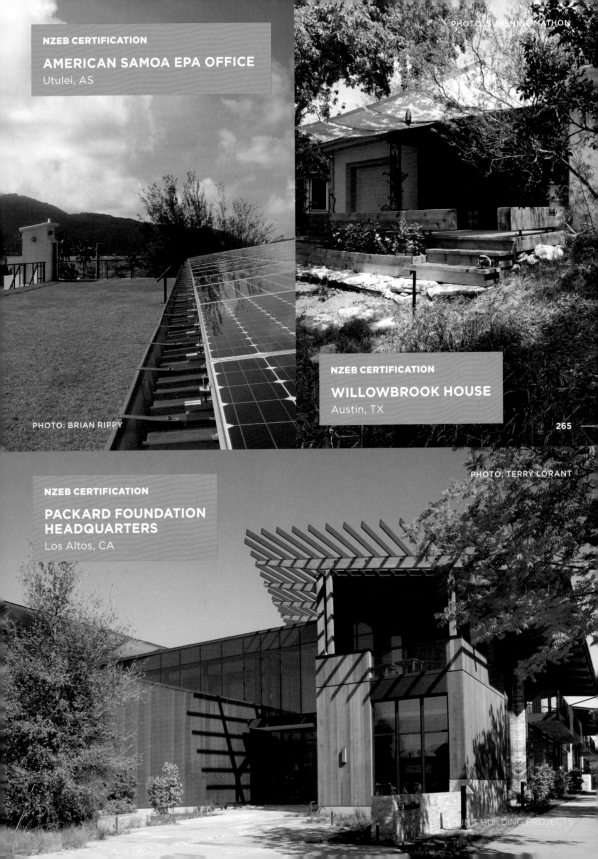

NZEB CERTIFICATION

AMERICAN SAMOA EPA OFFICE
Utulei, AS

NZEB CERTIFICATION

WILLOWBROOK HOUSE
Austin, TX

NZEB CERTIFICATION

PACKARD FOUNDATION HEADQUARTERS
Los Altos, CA

LIVING BUILDING PROJECTS

266
PHOTO: COURTESY OF WRNS STUDIO

PHOTO: MARK LUTHRINGER
COURTESY OF HARLEY ELLIS DEVEREAUX

PHOTO: ANA DERMER ON BEHALF OF ARROW INTERNATIONAL

NZEB CERTIFICATION

MISSION ZERO HOUSE
Ann Arbor, MI

PHOTO: KEVIN MIYAZAKI

NZEB CERTIFICATION

ZERO ENERGY HOUSE
Auckland, NZ

PHOTO: TODD EYRE

PHOTO: MICHAEL MATHERS

NZEB CERTIFICATION

HOOD RIVER MIDDLE SCHOOL MUSIC + SCIENCE BUILDING
Hood River, OR

TRIM TAB MAGAZINE

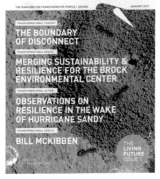

trim tab

TRANSFORMATIONAL THOUGHT
THE BOUNDARY OF DISCONNECT

TRANSFORMATIONAL DESIGN
MERGING SUSTAINABILITY & RESILIENCE FOR THE BROCK ENVIRONMENTAL CENTER

TRANSFORMATIONAL ACTION
OBSERVATIONS ON RESILIENCE IN THE WAKE OF HURRICANE SANDY

TRANSFORMATIONAL PEOPLE
BILL MCKIBBEN

THE LIVING FUTURE ISSUE 1

trim tab

TRANSFORMATIONAL THOUGHT
URBAN AGRICULTURE AND LIVING BUILDINGS

TRANSFORMATIONAL DESIGN
THE HAWAII PREPARATORY ACADEMY ENERGY LAB: HAWAII'S FIRST LIVING BUILDING CHALLENGE PROJECT

TRANSFORMATIONAL PEOPLE
BOB BERKEBILE
AN ENVIRONMENTAL LEADER ON WHAT INSPIRES HIM

ALSO
THE FOREST CERTIFICATION WARS: WHO ARE THEY REALLY FOR?

trim tab

TRANSFORMATIONAL THOUGHT
OUR CHILDREN'S CITIES: The Logic & Beauty of a Child-Centered Civilization

TRANSFORMATIONAL DESIGN
CHALLENGING A 'MISSION IMPOSSIBLE': The Hawai'i Preparatory Academy Energy Lab

TRANSFORMATIONAL ACTION
Disconnecting From Sewers, Reconnecting To Nature

TRANSFORMATIONAL PEOPLE
MARGARET WHEATLEY: The Power of Community

trim tab

TRANSFORMATIONAL THOUGHT
THE BUCKMINSTER SCHOOL OF THOUGHT

TRANSFORMATIONAL DESIGN
SMITH COLLEGE BECHTEL ENVIRONMENTAL CLASSROOM TAKES ON THE CHALLENGE

TRANSFORMATIONAL PEOPLE
JANINE BENYUS

ALSO IN THIS ISSUE
DECLARE: THE INGREDIENTS LABEL FOR BUILDING PRODUCTS

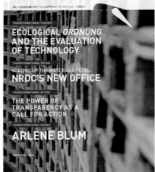

trim tab

TRANSFORMATIONAL THOUGHT
ECOLOGICAL *ORDNUNG* AND THE EVALUATION OF TECHNOLOGY

TRANSFORMATIONAL DESIGN
SCALING UP THE MATERIALS PETAL:
NRDC'S NEW OFFICE

TRANSFORMATIONAL ACTION
THE POWER OF TRANSPARENCY AS A CALL FOR ACTION

TRANSFORMATIONAL PEOPLE
ARLENE BLUM

trim tab

TRANSFORMATIONAL THOUGHT
THE HABITAT OF HUMANITY:
A WILD TO CLINICAL CONTINUUM

TRANSFORMATIONAL DESIGN
EQUITY AND THE LIVING BUILDING CHALLENGE

TRANSFORMATIONAL ACTION
#OURLIVINGFUTURE

TRANSFORMATIONAL PEOPLE
WITNESS CHANGE WITH ROBIN HAMMOND

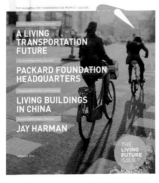

trim tab

A LIVING TRANSPORTATION FUTURE

PACKARD FOUNDATION HEADQUARTERS

LIVING BUILDINGS IN CHINA

JAY HARMAN

THE LIVING FUTURE ISSUE

trim tab

JUST: THE SOCIAL JUSTICE LABEL

EDUCATION AND LABOR: BEREA COLLEGE'S NEW STUDENT RESIDENCE HALL

EAST MEETS WEST: SOCIALLY RESPONSIVE DESIGN

PLINY FISK III

OCTOBER 2013

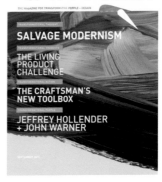

trim tab

SALVAGE MODERNISM

THE LIVING PRODUCT CHALLENGE

THE CRAFTSMAN'S NEW TOOLBOX

JEFFREY HOLLENDER + JOHN WARNER

LABELS

REVEAL.
THE ENERGY EFFICIENCY LABEL

Project Name: Bullitt Center
Project Owner: The Bullitt Foundation
Architect: MIller Hull
MEP Engineer: PAE Engineers Consulting
Building Type: Commercial Office
Location: Seattle, WA
Climate Type: Marine
Square Footage: 50,798
Time stamp: 2015-2017

EUI
(kbtu/SF/yr)

Energy use compared to average building of its type

74%
reduction from baseline
ASHRAE 90.1 – 2007

+159%
renewable production
% of energy use

INTERNATIONAL **LIVING FUTURE** INSTITUTE℠ living-future.org

Declare.

SD Nylon Modular Carpet Tiles with Accent Yarn

Mohawk Group

Final Assembly: Glasgow, VA, USA
Life Expectancy: 15 Years
End of Life Options: Take Back Program, Recyclable 100%

Ingredients:

Coal Fly Ash (Juliette, GA), **Nylon 6** (Dalton, GA), **Nylon 6,6** (Camden, SC), **Sodium Lime Glass** (Cornelius, NC), **Limestone** (Buchanan, VA), **Polyolefin Polymer, Hydrocarbon Resin, Butadiene Acrylate Polymer, Polyethylene Terphthalate & Polypropylene, Polyethylene Terephthalate & Polyamide, 2,5 Furandion Modified Ethylene/Hexane-1-Polymer, Glass/ Mineral Fiber, Calcium Oxide, Soy Lecithin, Amorphous Carbon Black, Ammonium Lauryl Sulfate, Sodium Polyacrylate, Colorant**

Living Building Challenge Criteria:

MHK-0004	EXP. 05/01/2015
LBC ZONE 3	09 68 13
Declaration Status	▣ LBC Red List Free
	☐ LBC Compliant
	☐ Declared

MANUFACTURER RESPONSIBLE FOR LABEL ACCURACY
INTERNATIONAL **LIVING FUTURE** INSTITUTE℠ declareproducts.com

---

Just.

Organization Name: Super Paint Corp.
Organization Type: LLC
Headquarters: Amherst, NJ
Satellite Facilities: Portland OR, Houston TX, Montreal CAN
Number of Employees: 3,220

Social Justice and Equity Indicators:

Diversity
■☐☐ Non-Discrimination
■■☐ Gender Diversity
■■☐ Ethnic Diversity

Worker Benefit
■☐☐ Worker Happiness
■■☐ Employee Health Care
■☐☐ Continuing Education

Equity
■■■ Full Time Employment
■☐☐ Pay-Scale Equity
■■☐ Union Friendly
■■☐ Living Wage
■☐☐ Gender Pay Equity
■☐☐ Family Friendly

Local Benefit
■■☐ Local Control
■■☐ Local Sourcing

Stewardship
■☐☐ Responsible Investing
■■☐ Community Volunteering
■☐☐ Positive Products
■■■ Charitable Giving
■☐☐ Animal Welfare

Safety
■☐☐ Occupational Safety
■☐☐ Hazardous Chemicals

THE SOCIAL JUSTICE LABEL
INTERNATIONAL **LIVING FUTURE** INSTITUTE℠

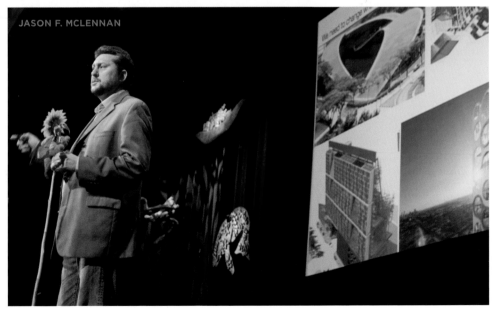

270

APPENDIX

TIMELINE

2003
McLennan launches Ecotone
Publishing Company
and includes an initial
challenge to the industry
to create Living Buildings

SPRING 2006
McLennan is named CEO
of the Cascadia Green
Building Council; Cascadia
agrees to "sponsor" the
Living Building Standard

SUMMER 1997
Jason F. McLennan joins
BNIM and begins working
with Bob Berkebile

2001 & 2002
Packard Sustainability
Matrix released (then
re-released the next year)
with a focus on Living
Buildings as the level
above LEED Platinum

AUGUST 2006
Cascadia has its first board
meeting with McLennan as
CEO; the Living Building
Standard becomes the
Living Building Challenge

APRIL 2009
The International
Living Building
Institute is formally
announced at
Living Future
in Portland

NOVEMBER 2006
McLennan formally
announces the Living
Building Challenge at
Greenbuild in Denver

AUGUST 2009
Living Building
Challenge Version
1.3 is released

SUMMER 1998
McLennan attends the
ACEEE conference in
Monterey and is inspired
by the metaphorical
resilience of a beach flower

1997 — **1998** — **1999** — **2001** — **2002** — **2003** — **2004** — **2006** — **20**

OCTOBER 1999
McLennan and Berkebile
publish "The Living Building"
in *The World and I*

2003
Green Dirt Farm
project begins, allowing
McLennan to test many
Living Building ideas

APRIL 2007
First Living Future
unConference is
held in Seattle

Living Building
Challenge Version
1.2 is released

1997
Jason F. McLennan
is added to the
EPICenter project team
in Bozeman, Montana
and the Living Building
concept begins to form

2004
McLennan's first book, *The Philosophy
of Sustainable Design*, is published

McLennan begins writing the Living
Building Standard

SUMMER 2007
Eden Brukman
joins Cascadia as
Living Building
Challenge Director

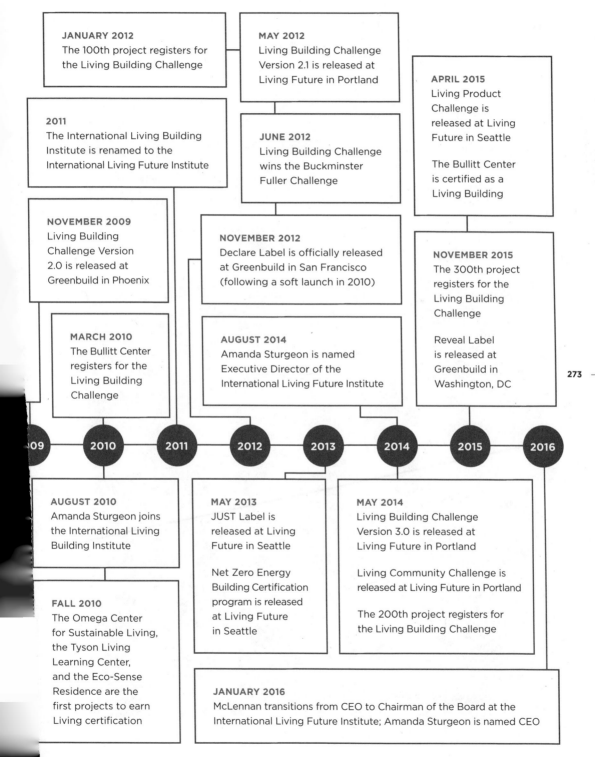

JANUARY 2012
The 100th project registers for the Living Building Challenge

MAY 2012
Living Building Challenge Version 2.1 is released at Living Future in Portland

APRIL 2015
Living Product Challenge is released at Living Future in Seattle

The Bullitt Center is certified as a Living Building

2011
The International Living Building Institute is renamed to the International Living Future Institute

JUNE 2012
Living Building Challenge wins the Buckminster Fuller Challenge

NOVEMBER 2009
Living Building Challenge Version 2.0 is released at Greenbuild in Phoenix

NOVEMBER 2012
Declare Label is officially released at Greenbuild in San Francisco (following a soft launch in 2010)

NOVEMBER 2015
The 300th project registers for the Living Building Challenge

Reveal Label is released at Greenbuild in Washington, DC

MARCH 2010
The Bullitt Center registers for the Living Building Challenge

AUGUST 2014
Amanda Sturgeon is named Executive Director of the International Living Future Institute

09   2010   2011   2012   2013   2014   2015   2016

AUGUST 2010
Amanda Sturgeon joins the International Living Building Institute

MAY 2013
JUST Label is released at Living Future in Seattle

Net Zero Energy Building Certification program is released at Living Future in Seattle

MAY 2014
Living Building Challenge Version 3.0 is released at Living Future in Portland

Living Community Challenge is released at Living Future in Portland

The 200th project registers for the Living Building Challenge

FALL 2010
The Omega Center for Sustainable Living, the Tyson Living Learning Center, and the Eco-Sense Residence are the first projects to earn Living certification

JANUARY 2016
McLennan transitions from CEO to Chairman of the Board at the International Living Future Institute; Amanda Sturgeon is named CEO

273 ——

SUMMARIES OF LIVING BUILDING CHALLENGE VERSIONS

LIVING BUILDING CHALLENGE 1.0

The 16 Prerequisites of The Living Building Challenge™

The Living Building Challenge is comprised of six performance areas, or Petals: Site, Energy, Materials, Water, Indoor Quality, and Beauty + Inspiration. Projects may apply for individual Petal designation by satisfying the requirements within that Petal, or for Living Building status by attaining all requirements within the standard.

Living Building designation is based on actual, rather than modeled or anticipated, performance. Therefore, buildings must be operational for at least Twelve consecutive months prior to evaluation.

PLACE	01. RESPONSIBLE SITE SELECTION
	02. LIMITS TO GROWTH
	03. HABITAT EXCHANGE
ENERGY	04. NET ZERO ENERGY
MATERIALS	05. MATERIALS RED LIST
	06. CONSTRUCTION CARBON FOOTPRINT
	07. RESPONSIBLE INDUSTRY
	08. APPROPRIATE MATERIALS/SERVICES RADIUS
	09. LEADERSHIP IN CONSTRUCTION WASTE
WATER	10. NET ZERO WATER
	11. SUSTAINABLE WATER DISCHARGE
INDOOR QUALITY	12. A CIVILIZED ENVIRONMENT
	13. HEALTHY AIR: SOURCE CONTROL
	14. HEALTHY AIR: VENTILATION
BEAUTY + INSPIRATION	15. BEAUTY + SPIRIT
	16. INSPIRATION + EDUCATION

The 20 Imperatives of the Living Building Challenge 2.1:
Follow down the column associated with each Typology
to see which Imperatives apply.

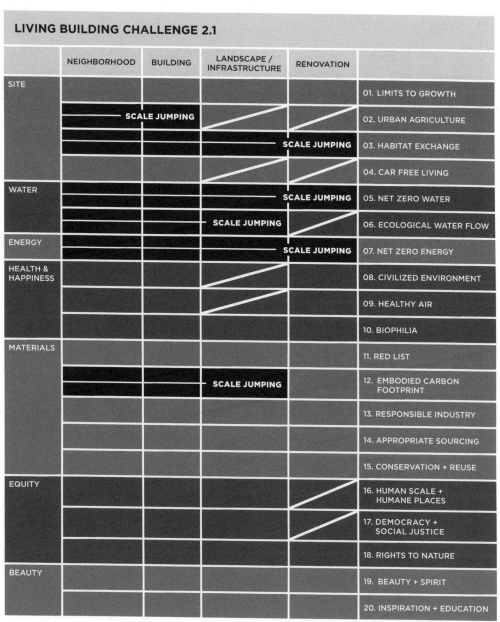

LIVING BUILDING CHALLENGE 2.1

	NEIGHBORHOOD	BUILDING	LANDSCAPE / INFRASTRUCTURE	RENOVATION	
SITE					01. LIMITS TO GROWTH
	SCALE JUMPING				02. URBAN AGRICULTURE
			SCALE JUMPING		03. HABITAT EXCHANGE
					04. CAR FREE LIVING
WATER			SCALE JUMPING		05. NET ZERO WATER
		SCALE JUMPING			06. ECOLOGICAL WATER FLOW
ENERGY			SCALE JUMPING		07. NET ZERO ENERGY
HEALTH & HAPPINESS					08. CIVILIZED ENVIRONMENT
					09. HEALTHY AIR
					10. BIOPHILIA
MATERIALS					11. RED LIST
		SCALE JUMPING			12. EMBODIED CARBON FOOTPRINT
					13. RESPONSIBLE INDUSTRY
					14. APPROPRIATE SOURCING
					15. CONSERVATION + REUSE
EQUITY					16. HUMAN SCALE + HUMANE PLACES
					17. DEMOCRACY + SOCIAL JUSTICE
					18. RIGHTS TO NATURE
BEAUTY					19. BEAUTY + SPIRIT
					20. INSPIRATION + EDUCATION

IMPERATIVE OMITTED
FROM TYPOLOGY

SOLUTIONS BEYOND PROJECT
FOOTPRINT ARE PERMISSIBLE

The 20 Imperatives of the Living Building Challenge 3.0:
Follow down the column associated with each Typology
to see which Imperatives apply.

LIVING BUILDING CHALLENGE 3.0

	BUILDINGS	RENOVATIONS	LANDSCAPE + INFRASTRUCTURE	
PLACE				01. LIMITS TO GROWTH
	SCALE JUMPING		SCALE JUMPING	02. URBAN AGRICULTURE
			SCALE JUMPING	03. HABITAT EXCHANGE
				04. HUMAN POWERED LIVING
WATER			SCALE JUMPING	05. NET POSITIVE WATER
ENERGY			SCALE JUMPING	06. NET POSITIVE ENERGY
HEALTH & HAPPINESS				07. CIVILIZED ENVIRONMENT
				08. HEALTHY INTERIOR ENVIRONMENT
				09. BIOPHILIC ENVIRONMENT
MATERIALS				10. RED LIST
			SCALE JUMPING	11. EMBODIED CARBON FOOTPRINT
				12. RESPONSIBLE INDUSTRY
				13. LIVING ECONOMY SOURCING
				14. NET POSITIVE WASTE
EQUITY				15. HUMAN SCALE + HUMANE PLACES
				16. UNIVERSAL ACCESS TO NATURE & PLACE
			SCALE JUMPING	17. EQUITABLE INVESTMENT
				18. JUST ORGANIZATIONS
BEAUTY				19. BEAUTY + SPIRIT
				20. INSPIRATION + EDUCATION

276

THE LIVING BUILDING CHALLENGE: ROOTS AND RISE OF THE WORLD'S GREENEST STANDARD

LIVING BUILDING CHALLENGE HEROES

2012

Skip Backus, CEO, Omega Institute

Bob Berkebile, Principal, BNIM

Eden Brukman, Vice President, International Living Future Institute

Mary Davidge, Principal, Mary Davidge Associates

Carolyn Aguilar-Dubose, Director of Department of Architecture, Universidad Iberoamericana

Ben Gates, Architectural Fellow, Housing Development, Central City Concern

Chris Hellstern and Stacy Smedley, KMD Architects

Brian O'Brien, Partner, Solearth Ecological Architecture

Warren Overton, Managing Director, VIRIDIS E3

Richard Piacentini, Executive Director, Phipps Conservatory and Botanical Gardens

Adam Robb, Teacher, Jasper High School

2013

Denis Hayes, President, Bullitt Foundation

Chris Rogers and Chris Faul, Founding Partners, Point 32

Joe David, Sustainability Program Manager, Point 32

Diane Sugimura, Director, City of Seattle's Department of Planning and Development

Dan Hellmuth, Principal, Hellmuth + Bicknese Architects

Bruce Coldham, Partner, Coldham&Hartman Architects

Jerome Partington, Sustainability Manager, Jasmax

2014

Joshua Berger, Captain, The Schooner Adventuress

Johanna Brickman, Director of Collaborative Innovation, Oregon BEST

Mary Casey, Board Chair, Living Future Institute Australia

Lance Jeffery, Project Manager,
University of Wollongong Sustainable Buildings Research Centre

Caroline Pidcock, Director, PIDCOCK - Architecture + Sustainability

Anthony Ravitz, Real Estate & Workplace Services Team Lead, Google

Pauline Souza, AIA, LEED Fellow, Partner and Director of Sustainability, WRNS Studio

Dr. Kath Williams, Founder, Kath Williams + Associates

2015

Tom Elliot and Barbara Scott, Owners, Desert Rain House

Anthony Guerrero, Chief Sustainability Officer,
Natural Resources Defense Council Offices

Michelle Johansson, Associate Architect, Jasmax

Alejandro Lirusso, Owner, BIOe, Buenos Aires

Tricia Love, ESD, Consultant and Owner, Tricia Love Consulting, Ltd.

Dale Mikkelsen, Director of Development, Simon Fraser University Community Trust

Charley Stevenson, Principal, Eco Strategy

Bill Updike, Interim Deputy Director, Urban Sustainability Administration,
District of Columbia's Department of Environment

ML Vidas, Architect and Owner, Vidas Architecture, LLC

CONTRIBUTORS

The author expresses her deep gratitude to the following individuals for generously sharing their time, recollections, and insights to help tell this story. Their contributions to this book — and to the Living Building Challenge itself — have been invaluable.

Carolyn Aguilar-Dubose	Universidad Iberoamericana
Skip Backus	Omega Institute
Ann and Gord Baird	Eco-Sense Residence
Tara Barauskas	A Community of Friends
Janine Benyus	Biomimicry 3.8
Bob Berkebile	BNIM
Clark Brockman	SERA Architects
Eden Brukman	Concenter Solutions
Jonathan Burgess	The Spinnaker Group
Mary Casey	Living Future Institute Australia
James Connelly	International Living Future Institute
Adib Dada	theOtherDada
Lorraine Doo	Doo Consulting
Rick Fedrizzi	U.S. Green Building Council
Pliny Fisk III	Center for Maximum Potential Building Systems
Mark Frankel	New Buildings Institute
Richard Graves	University of Minnesota
Debra Guenther	Mithun
Denis Hayes	Bullitt Foundation
Beth Heider	Skanska USA
Dan Hellmuth	Hellmuth + Bicknese Architects
Chris Hellstern	The Miller Hull Partnership
Kevin Hydes	Integral Group
Francis Janes	International Living Future Institute
Amy Jarvis	ZGF Architects
Brad Kahn	Groundwork Strategies

David Korten	Author, activist
Hilary LaRose	International Living Future Institute
Gerard Lee	HMC Architects
Brad Liljequist	International Living Future Institute
Nadav Malin	BuildingGreen
Sunshine Mathon	Foundation Communities
David McConville	Buckminster Fuller Institute
Jason F. McLennan	International Living Future Institute
Dale Mikkelsen	SFU Community Trust
Stacia Miller	International Living Future Institute
Michelle Moore	Groundswell
Paola Moschini	Macro Design Studio
Greg Norris, Ph.D.	International Living Future Institute, Harvard University
Jerome Partington	Jasmax
Lisa Petterson	SRG Partnership
Richard V. Piacentini	Phipps Conservatory and Botanical Gardens
Robert Peña	University of Washington
John Reynolds	University of Oregon
Stacy Smedley	Skanska USA
Amanda Sturgeon	International Living Future Institute
Sim Van der Ryn	Ecological Design Collaborative
Drew Wenzel	Google
Bill Wiecking	Hawaii Preparatory Academy
Sandy Wiggins	Consilience
Kath Williams	Kath Williams + Associates
Mary Tod Winchester	Chesapeake Bay Foundation
Jessica Hale Woolliams	First Cascadia British Columbia Director

Contributors are listed here and in quotes throughout the previous pages with the organizations with which they were affiliated at the time of this book's publication. Some individuals worked elsewhere while involved in the projects to which they refer in their comments.

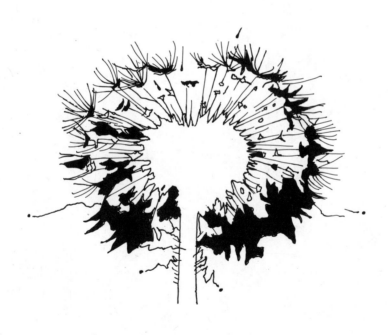

WWW.LIVING-FUTURE.ORG